OUTDOOR WOODWORK

S T E P - B Y - S T E P   P R A C T I C A L   G U I D E S

OUTDOOR WOODWORK

16 Easy-To-Build Projects for Your Yard & Garden

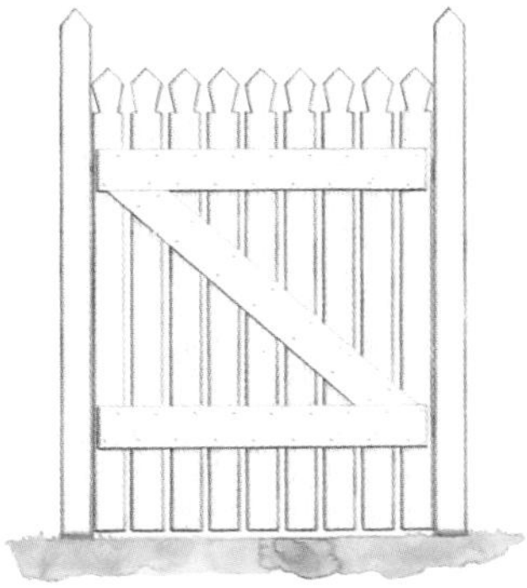

A L A N   &   G I L L   B R I D G E W A T E R

STOREY

The mission of Storey Publishing is to serve our customers by publishing practical information that encourages personal independence in harmony with the environment.

United States edition published in 2002 by Storey Books,
210 MASS MoCA Way, North Adams, MA 01247

First published in 2002 by New Holland Publishers (UK) Ltd
London • Cape Town • Sydney • Auckland

Garfield House, 86–88 Edgware Road, London W2 2EA, United Kingdom
80 McKenzie Street, Cape Town, 8001, South Africa
Level 1, Unit 4, 14 Aquatic Drive, Frenchs Forest, NSW 2086, Australia
218 Lake Road, Northcote, Auckland, New Zealand

ISBN 1-58017-437-X

Editorial Direction: Rosemary Wilkinson
Project Editor: Clare Johnson
Production: Hazel Kirkman
Professional Assistance: Bob Moran

Designed and created for New Holland by AG&G BOOKS
Designer: Glyn Bridgewater
Illustrator: Gill Bridgewater
Project design: Alan and Gill Bridgewater
Photography: AG&G Books and Ian Parsons
Editor: Fiona Corbridge
Woodwork: Alan and Gill Bridgewater, William Del Tufo and Richard Cope

Reproduction by Pica Digital Pte Ltd, Singapore
Printed and bound in Malaysia by Times Offset (M) Sdn. Bhd.

A note on measurements:
To accommodate standard sizes of building materials, the metric and imperial conversions in this book are not exact. It is important to use only one system of measurement for a project and not a combination of both.

Library of Congress Cataloging-in-Publication Data
Bridgewater, Alan.
Outdoor Woodwork: 16 easy-to-build projects for your yard & garden / Alan & Gill Bridgewater.
p. cm.
Includes index.
ISBN 1-58017-437-X
1. Woodwork. 2. Garden ornaments and furniture. 3. Garden structures. I. Bridgewater, Gill. II. Title.

TT180.B754 2002
84.1'8—dc21

2001031440

Contents

Introduction

One fine summer's day, Gill and I were busy in the workshop enjoying our woodwork, but at the same time desperately wishing that we could be outside in the garden soaking up the sun. Then we realized that we could have the best of both worlds: we could in fact be outside building really adventurous woodworking projects for the garden. We put down our tools and wandered around the garden considering the possibilities. I immediately thought about constructing a picnic table I had been dreaming about, and Gill had a Victorian tool shed in her sights. Better still, garden woodwork would be able to make use of relatively low-cost, rough-sawn wood straight from the sawmill, and we would require only basic tools.

The ambition of this book is to share with you all the delights of working with wood to build beautiful creations for the yard and garden. Each project follows the steps of collecting tools and materials, considering the design, and building. We describe how the component parts are cut and fitted, colorwash illustrations show how the structures are built, and photographs demonstrate how best to achieve the step-by-step procedures; in fact, we take you through all the stages of designing, making, and finishing.

So, if you like the idea of spending time out in your yard or garden doing woodwork that will add interest and functionality, you will get a lot of enjoyment from this book. You may have ambitions to sit on your very own bench to have a cup of coffee, to eat lunch on a picnic table, or to nestle under a romantic arch. You may long for an arbor where you can canoodle with your partner, or perhaps your children have always nagged you for a playhouse. Try one or two projects during the summer, then dream about all the garden woodwork that you are going to build next year!

Best of luck.

Alan & Gill

HEALTH AND SAFETY

Many woodworking procedures are potentially dangerous, so before starting work on the projects, read through the following list:

- Make sure that you are fit and strong enough for the task ahead. If you have doubts, ask your doctor for specific advice.
- When you are building sheds, arbors, pergolas, and other large structures, you will need to ask others to help you assemble the components towards the end of the project.
- When operating power tools, read the safety instructions supplied with the tool and wear the appropriate protective gear. A dust-mask and pair of goggles are usually adequate, and if the machine is noisy, wear ear protectors.
- Never operate electric tools, such as a drill or saw, if you are tired.
- Use power saws extremely carefully. Keep your fingers well away from the blade and use a stick of scrap wood for holding or pushing through short lengths of wood.

Part 1: **Techniques**

Designing and planning

Whatever the size or situation of your yard or garden, a well thought-out woodwork project will undoubtedly make it a more exciting and dynamic place. You don't have to have loads of experience as a woodworker in order to complete our projects successfully: if you have the correct tools, choose your wood with care, and spend time carefully designing and planning the whole exercise, you will be sure to get good results.

FIRST CONSIDERATIONS

- Will your lumber supplier deliver small quantities of wood, or are you going to pick it up yourself? Do you have a trailer or a suitable rack on the roof of your car?
- Do children and pets use your yard, and if so, is their presence going to affect your choice of project?
- Where are you going to do the woodwork? Will you work close to the house, perhaps on a patio, or are you going to work some distance away on the lawn?
- If you are building a structure such as a shed or arbor, are you going to set it up on levelled blocks or bricks, or are you going to lay a concrete slab?
- Will your neighbors be concerned about the location of a project? If this is a possibility, it's a good idea to involve them at the planning stage.
- Are you going to need help with lifting? If you plan to build the Victorian Tool Shed (see page 108), will you do the construction close to the site, or will you get help to move the panels once they have been built?

Choosing a suitable project

When you have decided what you'd like to build, the next step is to consider the project in terms of the site you have in mind. Is your chosen project a suitable size for the site? Will you have to move a drain? Will the project upset the way that you and the family currently use the garden?

Are there any narrow gateways that might restrict access when installing a project that you have built away from its eventual site? Are there any shrubs that need to be cut back to allow the project to be put in position? Would it be a good idea to mend and paint your fences before you build a shed? Are there any local restrictions related to the building of sheds?

So, our advice is to choose your projects with great care, and to involve your family (and neighbors if the projects could conceivably affect them, for example the height of your planned structure may obstruct their views) in decision-making, before going ahead and enjoying the building experience.

Planning the project

Whatever your choice of project, whether it is the Rabbit Hutch (see page 94) or the Classic Pergola (see page 100), it is vital to plan it out to the last detail, otherwise you can be caught by unforseen difficulties. If you are thinking about building a large, fixed project such as the Victorian Tool Shed (see page 108), draw a plan of your yard complete with the house, paths, flowerbeds, trees, and hedges. Mark in the trajectory of the sun as it arcs across the yard. Will the new shed cast shadows that will affect the flowerbeds? Will it necessitate the building of a new path so the shed can be reached easily from the house?

Keep asking yourself questions. If you have any doubts about how the shed will look when it has been erected, it's a good idea to stake out the site and build a large batten, board and string framework to the size of the shed. When the mock-up is in position, walk around it and consider how it relates to the rest of the yard. Live with it for a few days and see if it affects your family's movement around the yard.

Before you dig deep holes or pound in spiked metal post supports (for a fence, gate, or pergola), it is important to avoid potential problems by studying site plans, testing the ground, or making trial holes. If you suspect that there might be an underground structure such as a water main, drain, or power supply, start by gently and carefully probing the ground with a metal rod. If it slides into the ground easily, the site is clear, but if it meets an obstruction, you must consider digging a trial hole to see what the problem is, or opt to move the project anyway.

Buying the right tools and materials

The best strategy, when building up a tool collection, is to get yourself a basic kit, and then buy specialist tools if the need arises.

When buying your materials, on no account consider using pre-packed, planed wood from the local DIY store. Not only would it triple your costs, but its smooth finish may make it unsuitable for the projects in this book. Whenever possible, buy rough-sawn wood from a local sawmill. Shop around for the best price and then order in bulk. When you go to the sawmill, ask to see their waste pile, just in case there is a bargain to be had. For example, with the bevel-edged boarding, we were able to cut costs dramatically by using wood from a heap of random lengths. When selecting your wood, make sure that the finish is suitable. For instance, you must not use pressure-treated wood for the playhouse, because of the toxic nature of some preservatives.

WOODWORK DESIGNS FOR THE YARD AND GARDEN

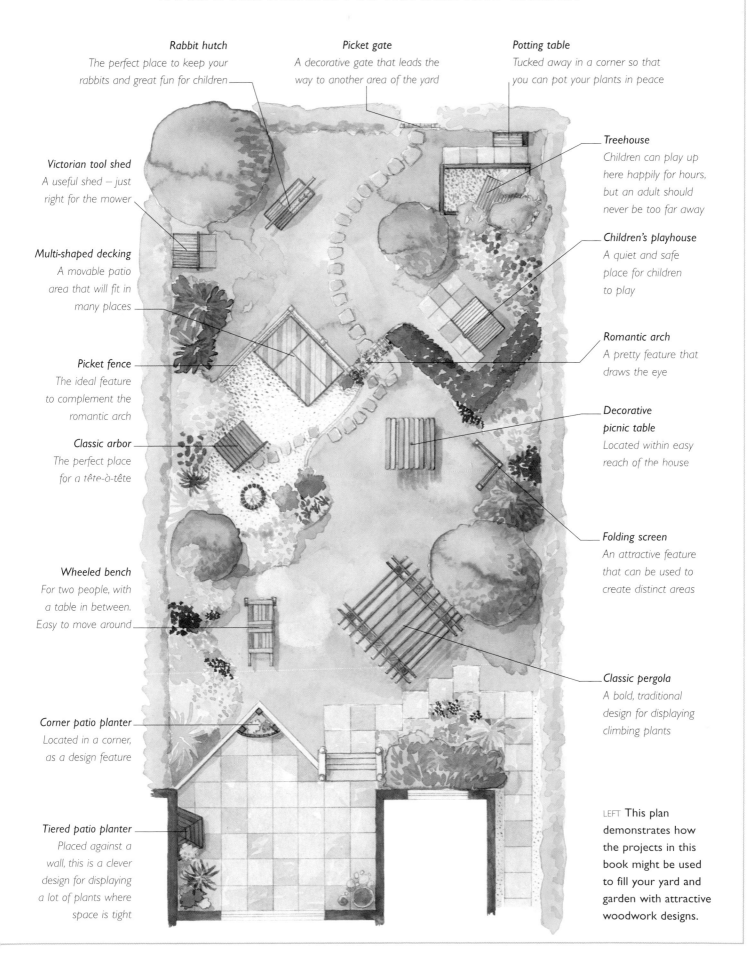

Rabbit hutch
The perfect place to keep your rabbits and great fun for children
Picket gate
A decorative gate that leads the way to another area of the yard
Potting table
Tucked away in a corner so that you can pot your plants in peace
Victorian tool shed
A useful shed – just right for the mower
Treehouse
Children can play up here happily for hours, but an adult should never be too far away
Multi-shaped decking
A movable patio area that will fit in many places
Children's playhouse
A quiet and safe place for children to play
Picket fence
The ideal feature to complement the romantic arch
Romantic arch
A pretty feature that draws the eye
Classic arbor
The perfect place for a tête-à-tête
Decorative picnic table
Located within easy reach of the house
Folding screen
An attractive feature that can be used to create distinct areas
Wheeled bench
For two people, with a table in between. Easy to move around
Classic pergola
A bold, traditional design for displaying climbing plants
Corner patio planter
Located in a corner, as a design feature
Tiered patio planter
Placed against a wall, this is a clever design for displaying a lot of plants where space is tight

LEFT This plan demonstrates how the projects in this book might be used to fill your yard and garden with attractive woodwork designs.

Tools

Always buy tools of the highest quality that you can afford. However, successful garden woodwork relies on controlling the wood while it is worked. To do this, you need a large space such as the lawn, two portable workbenches, and a sheet of plywood on which to set out the component parts.

TOOLS FOR MEASURING AND MARKING

Measuring rule

Carpenter's level

Square

Carpenter's pencil

Tape measure

Compass

Engineer's protractor

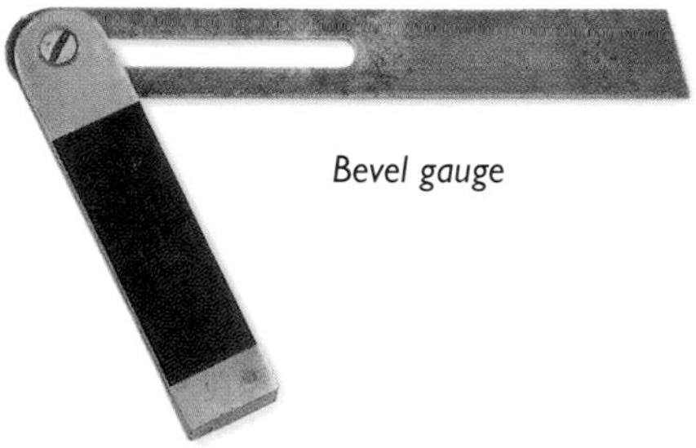

Bevel gauge

Measuring

You need two measuring tools: a wood or metal measuring rule for sizing and marking joints, and a flexible tape measure for setting out the site plan for large projects (such as the Victorian Tool Shed on page 108) and for measuring long lengths of wood. We use a 25-foot tape for all the projects. If you can afford to spend a little extra, it's a good idea to use a fiberglass tape for trailing about the garden, because it is more resilient to the wear and tear of working on wet grass and with damp wood. Always wipe your measuring tool after use and put it away clean and dry.

Marking out

The tools for this are: a square for laying out right angles, a bevel gauge for laying out approximate angles, an engineer's protractor for laying out precise angles, a compass for drawing circles, and several good-quality carpenter's pencils for drawing on the wood. The flat lead in a carpenter's pencil not only keeps its point longer, but the rectangular section of the lead resists breaking – a really good idea when working on rough-sawn wood. Before you put your tools away, wipe them over with thin oil in order to protect them against damp and corrosion. We use olive oil, but alternatively you could use very thin engine or bicycle oil. On no account use old engine oil.

Levelling

For a project such as a shed, where the ground must be level, you require three tools: a flexible tape for laying out the site, a spade for digging away the earth, and a carpenter's level for checking vertical and horizontal levels. If you are going to get involved in building a concrete slab, you will also need a shovel and a garden rake.

TOOLS FOR CUTTING WOOD

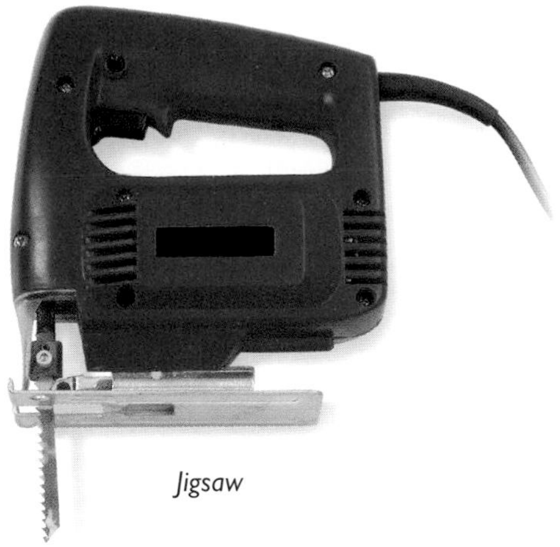

Jigsaw

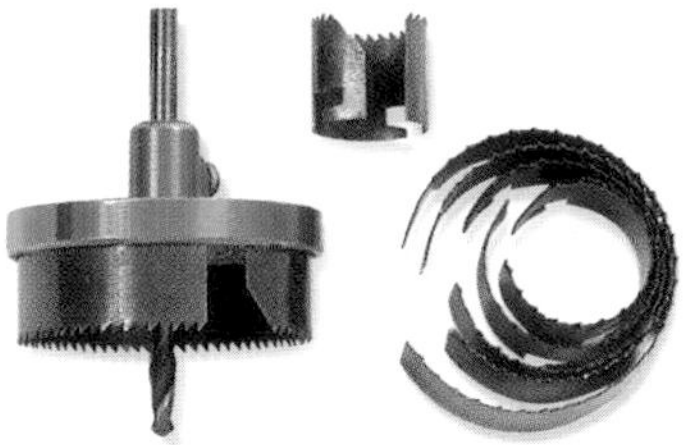

Hole saw

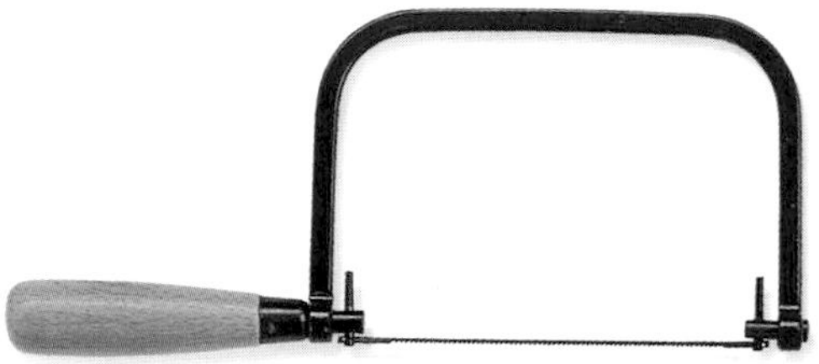

Coping saw

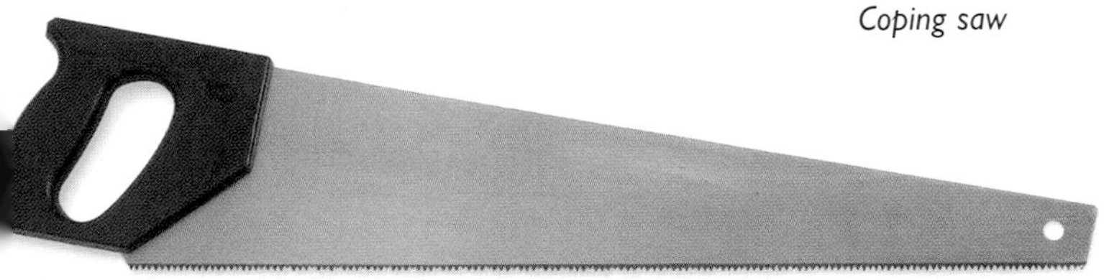

Crosscut saw

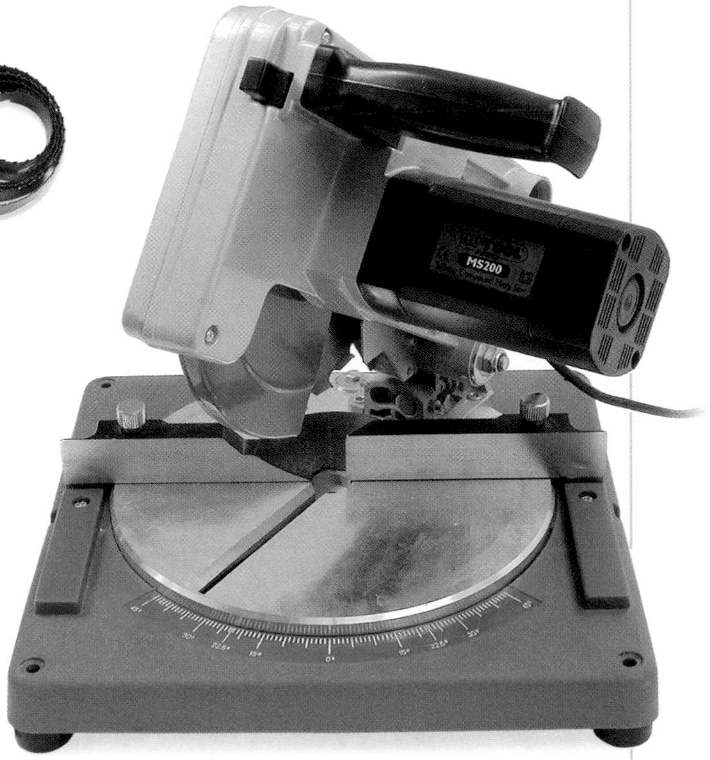

Compound miter saw

Sawing to size

Assuming that you purchase all your wood ready-sawn to a section size (sawn to the desired width and thickness), all you really need for the projects is a top-quality, hard-toothed, crosscut saw. Buy one that is described as "trade quality", and do not attempt to save money by opting for a bargain or secondhand saw. We purchased ours directly from the sawmill. Sawmill wood is generally green, wet, sappy, and sometimes dirty, so it is best to get two crosscut saws – use one for cutting wood to length, and keep the other for cutting joints. To help ensure that the saw blades last, remove sticky sap with mineral spirits at the end of a day's work, and wipe the blade with olive oil or thin machine oil.

CAUTION

The electric compound miter saw is potentially an extremely dangerous tool. Never leave it unattended. If you have children, pull out the plug and lock the blade into the "down" position when the saw is not in use.

Sawing angles

While you can certainly make all straight and angled cuts with the crosscut saw already described, you can make life much easier – especially when cutting repeat angles – by obtaining an electric compound miter saw. Not long ago, such saws were quite expensive, but now they are within reach of most people.

To use a compound miter saw, set it on a level surface, either on a workboard or clamped in the jaws of a portable workbench. Adjust the blade to the desired angle, position the workpiece against the backstop, and then switch on the power and lower the blade to make the cut. Compound miter saws are great tools for tasks such as cutting the tops of the pickets in the Picket Fence project (see page 42). When using a power tool such as this, always read the manufacturer's literature, follow all the safety rules, and work with a helper close at hand.

Sawing curves

The projects use three tools for cutting curves: a hand coping saw for small, tight curves in thin wood; an electric jigsaw for broad curves in thick wood; and an electric drill with a saw-toothed cutter (hole saw) for cutting large-diameter holes. We particularly enjoy using the jigsaw – it is an uncomplicated, very efficient, low-cost tool. To use it, you set the blade close to the start of the cut, with the bed of the tool resting flat on the wood, switch on the power, and then slowly advance the tool so that the cut runs slightly to the waste side of the drawn line. Remember not to snatch the tool from the workpiece while the blade is still moving. When you have made the cut, switch off the power, wait until the blade has come to a standstill, then lift the tool away. Always wear a dust-mask and a pair of safety goggles.

We used an electric drill with a saw-toothed cutter for cutting large-diameter holes in thick wood, but it wasn't an experience that we enjoyed. This tool combination does get the job done, but it is extremely noisy and juddery, and generates a lot of dust. If you feel nervous about using any of the power tools, it's a good idea to ask friends to help you.

TOOLS FOR MAKING JOINTS

Tenon saw

Axe

Chisel

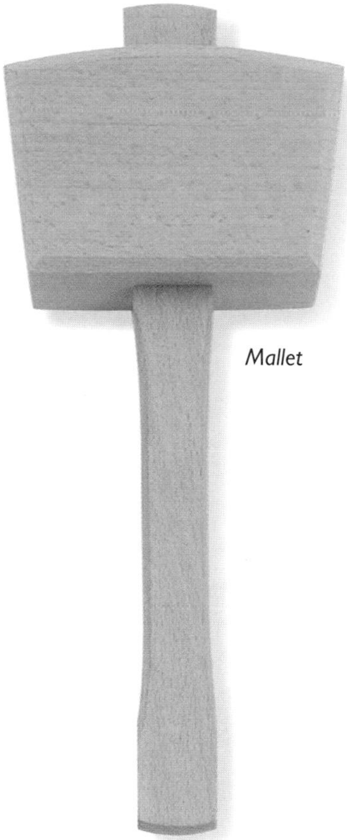

Mallet

Marking gauge

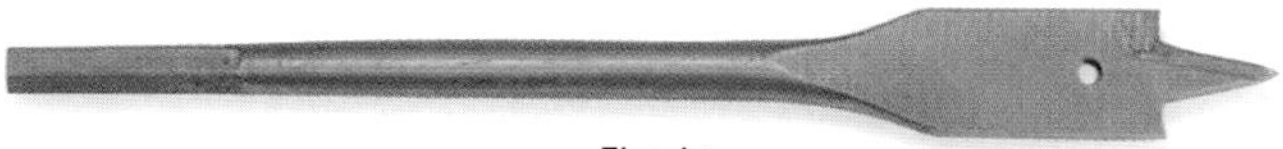

Flat bit

Marking out and cutting joints

When working outside cutting swift, basic joints in rough-sawn wood, you need these basic tools: a marking gauge, tenon saw, flat drill bit, chisels, mallet, and axe.

A large, single-spike marking gauge is used for laying out the joints on the wood, a tenon saw for removing the bulk of the waste, and a flat drill bit for clearing the mortises. When purchasing the marking gauge, get a good, basic model, which will stand up to wear and tear in the garden.

Once you have rough-cut the joint with the saw and drill, you need a selection of bevel-edged chisels for shaving the wood down to the mark. Again, choose good-quality solid chisels. Avoid those with cheap wooden handles that are likely to split, and select tools with solid plastic handles molded to the shank.

CAUTION

Although chisels and axes are potentially dangerous tools, you can cut the risks to almost zero by always holding the tool with a firm grip, cutting away from your body, and applying full concentration to the job.

For large basic joints we also use a mallet and a small axe. The axe is a particularly useful tool. Apart from all manner of splitting and shaving tasks, such as cutting dowels for pegging joints and trimming the bottoms of posts, the axe can also be used in much the same way as a wide-bladed chisel. A tenon is sawn to the waste side of the shoulder-line, and then the blade of the axe is set on the end-grain mark and driven home with a blow from the mallet. Choose a good, heavy-duty axe, with a thin blade that has a bevel on both sides. Avoid the thick-bladed, stainless-steel axes sold for splitting kindling, opting instead for a hand-forged black iron axe. Pay careful attention to safety considerations when using an axe. Always make sure that your body (and anyone else's) is well clear of the path of swing. Do not use your free hand to hold the wood in position.

TOOLS FOR SCREWING AND NAILING

Electric drill

Drill bit for wood and metal

Phillips screwdriver

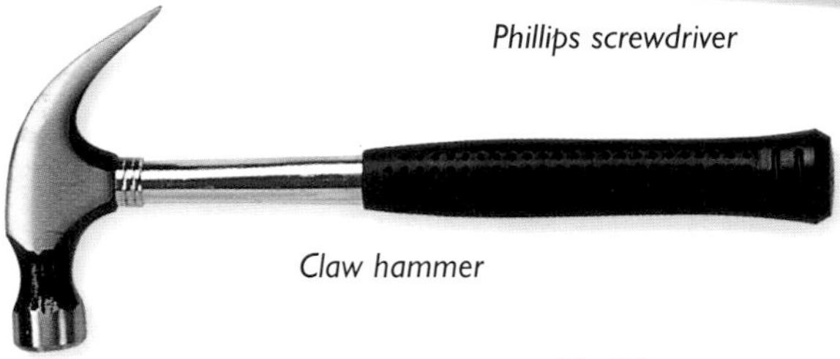
Claw hammer

Cordless drill/driver

Screwing

Before a screw is driven into wood, it is best to drill a pilot hole with a twist drill bit. (In most cases, the holes do not need to be countersunk with a pilot-countersink bit: the pine used for the projects is so soft that the screwhead will cut its own countersink.) Then use a variable-speed cordless drill fitted with a Phillips screwdriver bit for driving in the screws. Set the torque on the drill to suit the thickness and hardness of the wood, and drive the screw home until the torque slips the clutch.

Nailing

The projects in this book use slender nails for fastening bevel-edged boards to frames, and flat-headed nails for roofing felt. To fasten the felt, you simply pound the nails home with a claw hammer. With bevel-edged boards, however, you need to drill pilot holes for the nails so that you do not split the fragile grain. Small staples are used for fastening rabbit wire. Make sure that all nails and staples are galvanized. Avoid nails and staples described as "black iron", because they bend and stain the wood.

OTHER ESSENTIAL TOOLS

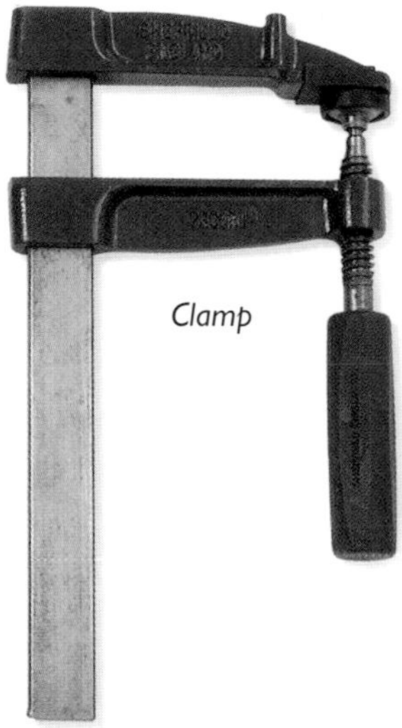
Clamp

Metal snips

Adjustable wrench

Sledgehammer

Electric sander

Utility knife

Paintbrush

Fastening and finishing

Some projects require a sledgehammer, but don't be tempted to buy the biggest one you can find, because a medium-weight one is more than adequate. When using the sledgehammer, make sure that your helper is standing on the opposite side of the post to be driven home, and that his or her hands are out of harm's way.

Once the woodwork is finished, the project is completed by sanding, painting, and preserving. You will need an electric sander for removing large splinters and for sculpting surfaces, a clamp for holding parts together, and a brush for applying paint or preservative. Depending upon the project, you might also need an adjustable wrench for tightening up nuts, a pair of metal snips for cutting wire mesh, and a utility knife for cutting roofing felt.

If you really need to cut costs on a project, and do not want to go to the expense of buying the tools we have described, see if you can borrow various items from friends and neighbors. You may also want to consider renting power tools. If you are going to use an unfamiliar tool, it is always a good idea to have a trial run on some scrap wood, just to make sure that you understand how the tool is best handled.

Materials

We obtained all the rough-sawn softwood for the projects from a local sawmill using three types of wood: wood that had been left in its natural state, wood that had been brush-treated to give it a brown finish, and wood described as "short ends and offcut waste".

USEFUL LUMBER SECTIONS

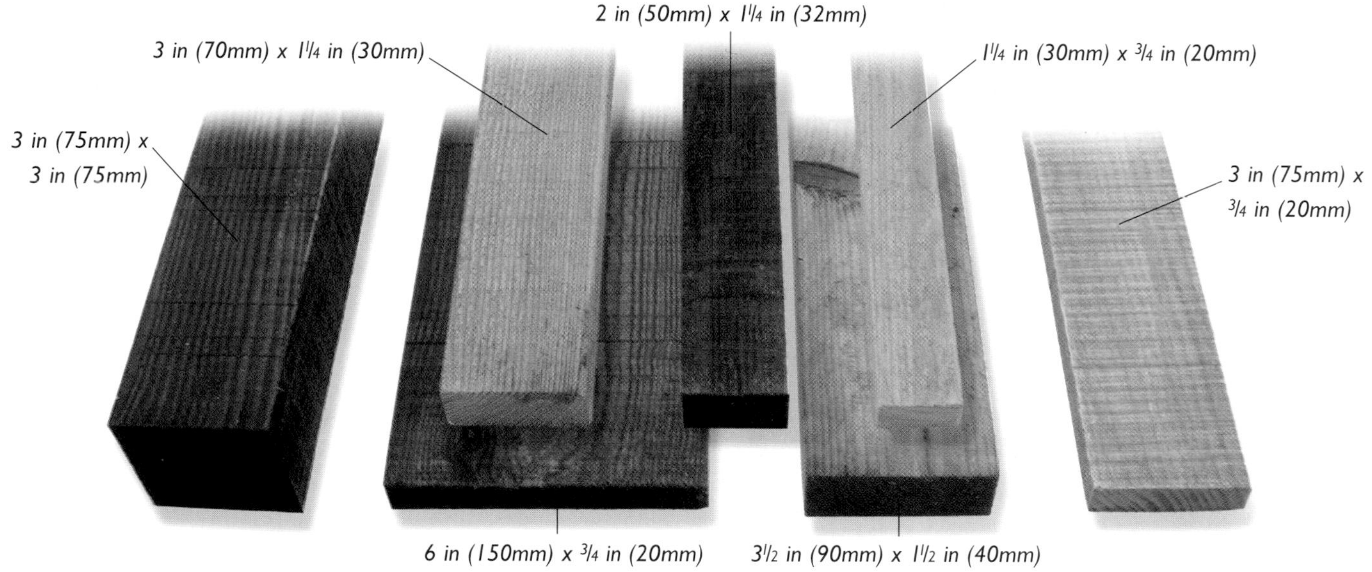
2 in (50mm) x 1¼ in (32mm)
3 in (70mm) x 1¼ in (30mm)
1¼ in (30mm) x ¾ in (20mm)
3 in (75mm) x
3 in (75mm)
3 in (75mm) x
¾ in (20mm)
6 in (150mm) x ¾ in (20mm)
3½ in (90mm) x 1½ in (40mm)

Posts, planks, and sticks

The sawmill supplied us with rough-sawn softwood intended for garden items such as fences, gates, sheds, and screens. We used sections ranging from roofing battens about 1¼ inches (30 mm) wide and ¾ inch (20 mm) thick, through to flat battens 3 inches (75 mm) wide and ¾ inch (20 mm) thick (sold to be used for pickets). We purchased posts 3 inches (75 mm) and 4 inches (100 mm) square, planks up to 6 inches (150 mm) wide described as "gravel boards", and all manner of smaller sections.

When you are buying wood, make allowances for inaccuracies in the measurements. For example, a plank described as being ¾ inch (20 mm) thick might actually measure anything from ⅝ inch (18 mm) through to ⅞ inch (23 mm). When you get the wood home, leave it propped up against a wall or fence to dry out for a couple of days, until it feels dry to the touch.

Choosing the right length and section

Most sawmills sell wood in lengths that are an even number of feet long. You will need to work out the most economical length for your chosen project. Most wood will be sold as rectangular sections, boards, planks, and posts. The projects assume that you won't need to cut the wood to a different section size. Be ready to modify the projects to suit the sections sold by your local sawmill. If you are not confident in your ability to adjust the requirements, take your plans to the sawmill and ask for advice.

BUYING TIPS

- Be flexible. If, for example, a project specifies a section 2 in (50 mm) square, but you are only able to get something 2 in (50 mm) wide and 1 in (25 mm) thick, you can screw two sections together.
- Always choose local softwood – it is cheaper and more forest-friendly.
- There are lots of bargains to be had. Go prepared with heavy boots and gloves, and be ready to search through piles of wood that are variously described as trimmings, short ends, offcuts, or waney-edged.
- Don't be talked into using imported hardwood or wood that has been overly planed or prepared.
- Remember that while pressure-treated woods are long-lasting, they are also highly toxic (to the extent that your skin might blister on contact). A good alternative is to buy sawn wood and then treat it with a suitable preservative or paint.
- If you are a woman, be prepared for the fact that most sawmills are run by men and may have a mainly male clientele. Try not to feel intimidated.
- We suggest that you do not take children to the sawmill. But do encourage them to help make the projects, because the planning and building are a good educational experience.

SIDING

Types of siding

While we decided to use bevel siding, some suppliers offer other options. There is ship-lap siding, which looks a bit like tongue-and-groove boarding, and log siding, which looks very much like half-logs. In our opinion, the bevel siding is the least expensive, the easiest to work and fit, and the most attractive. The bevel is also more traditional, and the layering gives a stronger structure.

Nailing bevel siding

We always use a jig made from two offcuts screwed together, which is butted against the lower edge of a board to ensure that it overlaps the next one by 1½ inches (35 mm). To avoid splitting the wood, the boards must be drilled prior to fastening, with the holes set so that the nail or screw misses the board that you are just about to lap.

Before fastening the siding, it is a good idea to have a trial dry run just to make sure that you have enough wood. Arrange each piece so that any knots or splits are clear of the nailing points. When you are driving the nails home, be careful that you do not force the wood to bend into a concave profile, so that it splits.

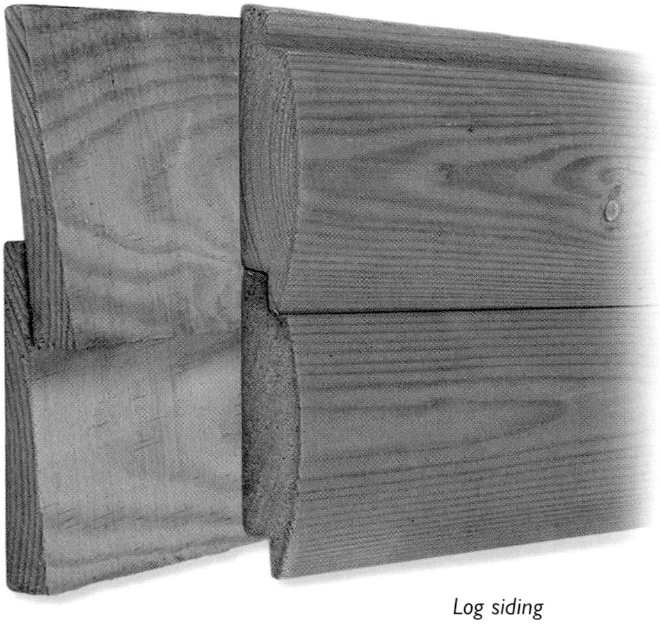

Log siding

Bevel siding

OTHER USEFUL SECTIONS AND READY-MADE ITEMS

Triangular section

Decking

Dowel

Ball

Trellis screen

Triangular section and decking

Triangular sections are designed to be used for fence rails. They run horizontally from post to post at the back of the fence and are used to support the vertical boards. The widest face of the section is fixed in contact with the fence. If a local sawmill is unable to saw these for you, substitute rectangular section stock.

Decking is available in several thicknesses and lengths. Avoid buying pressure-treated wood because of its cost and the toxic nature of the preservative, but decking is an exception. Do not let children play on newly-treated timber, to prevent skin coming into contact with the wood. However, decking is subjected to the full blast of the weather, which soon dispenses with the hazard.

Dowels and balls

Dowelling is bought according to requirements. Finial balls come in all shapes and sizes. Those with a screw attached just need a pilot hole in the post so the ball can be screwed in place. Some balls require a double-ended screw (half the screw goes into the post and the other end into the ball).

Trellis screens

It is possible to make trellis screens from thin lathes, but they are so tricky to make that it is best to purchase them ready-made. Buy your screens before you buy anything else, and then modify all the other measurements to suit.

FASTENERS AND FITTINGS

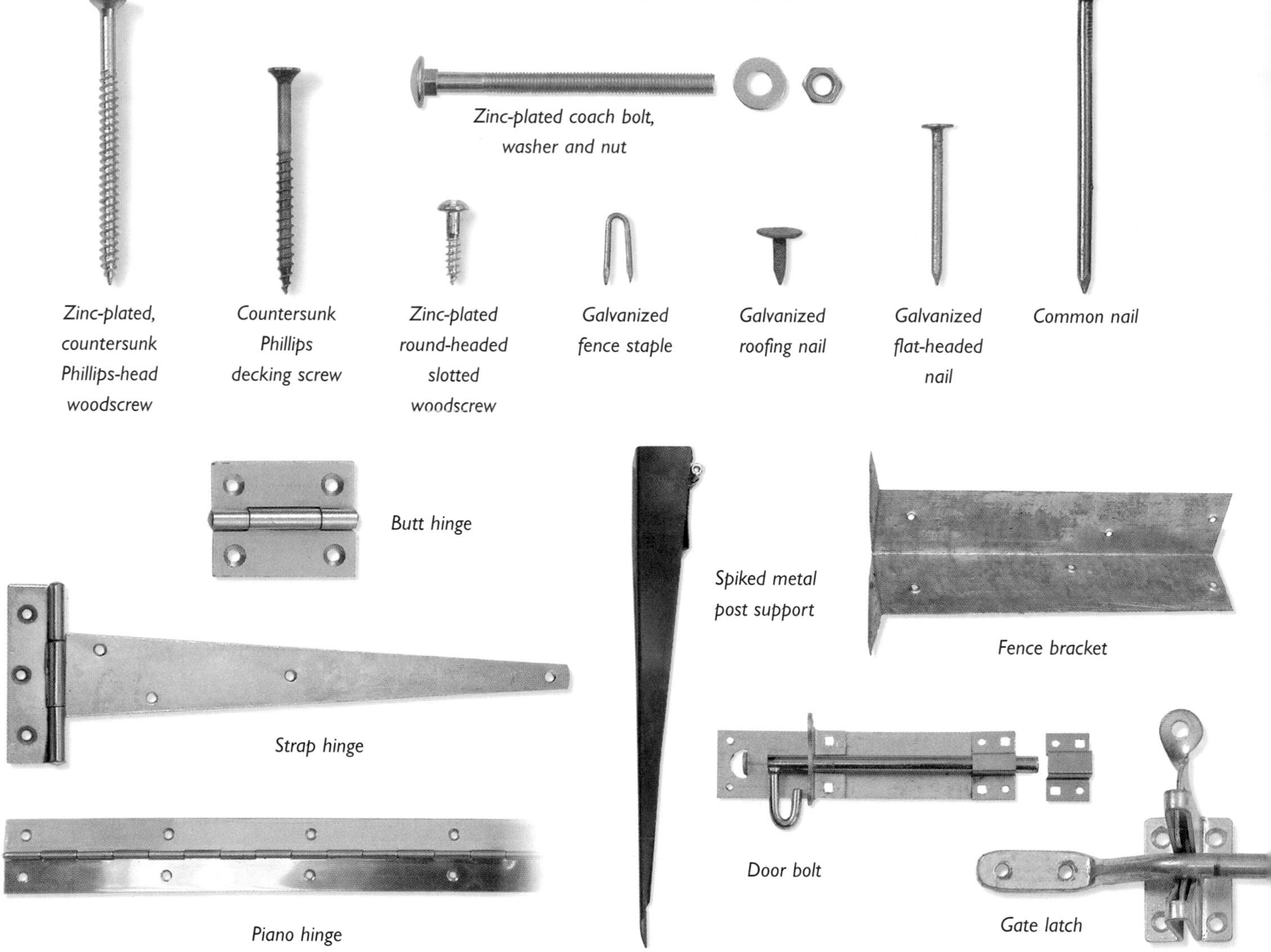
Zinc-plated coach bolt, washer and nut
Zinc-plated, countersunk Phillips-head woodscrew
Countersunk Phillips decking screw
Zinc-plated round-headed slotted woodscrew
Galvanized fence staple
Galvanized roofing nail
Galvanized flat-headed nail
Common nail
Butt hinge
Strap hinge
Piano hinge
Spiked metal post support
Fence bracket
Door bolt
Gate latch

Screws, bolts, nails, and staples

We use best-quality, exterior-grade, galvanized, or zinc-plated Phillips screws throughout – because they stay bright and can easily be driven home with a variable-speed, cordless electric drill fitted with a screwdriver bit. Buy boxes of 100 or 200 screws at a time: it is cheaper, and you won't run short of screws.

Carriage bolts, with washers and nuts to fit, are used for projects such as the Picket Gate (see page 46). A hole to fit the shank is drilled, the bolt is tapped home until the square section just under the head bites into the hole, and then it is tightened with a washer and nut.

We buy nails and staples by weight because it is more cost-effective. Always specify that they should be galvanized, or at least plated, so you won't have to worry about rust staining the wood.

Hinges, gate bolts, and latches

We use butt door hinges for the Folding Screen (see page 38) and the Rabbit Hutch (see page 94), piano hinges for the Children's Playhouse (see page 120), T-strap hinges for the Victorian Tool Shed (see page 108), and heavy-duty reversible hinges for the Picket Gate (see page 46). The advantage of using piano hinges on a door that children will play with is that the continuous body of the hinge prevents the child from trapping his or her fingers between the door and doorpost. The heavy-duty reversible hinges for the gate are designed to be fastened with both screws and carriage bolts, making them even more sturdy.

We also use a latch for the gate and a sliding gate bolt for the tool-shed door. Don't try to cut costs by using cheap hardware. If you have gone to a lot of trouble to build an item, it is a false economy to skimp on the fasteners and fittings: always specify that they are galvanized (or at least plated), and always buy the items complete with galvanized bolts and screws to fit.

Post and fence hardware

We use spiked metal post supports for fenceposts and gateposts, because they are very efficient and easy to use. The spike is put in position, an offcut is placed on top of the spike, and it is pounded home with a sledgehammer. The post is then slid into the containment and held by clamping nuts. The metal brackets for post rails are also easy to use. One half is screwed to the triangular-section rail and the other to the post itself. Rectangular section brackets are available as well as those for triangular section.

OTHER MATERIALS

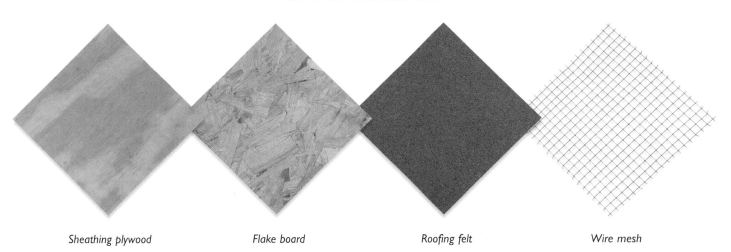

Sheathing plywood

Flake board

Roofing felt

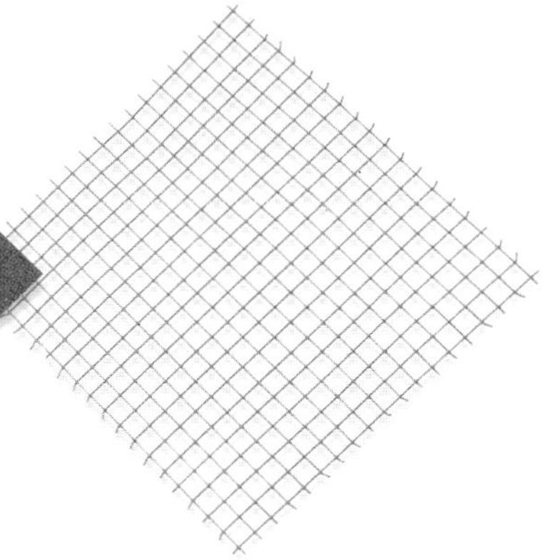

Wire mesh

Plywood, stirling board, and felt

To make a board and felt roof, first cover the roof with a sheet of exterior-grade sheathing plywood. Nail the first sheet of felt in place on the plywood, paint felt adhesive over the nails, stick the second sheet of felt in place, and so on. The idea is that on the top of the roof at least, the nailed edge of one piece of felt is always covered by the glued edge of the neighboring piece. It is rather like a tiled roof, where the nailed head end of one tile is covered and protected by the tail end of the neighboring tile.

Wire mesh and window plastic

We used welded galvanized wire "grid" mesh for the Rabbit Hutch (see page 94) rather than woven fence wire, because it keeps its shape and is easier to cut and fit. It is important to buy mesh that is specifically described as being suitable for rabbit cages.

For safety reasons, the window of the Children's Playhouse (see page 120) is glazed with polycarbonate sheet rather than glass. To cut the sheet, score the line of cut with a utility knife – on both sides – and then fold it so that it breaks on the line.

PAINTS, STAINS, AND PRESERVATIVES

Red stain/preservative on pine

Mauve paint/preservative on pine

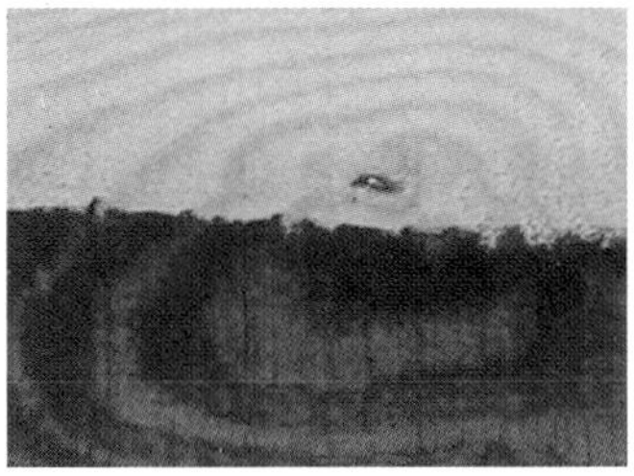

Blue stain/preservative on pine

Creosote on pine

Pressure-treated wood

Pressure-treated wood undoubtedly gives the best protection, but it is both expensive and highly toxic. It is fine for projects such as the Victorian Tool Shed (see page 108) and the Multi-shaped Decking (see page 52), but we wouldn't use it for "close-contact" projects such as the Decorative Picnic Table (see page 56), Rabbit Hutch (see page 94), or Children's Playhouse (see page 120). The subject is open to debate, but we would not like a child to sleep in a playhouse made from pressure-treated wood.

Exterior paints and stains

We favor using exterior-grade water-based paint, because the colors can be blended, and the paint can be diluted to give a thin wash or stain. We usually color the wood with a thin wash, and then protect the whole thing with a coat of clear preservative. Always read the labels on the cans and then you will be able to make a value judgement about the best treatment for your project.

CAUTION

Always wear gloves when you are handling preservatives and paint. Read the labels carefully. If you are worried, get specific advice.

Preservatives

A variety of wood preservatives have replaced old-fashioned creosote for all but utility poles. These preservatives are available with or without wood stain. Use them with caution, and only where skin contact with the treated wood will be minimal. For applications where contact cannot be avoided, use a naturally rot-resistant wood like red cedar.

Working with wood

Immersing yourself in creative woodwork outdoors is an exciting and therapeutic activity. A pile of sawn sections can be transformed into attractive and useful items, such as a picnic table or tool shed, in the space of a weekend. If you can use a saw and drive in a screw, you are capable of making all the projects in this book.

STRAIGHT CUTS

ABOVE Use a square for marking 90° cuts. Hold the wooden handle against the edge of the piece of wood and draw a pencil line.

To make a straight cut (at right angles to the face or edge of the wood), take a square and pencil and mark the wood. Let's say you want to cut a 3-foot (600 mm) length off a 6-inch-wide (150 mm) plank. Hold the handle (or "stock") of the square against the workpiece, and run a pencil line against the edge of the steel blade. Repeat on all faces and edges of the plank, so the line encircles the wood. Clamp the workpiece in a workbench, take a crosscut saw and place the teeth to the waste side of the drawn line. Perform a few short, strokes, and then use the full length of the saw to make the cut. At the end of the cut, use your free hand to support the waste, making lighter strokes until the wood is sawn through.

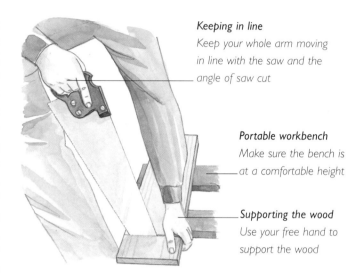

Keeping in line
Keep your whole arm moving in line with the saw and the angle of saw cut
Portable workbench
Make sure the bench is at a comfortable height
Supporting the wood
Use your free hand to support the wood

ABOVE After marking the length of a piece of wood, use a crosscut saw (for cutting across the grain) to cut it to length. Support the wood on a workbench and saw to the waste side of the pencil line.

ANGLED CUTS

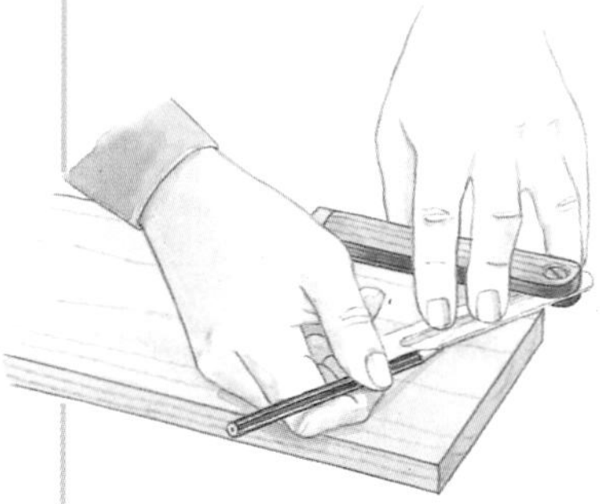

ABOVE Use a bevel gauge for drawing angled lines. Set the gauge to the required angle, and use in the same way as a square (shown above).

To make an angled cut (a straight cut that runs at an angle to the edge of the wood), you can use a crosscut saw or an electric compound miter saw. For example, imagine that you want to cut an angle across a picket. If you are going to use the hand saw, take a bevel gauge, set the angle to suit your needs, hold the handle up against the edge of the wood and draw a line against the steel blade. Clamp the workpiece in the workbench and use the crosscut saw to make the cut as already described. To use the compound miter saw, first set the blade of the saw to the desired angle and lock it into position. Hold the workpiece against the fence, repeatedly lower the blade and nudge the wood until the blade is just to the waste side of the drawn line. Raise the blade, switch on the power, lower the blade and make the cut.

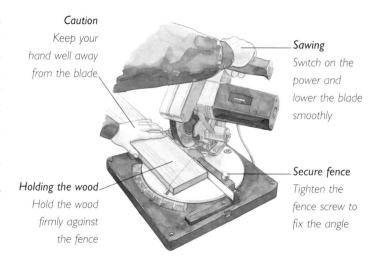

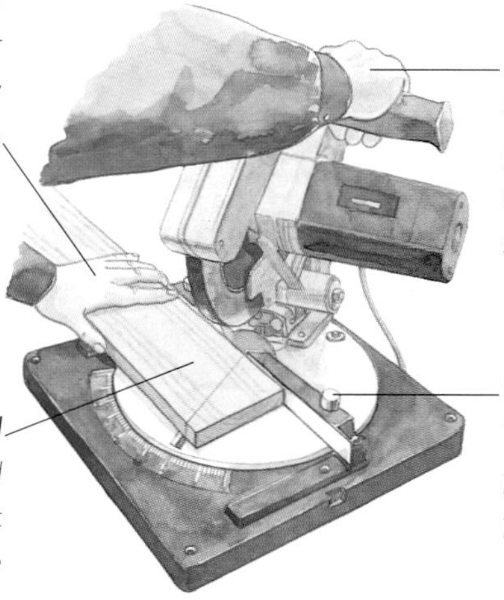
Caution
Keep your hand well away from the blade
Sawing
Switch on the power and lower the blade smoothly
Holding the wood
Hold the wood firmly against the fence
Secure fence
Tighten the fence screw to fix the angle

ABOVE After marking a straight or angled line, use the compound miter saw to cut the wood quickly and accurately. The blade can be tilted as well as rotated, so you can also cut compound angles (for example a cut that is 30° across a plank and 20° through it). The saw is especially useful for cutting lots of wood to the same size.

CUTTING CURVED SHAPES

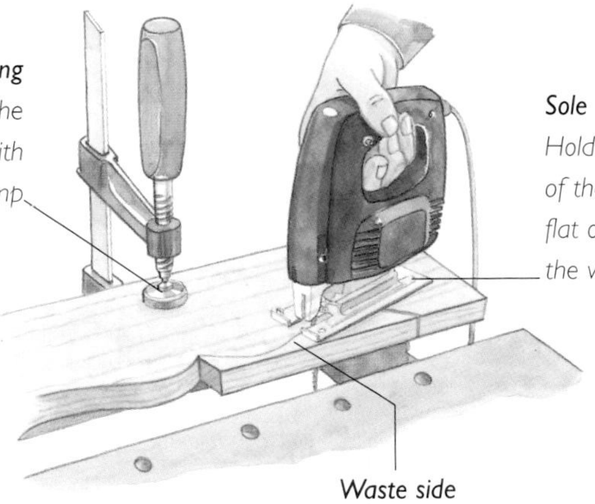
Clamping
Secure the wood with a clamp
Sole
Hold the sole of the saw flat on the wood
Waste side
Make sure that you saw to the waste side of the line

ABOVE The jigsaw is designed for cutting curves in wood. The narrow blade enables the saw to be rotated to follow tight curves in decorative designs. The sole can be locked in a tilted position to produce an angled, curved cut. Always rotate the saw in the direction of a curve rather than forcing the blade sideways.

We use two procedures to draw curved shapes. For shapes that are made of circles and part-circles, we simply use a compass. For symmetrical cyma curves (the ones that look a little like stylized lips) we draw half of the shape freehand, cut it out, and use this as a template to draw the other half. This way of working ensures that the shape is perfectly symmetrical and also means that you can create your own designs and shapes to fit your project.

To cut curves, you can use two types of saw – either a coping saw for cutting small, tight curves on or near the edge of thin wood, or a power jigsaw for broad curves in thick wood. Tighten up the blade until it "pings" when plucked. Secure the workpiece in the jaws of a portable workbench, position the blade to the waste side of the drawn line, and work with a steady stroke to make the cut.

To use the power jigsaw, first bridge the workpiece across a couple of workbenches. Set the sole of the saw on the workpiece (so that the blade is just clear of the wood), switch on the power and slowly advance the tool so that the line of cut runs slightly to the waste side of the drawn line. Hold the tool with a firm grip, in order to prevent juddering and vibrating.

CUTTING MORTISE AND TENON JOINTS

Mortise and tenon joints are made up from two mating halves: the mortise (or hole) and the tenon that fits into the hole. The ideal is a joint that is a tight push-fit.

Procedure to cut a mortise

1 Use a pencil, ruler, square and marking gauge to carefully lay out the lines that make up the mortise.

2 Select a drill bit size that fits within the width of the mortise, and bore out one or more holes to remove the bulk of the waste. Hold the drill upright so that the drilled holes are at right angles to the face of the wood. There are various types of mortise. If it is a through mortise (one that goes right through the thickness of the wood), drill the holes completely through. If it is a blind or stopped mortise (the hole doesn't go through the wood), put a piece of masking tape around the drill bit to mark the depth you want to drill to, and stop when the hole reaches that depth.

3 Use a chisel to pare back the sides of the hole to the drawn lines. Work with a series of skimming cuts.

Procedure to cut a tenon

1 Use a square, rule, pencil, and gauge to draw a tenon that is a tight push-fit for the mortise.

2 Secure the workpiece in the portable workbench at an angle of about 45°. Use the saw to cut down to the shoulder-line. Repeat this procedure for both cuts on both sides of the joint.

3 Set the workpiece flat on the bench and saw down the waste side of the shoulder-line, so that the piece of waste falls away. Do this on both sides of the tenon.

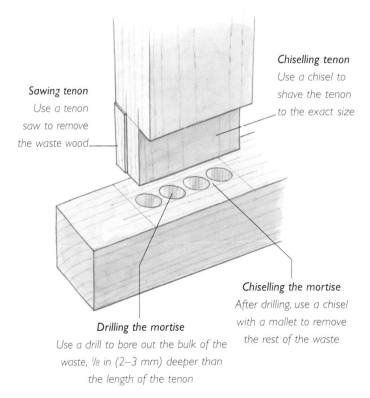

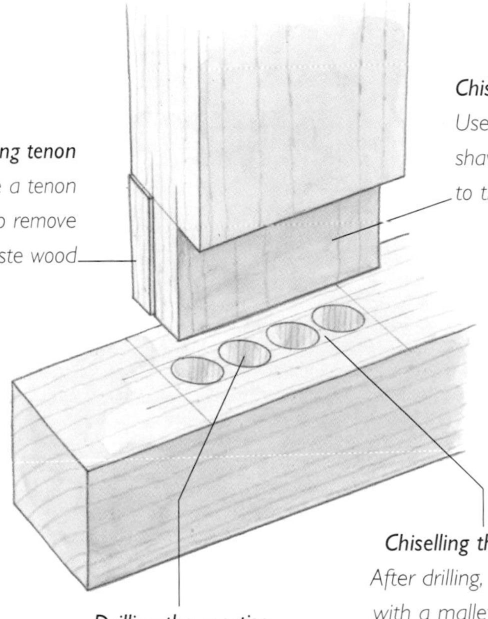
Sawing tenon
Use a tenon saw to remove the waste wood
Chiselling tenon
Use a chisel to shave the tenon to the exact size
Chiselling the mortise
After drilling, use a chisel with a mallet to remove the rest of the waste
Drilling the mortise
Use a drill to bore out the bulk of the waste, 1/8 in (2–3 mm) deeper than the length of the tenon

ABOVE The mortise and tenon is a traditional joint for joining two pieces of wood, usually at right angles as shown here. Cut the mortise first with a drill bit and chisel(s), and then cut the tenon with a tenon saw. Mortise and tenon joints are hard work to cut by hand but are often stronger, cheaper and more attractive than fixing with screws or special hardware.

Fences and gates

In the Koran it says, "A fence without a gate is a prison, while a fence with a gate is a paradise". This section shows you how to create your own "paradise" by constructing a fence with an integral gate. Strength and stability are watchwords for both items: they must be able to stand up to both the weather and general wear and tear. Gates must be functional and appropriate for their situation and should open and close without undue hindrance.

SETTING POSTS

Traditionally, wooden fenceposts and gateposts had half their length set below ground, with the below-ground section first charred or tarred, and then supported with a mix of well-tamped clay and rubble. However, the posts in our projects are best supported with concrete, or with a metal post support spike. When digging holes or pounding in metal spikes, bear in mind that there may be underground power cables, water and drainage pipes lurking in the earth, so dig cautiously.

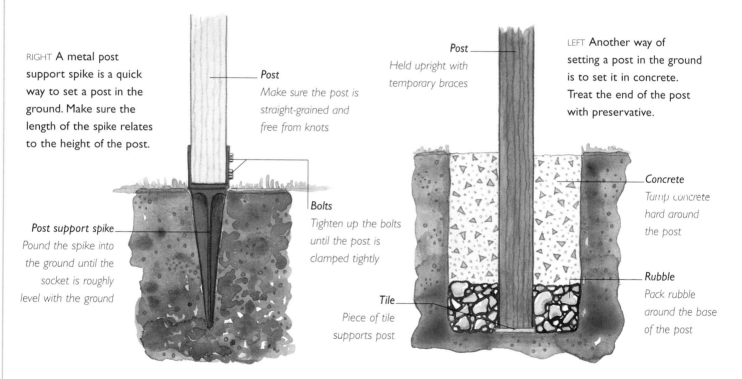

RIGHT A metal post support spike is a quick way to set a post in the ground. Make sure the length of the spike relates to the height of the post.

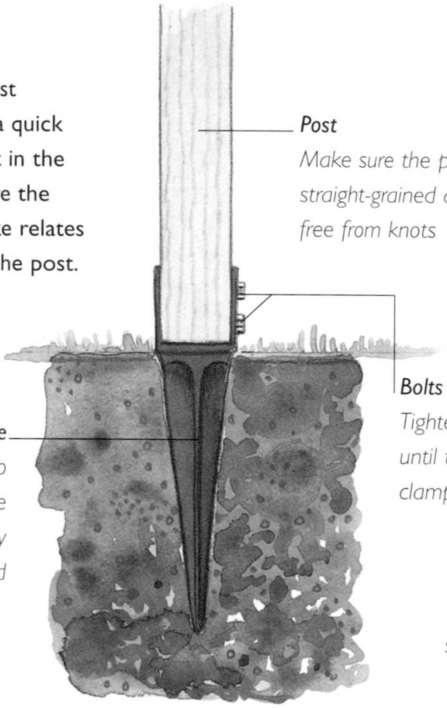
Post
Make sure the post is straight-grained and free from knots
Bolts
Tighten up the bolts until the post is clamped tightly
Post support spike
Pound the spike into the ground until the socket is roughly level with the ground

LEFT Another way of setting a post in the ground is to set it in concrete. Treat the end of the post with preservative.

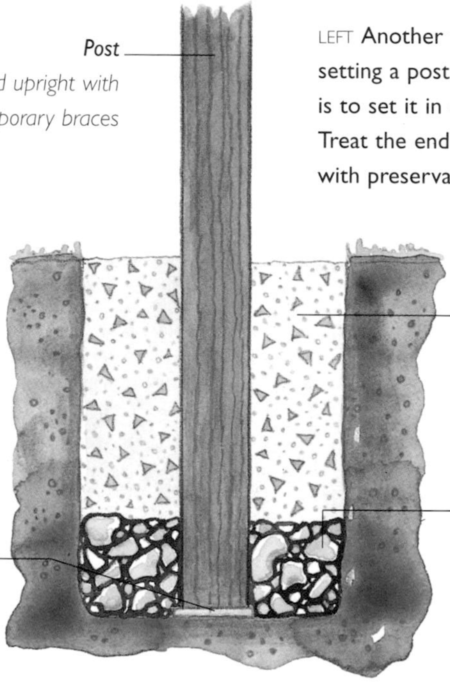
Post
Held upright with temporary braces
Concrete
Tamp concrete hard around the post
Rubble
Pack rubble around the base of the post
Tile
Piece of tile supports post

Procedure for setting a post support spike

1 Buy a metal post support spike to suit the length and square section of your post. The taller the post, the longer the length of spike required. Make sure that the spike has a strong bolt-clamp fitting, and that the metal is well protected by being galvanized or painted.

2 Set the support spike on the mark, slide an offcut from your post into the socket at the top of the spike, and give it a little tap with a sledgehammer to insert it just into the ground.

3 Adjust the spike so that it is upright, and pound it down into the ground with the sledgehammer. Continue until the bottom of the socketed top is positioned just above ground level.

4 Finally, set the post in the socket, make adjustments until it is vertical, and tighten the bolts with a wrench.

Procedure for setting a post with concrete

1 Use a spade to dig a hole about 16 inches (400 mm) deep and 12 inches (300 mm) square. Remove the waste earth from the site.

2 Put a piece of broken tile into the bottom of the hole, position the post on the tile, and tamp a small amount of rubble around the bottom 4 inches (100 mm) of the post.

3 Prop the post upright with three temporary braces (nail the braces near the top of the post and angle them down to make a tripod) and make adjustments until the post is perfectly vertical. Check with a level.

4 Make a concrete mix of 1 part Portland cement, 2 parts sharp sand, and 3 parts coarse aggregate (gravel). Tamp it into the hole.

5 Remove the temporary battens after four days. The concrete will not achieve its full strength until about three weeks later.

TYPES OF FENCE

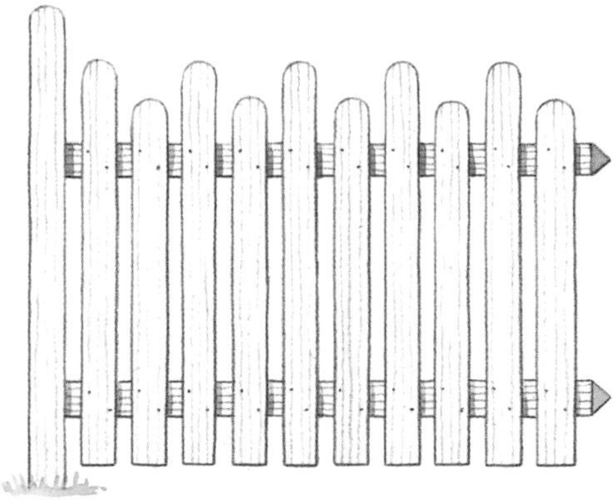

ABOVE A traditional picket fence with rounded ends. The gap between the pickets should be no greater than the width of a picket.

ABOVE A closeboard fence – bevel-edged boards framed by the posts, capping rail and bottom board.

ABOVE A diamond trellis (overlapping lathes contained within a batten frame) set between capped posts.

There are various things to take into consideration when planning a fence. Do you need to keep children or livestock in, or wildlife out? Would you like the fence to look attractive and welcoming? Do you want a strong fence that discourages invaders, or a tall fence that prevents prying eyes?

In this book we show you how to make a traditional picket fence (see page 42). The word "picket" comes from the French word *piquer*, meaning "to prick". A picket fence has now come to mean a fence made up from a number of pointed slats; however the word once meant the pointed part of a palisade or wicket. From one country to another, the terms picket, wicket, and palisade are more or less interchangeable and loosely used to describe many other types of wooden fence. There are closeboard fences made up from overlapping bevel-edged boards, trellis fences made from a woven web of thin sections, and woven willow fences. Ranch-style fences are made from large-section split wood, and the rails are dominant; chestnut fences are made from split sticks and the posts are dominant.

TYPES OF GATE

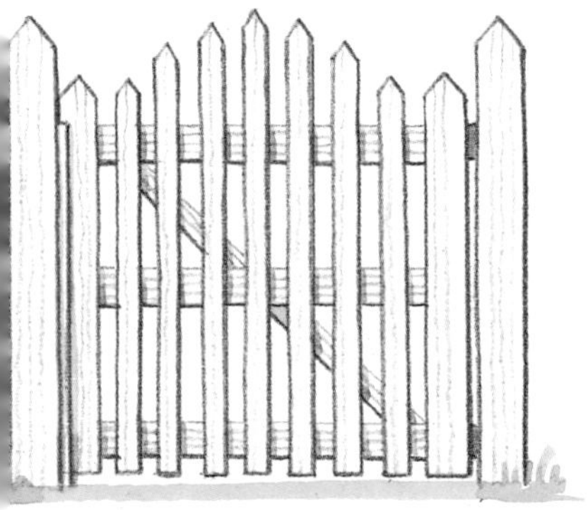

ABOVE A traditional picket gate in an arched pattern, held together with three horizontal rails and a diagonal brace.

ABOVE A gate made from riven wood (split, not sawn) is a good choice for an informal rustic garden. The split wood has a rough texture and varies in width and thickness, giving the gate an unmistakable hand-crafted appearance.

ABOVE Closeboard gates such as this are long-lasting and will prevent pets wandering in and out of your garden.

Gates have much the same history and design variations as fences, but they are more complex structures in that they have additional members such as stiles, braces, and posts. Within the basic gate, the vertical side members are called stiles, the horizontal members are called rails, and the diagonal member is called a brace (and of course the gate frame is covered with additional vertical or horizontal members).

The gate is set between two posts – hinged to one and latched to another. Though designs vary, the one constant is that the brace always runs uphill from the hinge side of the gate to the latch side. If the brace were to be set the other way around, the gate would sag down from the hinge side. A main factor in the strength of a gate is its hinges, and the hinge stile and the hinge post are often built from large-section wood.

Benches, chairs, and decking

Every yard needs benches and seats scattered around so that you can enjoy the changing seasons throughout the year. If the designs include decorative touches, these items are elevated from objects of practicality to aesthetically-pleasing outdoor features. If your yard is in need of small, firm areas for standing, wooden decking is a good-looking solution, which can create a softer effect than stone or concrete.

SEATING CONSIDERATIONS

Wooden seats must be attractive and well built, and should be positioned to take advantage of sun or shade as required. They can be made to a variety of designs to suit a selection of purposes. We have chosen three different options: a Decorative Picnic Table (see page 56), a Wheeled Bench (see page 68) and a small bench seat set within a Classic Arbor (see page 62). The picnic table can be used for family meals or entertaining. The wheeled bench can be moved with ease and has an integral table, which is a useful place to put a drink. The arbor provides a sheltered spot to sit.

TYPES OF SEATING

ABOVE A straightforward picnic table with the added feature of flip-up seats, which allows them to remain dry during a shower of rain.

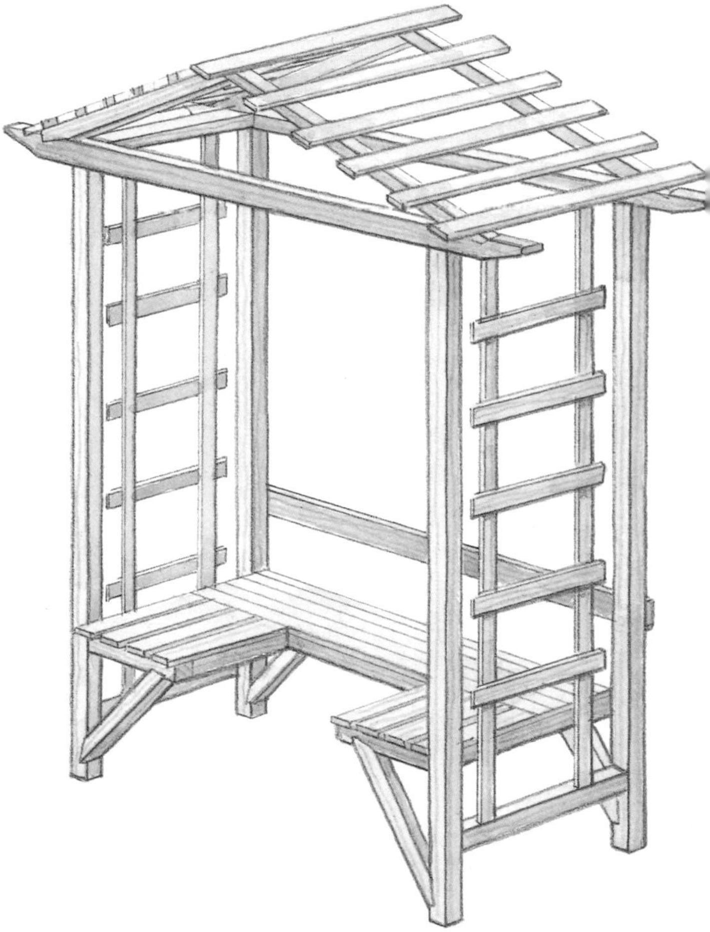

ABOVE Bench seating and trellis combine to form a cozy arbor (see also page 27). Climbing plants can be grown up it to provide shade in the hot weather.

TYPES OF CHAIRS

ABOVE A traditional painted pine chair with slatted seat and strong mortise and tenon joints.

ABOVE An oriental-style teak chair, ideal for outdoor dining and general use. Heavyweight and long-lasting.

ABOVE A folding chair for occasional use, which can be brought in from the garden during wet weather.

DECKING

Wooden decking is a great idea for the garden – perfect when you want a level patio without going to all the time, trouble, and expense of laying a concrete or stone paved area complete with a massive crushed stone and concrete foundation. Furthermore, if you might conceivably want to move the patio from one year to the next, or you have a difficult sloping site, wooden decking is a good choice. There are also aesthetic considerations – perhaps you enjoy the sight and feel of wood – a decked area feels alive and springy, quite different from stone or brick. Also, by building a raised deck, you can achieve an area that gives the impression of a balcony or jetty, which extends and enhances your home.

Procedure for levelling decking

1 Rake the site smooth and cover it with a plastic membrane.
2 Rake a layer of gravel or bark chippings over the plastic, completely covering it to a thickness of about 4 inches (100 mm).
3 Mark the position of the decking legs on the ground, set each paving slab on a bed of mortar, and wait for the mortar to set.
4 Lift the decking module into position, with each leg resting on a slab. Test to see whether it is level with a carpenter's level, selecting one leg to become a constant reference point.
5 Make adjustments by adding pavers under one or all of the remaining legs, to make the decking level.

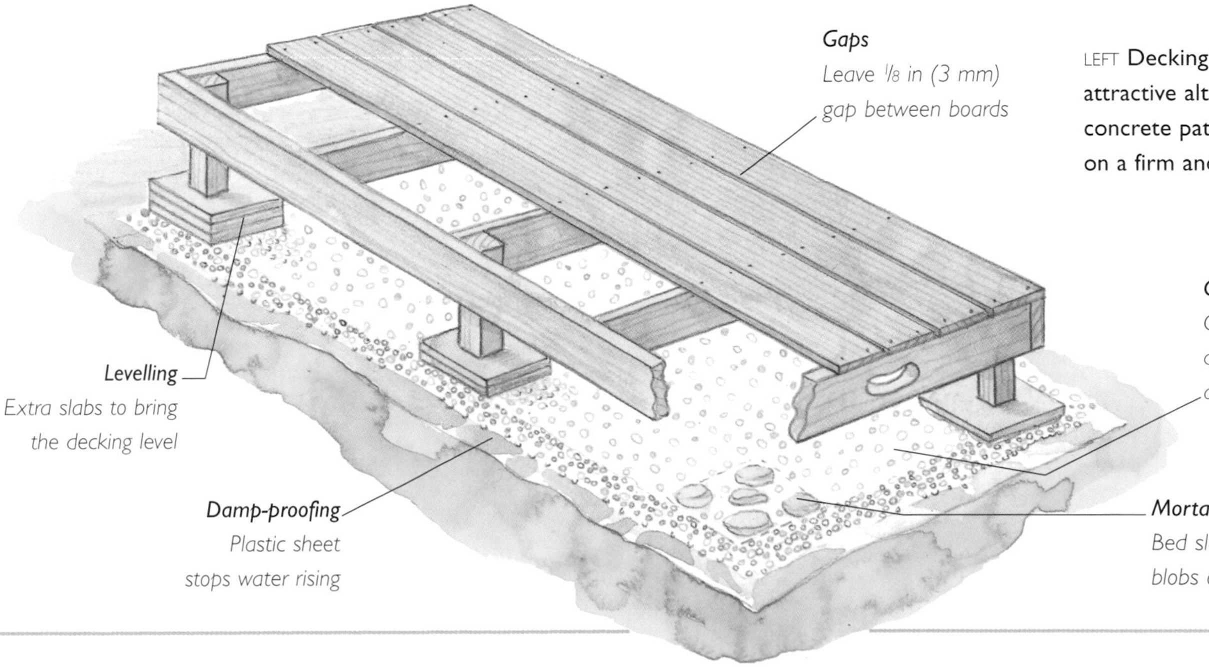

Gaps
Leave 1/8 in (3 mm) gap between boards
Gravel or bark
Gravel holds plastic down and improves appearance
Levelling
Extra slabs to bring the decking level
Damp-proofing
Plastic sheet stops water rising
Mortar
Bed slabs on blobs of mortar

LEFT Decking provides an attractive alternative to concrete patio areas. Set it on a firm and level base.

Sheds, houses, and arbors

A shed is invaluable for storing all the paraphernalia required for tending the yard and garden. Summerhouses and arbors are beguiling and exciting structures which can enhance a yard or garden, adding texture to the backdrop of plant life. They are functional too, providing a sheltered spot to sit. You can sit and enjoy looking at a cheerful display of bulbs on a fresh spring morning, or appreciate blazing leaf colors on a chilly autumn afternoon.

FOUNDATIONS

All these structures require firm foundations, although you do not necessarily need to go to the trouble of laying a concrete base slab, which involves lots of digging, tamping crushed stone, mixing concrete and so on. If the ground is wet and boggy, there is no option other than to lay concrete; otherwise a base made from concrete paving slabs set on a bed of sand is more than adequate.

Procedure for laying a concrete base

1 Skim off the topsoil to a depth of about 4 inches (100 mm).
2 Position, mark out and level a foundation frame made from rough-sawn wood 3 inches (80 mm) wide and 1 inch (25 mm) thick.
3 Fill the area within the frame with builder's crushed stone to a depth of about 4 inches (100 mm).
4 Top up the frame with concrete (1 part Portland cement, 2 parts sharp sand, 3 parts aggregate, water); level and tamp with a plank.
5 Remove the wooden frame and rub the sides of the slab with a piece of scrap wood to remove the sharp edges.
6 When dry, lay pads of heavy-duty plastic or felt on the concrete to go under the shed's base bearers.

Procedure for laying concrete pavers

1 Dig away the topsoil to a depth of about 4 inches (100 mm).
2 Fill the recess with a layer of sharp sand, to a depth of 4 inches (100 mm), then rake it smooth and level it off.
3 Set the concrete paving slabs on generous wedges of mortar (1 part Portland cement, 6 parts building sand, 1 part hydrated lime, water). Level the first paver and then make sure that all subsequent pavers relate to it.
4 When the mortar has set (two days to harden completely), set the shed's base bearers on pads of heavy-duty felt or plastic sheet.

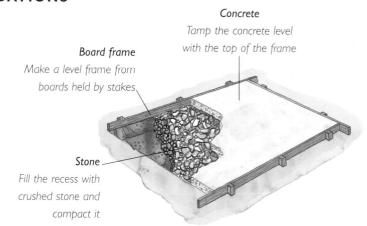

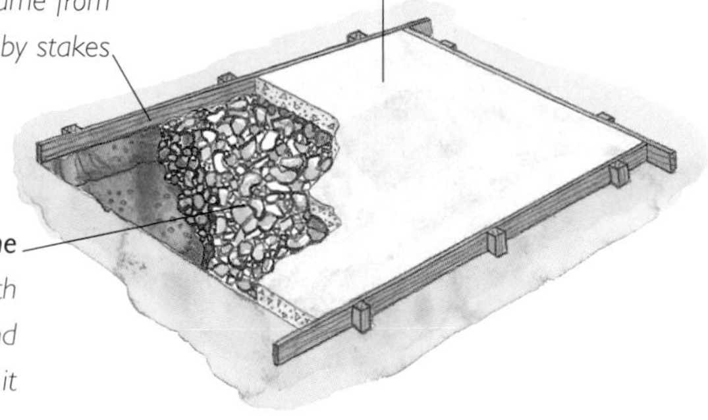
Concrete
Tamp the concrete level with the top of the frame
Board frame
Make a level frame from boards held by stakes
Stone
Fill the recess with crushed stone and compact it

ABOVE If the ground is unstable, sheds, garden houses, and arbors require a foundation consisting of crushed stone and concrete.

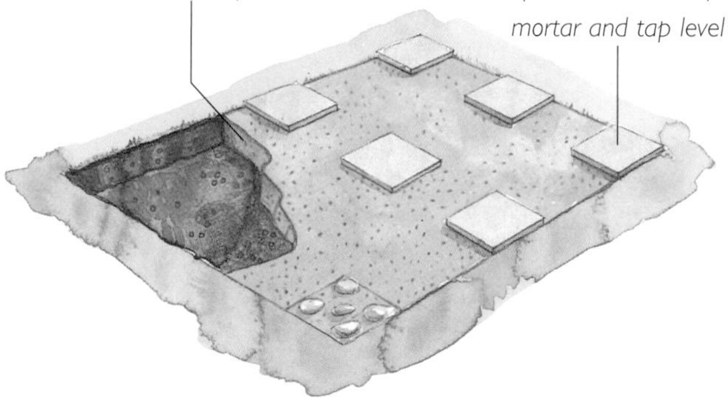
Sand
Fill the recess with sand and compact it
Pavers
Set the concrete pavers on blobs of mortar and tap level

ABOVE Where the ground is stable, concrete pavers are an adequate foundation for sheds, arbors, and other lightweight structures.

TYPES OF SHEDS

Sheds are defined and described by the shape of their roof. There are two basic types: the gable roof, which slopes down from a central ridge board, and the shed roof, which has a single gentle slope. A shed roof is much cheaper and easier to build than a gable roof, because it can be made from large sheets of board. When you are planning a shed, you need to consider the head height required inside the shed, and the way the roof sits in relation to the door. For example, some structures are designed with the slope of the roof running forwards rather than backwards. Certainly the rain drips off at the front, so you get wet going in and out, but on the other hand, the low front prevents driving rain from getting inside the shed.

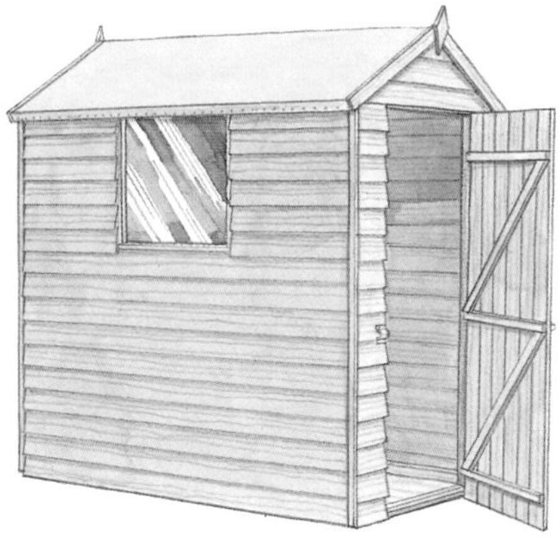

LEFT A simple, small garden tool shed with a gable roof.

LEFT A shed-roofed shed (the roof is a single slope).

SUMMERHOUSES AND OUTDOOR ROOMS

A summerhouse is a retreat, which allows you to get away from your everyday home. It is an opportunity to let your imagination run wild. If you have always harbored fantasies about living in a Wild West cowboy bunkhouse, Swiss cottage, or log cabin, your summerhouse is an opportunity to satisfy these urges. Basically, there are two types of summerhouses: the small day room that is just big enough for a couple of chairs and a table, and the room that is large enough to double up as a spare guest room.

ABOVE A Swiss-style summerhouse complete with fancy gable boards, double doors, and integral matching window boxes.

ABOVE This Victorian-design octagonal summerhouse has arched windows and a roof vent.

ABOVE An elaborate summerhouse with a lovely veranda, thistle-pattern banister rails, and decorative woodwork on the gable.

ARBORS

Generally speaking, an arbor is no more than a roof supported on poles – an open-sided structure that is just about big enough for a couple of seats. Arbors are very similar to gazebos in that they are often used to support scented climbing plants such as honeysuckle. Our Classic Arbor (see page 62) has a solid back and a waterproof roof, the idea being that it can be built in a small garden and pushed up against a wall or fence to be used as a bower, rather like a miniature summerhouse.

LEFT An arched arbor in an American design of the early nineteenth century.

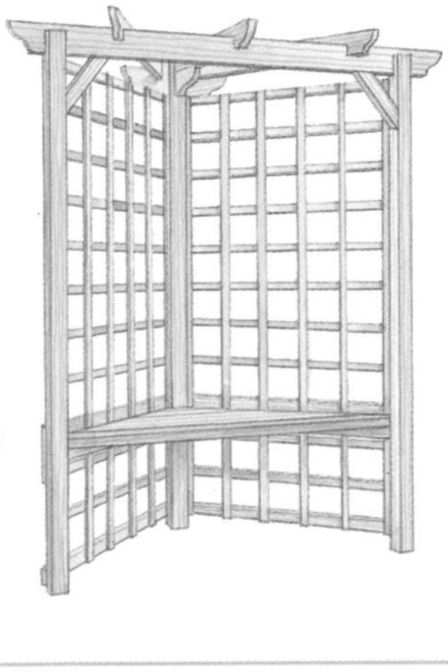

LEFT A corner arbor with pergola beams and trellis sides.

LEFT A Victorian-style arbor with plenty of ornate details.

Pergolas, trellises, and planters

If you want to add an eye-catching feature to your yard, you will find this section useful. Pergolas and trellises provide a support for plants and add a vertical dimension to the geography of the yard. If you would like to create stunning seasonal displays of flowers, our two patio planters (see pages 34 and 82) provide solutions.

TYPES OF PERGOLAS

A pergola is best defined as a pattern of beams supported by a collection of posts, rather like a basic hut frame. In essence, there are four types of pergola design. A traditional rustic frame is made from poles cut straight from the tree and nailed together. A straightforward pergola is made from sawn square sections notched and screwed together. A slightly more elaborate variation on this has the ends of the crossbeams shaped and profiled. Finally, a lean-to pergola is designed to be built up against a wall.

The rustic pergola is exciting to build, but the actual jointing is made more difficult by the fact that the sections are round. Our design for the Classic Pergola (see page 100) is something of a hybrid, with the cross beams made by laminating pairs of planks.

Whatever the design, the structure must be strong and stable enough to withstand high winds. The best way to do this is to fasten it with screws, wait for the structure to settle, and then run galvanized bolts through the primary joints.

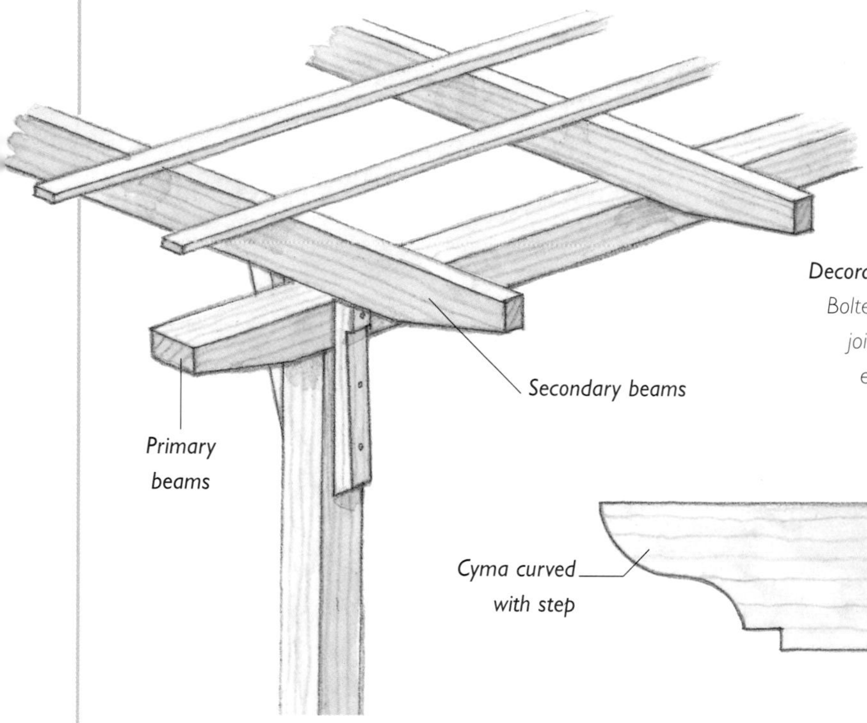
Secondary beams
Primary beams

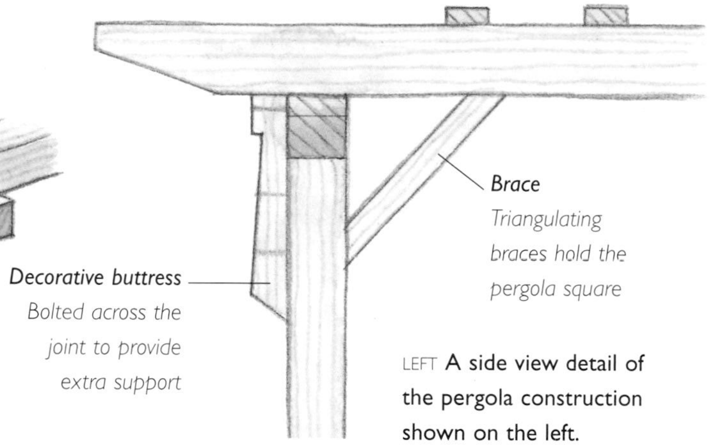
Brace
Triangulating braces hold the pergola square
Decorative buttress
Bolted across the joint to provide extra support

LEFT A side view detail of the pergola construction shown on the left.

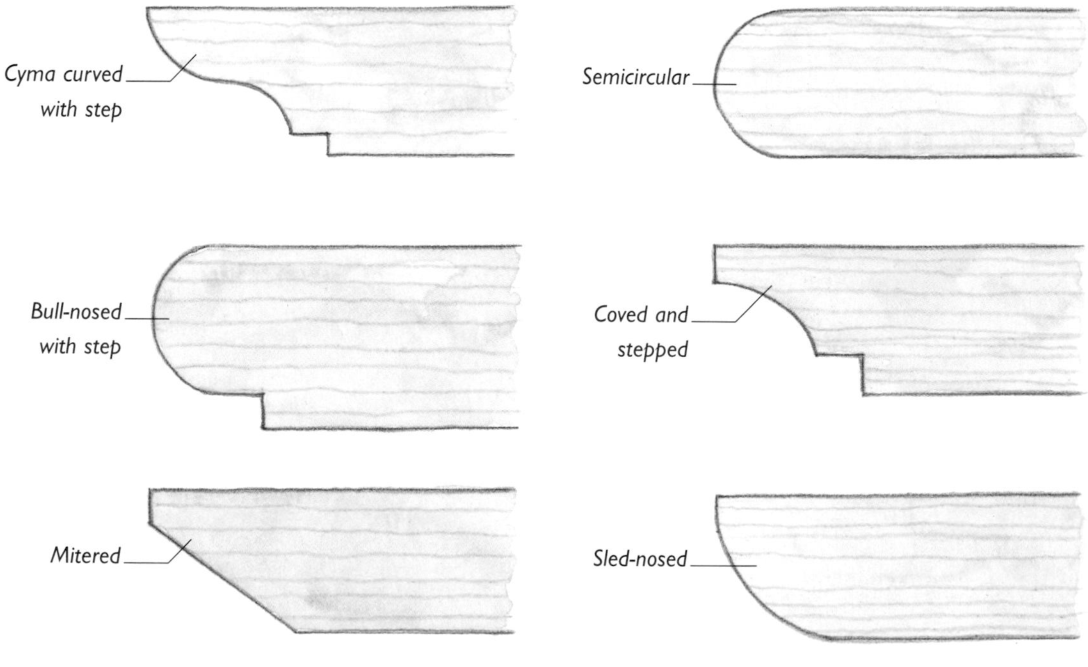
Cyma curved with step
Semicircular
Bull-nosed with step
Coved and stepped
Mitered
Sled-nosed

ABOVE A corner detail of a traditional pergola construction with square-section posts, beams and braces.

RIGHT Details of a variety of pergola beam-end designs. Classic profiles not only look good, but are also easy to cut.

TRELLISES

Trellises are traditionally made from sawn lathes arranged in a square or diamond grid pattern. The trellis is either contained within a frame or fixed to a stronger support, and then mounted on a wall, used as a space filler between two posts, or fixed between a wall and a post.

Naked trellis can be used as an effective design motif, but it is mostly used as a support for climbing plants. If you want to use trellis as a plant support, make sure, when purchasing, that it has been treated with a plant-friendly preservative. Some trellises are painted with toxic preservatives that kill plants on contact. Perhaps the most attractive type of trellis is one described as "riven", which means that the lathes are split rather than sawn, giving the structure a curvy appearance. The highest quality of trellis you can buy is made by hand from riven hardwood such as oak or hazel, and the intersections are fixed with bent and clinched copper nails.

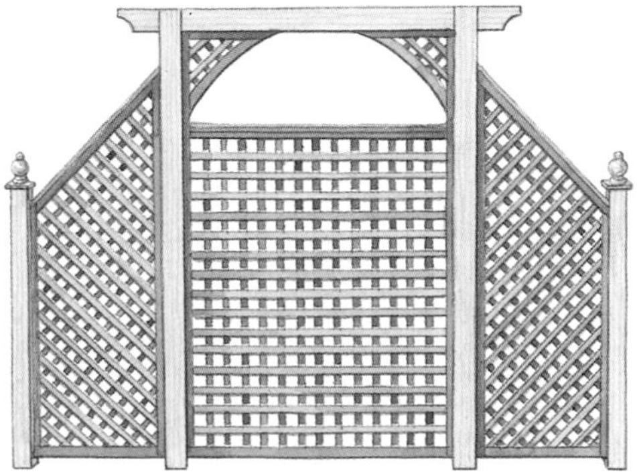

ABOVE A Victorian patio trellis with neo-Japanese beam design. Trellises of this type were traditionally used as freestanding backdrop features at the end of walkways.

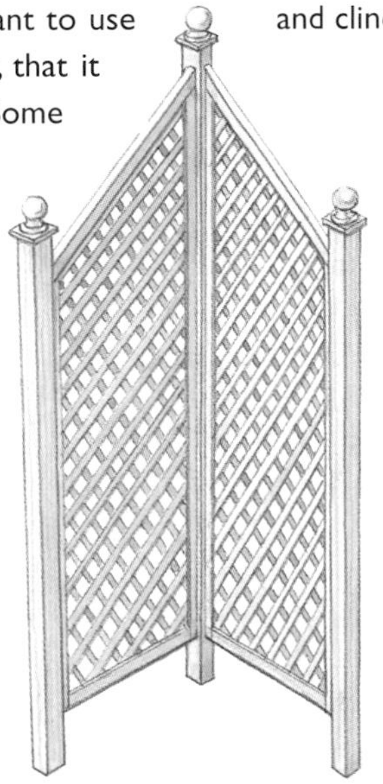

ABOVE Book-fold trellis – this is designed to be used in a corner area.

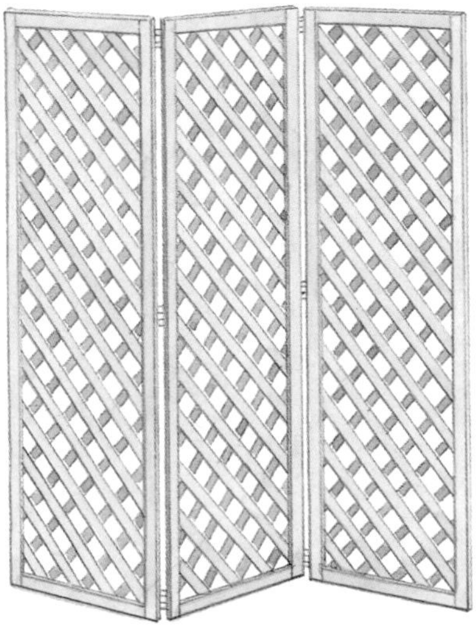

ABOVE A traditional folding trellis: this can also be used in a conservatory.

PLANTERS

Planters are best defined as self-contained plant-holders. The plants within them have no contact with the ground underlying the planter. Some planters hold earth, but our Corner Patio Planter (see page 82) is designed as a repository for a number of potted plants. Position it on your patio, balcony, or conservatory. The air space underneath the planter ensures that the structure remains sound and free from rot. When individual plants have passed their best, or you would like a change, remove or add plants as desired. The Tiered Patio Planter project (see page 34) gives you the opportunity to create a really dramatic display.

ABOVE A planter with integral trellis and finial posts is a stylish structure.

ABOVE A traditional English design, usually displayed in pairs by a doorway.

ABOVE Pickets are adaptable components, which can be used for constructing various planters. Small ones are suitable for window boxes; larger versions are good for grander patio containers.

Finishing

In the context of outdoor woodwork, the term "finishing" has very little to do with bringing the surface of the wood to a smooth, shiny finish – as you would do when building fine furniture. Rather, it is the procedure of finishing a project by ensuring a satisfactory color and surface texture that is suitably protected or preserved.

SANDING

Sanding or rubbing down is the process of using sandpaper to smooth wood to a textural finish that suits your requirements. The degree of sanding is a matter of personal choice. For example, while you might want to sand the handles and arms of the Wheeled Bench (see page 68) to a really butter-smooth finish, you might well do no more than remove large splinters from the sides of the Classic Arbor (see page 62). We employ a power sander because it is so quick and easy to use. When fitted with a coarse sandpaper, it is possible to sculpt wood to shape – as shown by the handles of the Rabbit Hutch (see page 94).

APPLYING PAINTS, STAINS, AND PRESERVATIVES

RIGHT Deciding how to paint and/or preserve outdoor woodwork is not always straightforward. Bright colors, although appealing, may be too dominant in your yard or garden, particularly in winter, so choose carefully. Always read the directions for applying paint and preservative and wear protective gloves.

Preserving
Most exterior woodwork should be treated with preservative
Color
Use exterior paint over a clear preservative, or choose a product that preserves and colors in one step
Application
For speed, use brush sizes that relate to the size of area you are painting – smelly preservatives can be applied using a brush attached to the end of a stick

Colorwashing

Colorwashing is the technique of diluting a water-based paint with water, and painting the resulting wash over the wood. This can then be rubbed through in places if desired, to reveal the underlying wood. We like this finish for many reasons – it is possible to mix an unlimited range of subtle colors, it is very cheap, it is non-toxic, and the finish blends in with nature. When choosing your paints, make sure that they are the water-based type specifically designed for exterior use.

Painting

Unlike interior painting, for which you nearly always need to sand wood to a smooth finish, or the exterior painting of woodwork such as windows, for which oil-based gloss paints are mostly used, painting outdoor woodwork involves little sanding and is done with water-based paints. All we do is rub down the wood to remove the worst of the splinters and then brush on the paint. The more textured the wood, and the thicker the paint, the more exciting the finish achieved. When the paint is dry, we favor rubbing through areas of paint to reveal the grain of the wood and create a worn and weathered appearance.

USEFUL TIP

If you want to avoid using paints and preservatives altogether, choose a long-lasting wood such as Western red cedar.

Preserving

Not so long ago, the only product for preserving outdoor woodwork was dark brown creosote. However, now there are many other options for treating your woodwork. You may be able to buy wood that has been pre-treated with a clear or colored preservative, or apply a preservative yourself. Alternatively, you can paint the wood and then give the item a coat of clear preservative. For items such as tables and benches, and particularly items the Treehouse or Children's Playhouse (see pages 114 and 120), you must ensure that a non-toxic preservative is used.

Maintenance

Maintenance is the procedure of keeping outdoor woodwork in good order and fit for its intended purpose. Every autumn and spring, make sure that fastenings are firm and have not rusted, check that wood is sound, and apply paint or preservative if necessary. You will then be able to enjoy your wooden items for many years to come.

REPAIRING AND REPLACING

Repairing and replacing

The forces of nature and normal wear and tear mean that outdoor woodwork is under constant attack. Metal may rust, wood may go moldy, or structures may break from misuse. If you want your projects to last for more than a couple of seasons, you do need to spend time repairing and replacing parts that are less than sound.

You will need to oil hinges and latches, make sure screws are free from rust, replace pieces of rotten or broken wood, renew torn or pierced roof felt, add more bolts, and so on. The best time to do these tasks is in the early spring (after the wind and rain of winter and before the peak garden season of summer) and then again in the autumn (after a summer's use and before the winter). By following this routine conscientiously, you can expect most of the projects to last for up to ten years.

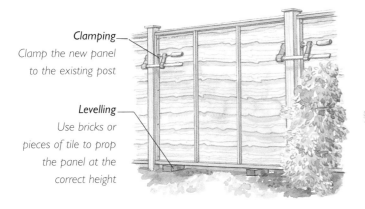

Clamping
Clamp the new panel to the existing post
Levelling
Use bricks or pieces of tile to prop the panel at the correct height

ABOVE Replacing a damaged fence panel. Fences made from thin wood, resembling this one, will need regular maintenance.

Procedure for mending a fence panel

1 Remove dying foliage and tie plants back so that you are able to move freely around the fence panel. Discuss the situation with your neighbor if it is a boundary fence.
2 Remove the broken panel along with any clips or fasteners, and make sure that both posts are sound and in good order. Give the posts a generous coat of a suitable preservative.
3 Take your replacement panel and position it between the two posts. Check the level and make height adjustments by standing the panel on bricks or tiles.
4 Clamp the panel in place. Drill holes from the edge of the panel through into the post and fasten with galvanized screws.

Procedure for mending bevel siding

1 Wedge the overlapping board out of the way, and use a pair of long-nosed pliers or a wire cutter to snip the nails or screws so that the damaged piece of wood falls away.
2 Buy a length of bevel siding to match the damaged piece and cut it to fit.
3 Ease the new board up under the overlapping board and use a clamp to hold it in place. Remove the wedge.
4 Drill pilot holes through the new board and its underlying piece and fasten in place with galvanized screws.

Procedure for mending a felt roof

1 Cut around the hole in the roof and remove the damaged felt, together with any accumulated grit and debris.
2 Daub a generous amount of felt adhesive in and around the hole and let it dry completely.
3 Daub more adhesive over the first layer, then stick a patch of new felt over the damage and fasten with flat-headed galvanized nails.
4 Finally, stick a larger patch of felt over the first patch, which covers all the nail heads with a generous overlap.

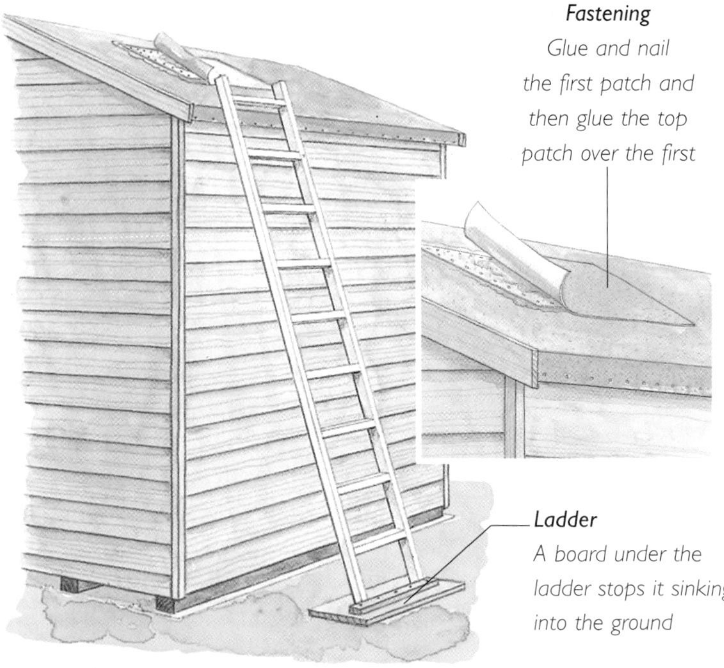
Fastening
Glue and nail the first patch and then glue the top patch over the first
Ladder
A board under the ladder stops it sinking into the ground

ABOVE Felt roofs can suffer after a bout of hot or severe weather. The double-patch procedure avoids nailing through the exposed felt.

Part 2: **Projects**

Tiered patio planter

If you have ever stared enviously at the stunning displays of flowers exhibited at professional flower shows and wondered how the designers manage to achieve such beautiful cascading tiers of blooms, this project tells you how. To create a similar effect, you need to display flowers on a specially built tiered planter.

TIME

Two days' work (about a day to mark out and cut the wood, and the rest of the time for putting together and finishing).

USEFUL TIP

An electric compound miter saw can be used instead of a miter saw. This is a relatively inexpensive tool, which is really good for cutting repeat angles in small-section wood.

EXPLODED VIEW OF THE TIERED PATIO PLANTER

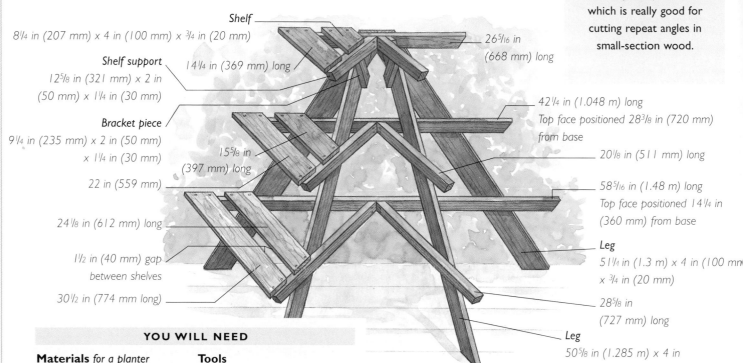

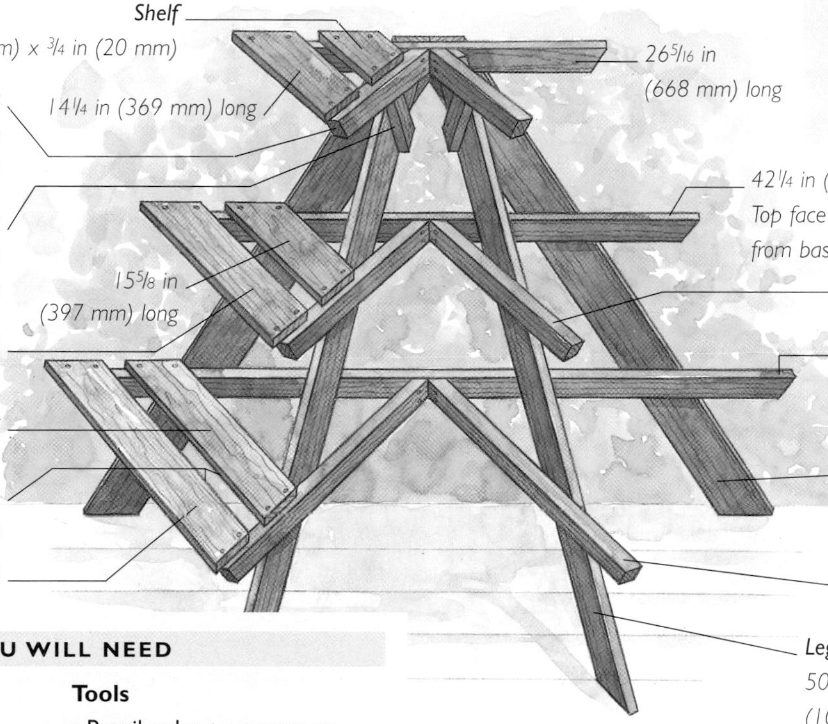

Shelf
8¼ in (207 mm) x 4 in (100 mm) x ¾ in (20 mm)
14¼ in (369 mm) long
26⁵⁄₁₆ in (668 mm) long
Shelf support
12⅝ in (321 mm) x 2 in (50 mm) x 1¼ in (30 mm)
42¼ in (1.048 m) long
Top face positioned 28⅜ in (720 mm) from base
Bracket piece
9¼ in (235 mm) x 2 in (50 mm) x 1¼ in (30 mm)
15⅝ in (397 mm) long
20⅛ in (511 mm) long
22 in (559 mm)
58⁵⁄₁₆ in (1.48 m) long
Top face positioned 14¼ in (360 mm) from base
24⅛ in (612 mm) long
Leg
51¼ in (1.3 m) x 4 in (100 mm) x ¾ in (20 mm)
1½ in (40 mm) gap between shelves
30½ in (774 mm long)
28⅝ in (727 mm) long
Leg
50⅝ in (1.285 m) x 4 in (100 mm) x ¾ in (20 mm)

YOU WILL NEED

Materials *for a planter 43⁵⁄₁₆ in (1.1 m) high, 59 in (1.5 mm) wide, and 27³⁄₁₆ in (690 mm) deep. (All rough-sawn pine pieces include excess length for wastage.)*

- Pine: 7 pieces, each 10 feet (3 m) long, 4 in (100 mm) wide, and ¾ in (20 mm) thick (shelves, legs and braces)
- Pine: 6 pieces, each 8 feet (2 m) long, 2 in (50 mm) wide, and 1¼ in (30 mm) thick (shelf supports)
- Zinc-plated, countersunk Phillips screws: 100 x 1½ in (38 mm) no. 8, 50 x 2 in (50 mm) no. 10,
- Acrylic paint, color to suit
- Clear preservative

Tools

- Pencil, ruler, tape measure, marking gauge, and square
- Portable workbench and C-clamp
- Plywood workboard about 4 feet (1 m) square
- Crosscut saw
- Cordless electric drill with a Phillips screwdriver bit
- Drill bits to match the screw sizes
- Electric compound miter saw
- Electric sander with a pack of medium-grade sandpaper
- Paintbrush: 1½ in (40 mm)

A HIGH-RISE DISPLAY

This planter is designed to be pushed against a wall, with the flowers being viewed from the front. However, the height of the stand and the fact that it is based on a hexagon also mean that the display will be cone-like in form – so if you were to arrange 50 potted plants on it, you would see a towering hill of blooms.

The tiered shelves enable you to design a display where the focus is directed towards the plants rather than their pots. We have painted the wood a rich red color, so that when there are gaps in the display and the supporting skeleton peeks through, it looks attractive. The structure stands well over 3 feet (1 meter) high, but even so, the splay of the legs allows it to be fully loaded without any danger of it tipping forward.

Because you are likely to be watering the plants daily, we have given the wood extra protection by sealing the paint with a coat of clear preservative. You may prefer to go for a brown color rather than the red we have used, but do not use a preservative that the plants will not like.

Step-by-step: **Making the tiered patio planter**

Workboard
Square the top support with the workboard

Parallel supports
Make sure that the three shelf supports are parallel to one another

1 Take the two legs that make the primary back frame and center them on top of the three primary shelf supports. Butt the legs together at the top, check the angles and squareness, and then drive 1½ inch (38 mm) screws through into the shelf supports.

Screwholes
Drill holes for the screws to avoid splitting the wood

Cordless driver
Charge the driver the day before you start the project

Supports
Butt the supports together so that they meet on the center-line

2 Turn the back frame over so that the shelf supports are uppermost, and screw the secondary supports in place with 2 inch (50 mm) screws – so that they angle out at 60° from the center. Take care: the structure is fragile at this stage.

Screwing
Position the screws to avoid knots

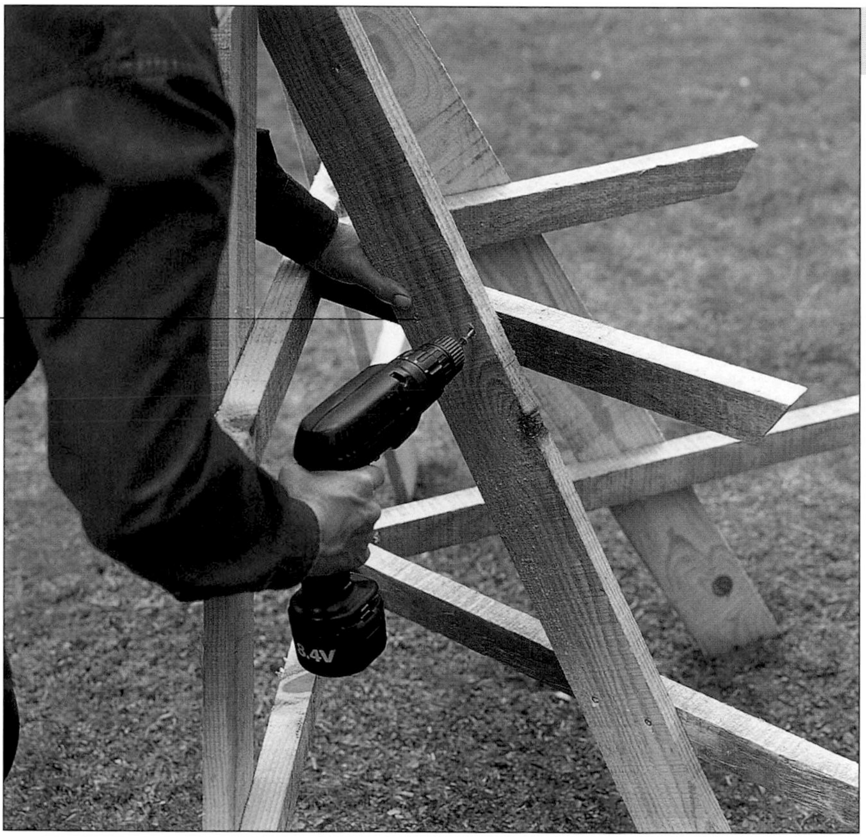

3 Set the secondary legs in place, so that they meet at top center, and screw them to the side of the supports with one 1½ inch (38 mm) screw at each intersection. Check the angles and positioning and then drive in the second screws.

Helpful hint

If you find that the whole structure is difficult to support while you work, either ask a friend to help you or secure the various components together with clamps.

Power cable
Make sure the power cable is clear of the saw

Caution
Switch off the power before moving the workpiece

4 Clamp the electric compound miter saw on the portable workbench, check that it is stable, and set the machine to cut at an angle of 60°. Cut all the shelves to length.

Screw position
Make sure you do not put a screw close to the end of the support

Shelf center
Align the ends of the shelves with the center-line of the supports

Shelf position
Butt the shelves together on the center-line

5 Starting at the bottom tier and working upwards, set the shelf boards in place on the supports, with the butted ends of the shelves meeting the center-line of the supports. Screw in place with $1\frac{1}{2}$ inch (38 mm) screws.

Screwdriver
You might need to use a hand screwdriver at this stage if your cordless driver is too big

6 Fasten the two bracket pieces in place in the angle on the underside of the top shelf, using 2 inch (50 mm) screws. Finally, rub down the wood to remove the splinters, give it a thin wash of acrylic paint and brush on the clear preservative.

Angled support
Drive the screw home so that the bracket is a tight fit

Folding screen

A folding screen is a very useful item for the yard or garden. It can be used to create a separate space or "room", which might be used for relaxing, for a dining area, or even for a children's play corner. If you yearn for somewhere to sneak off to and read a book, find a nice quiet area, preferably by lots of flowers or a favorite plant, and site the screen so that you have your own private space. Even greater privacy is available if you clothe the screen in climbing plants.

TIME

Two long days' work (most of the time for building the screen, and about an hour to get it sited).

USEFUL TIP

If you decide to open the screen wider than 90°, it will need to be secured with pegs or spiked post supports.

YOU WILL NEED

Materials *for a screen 46¼ in (1.174 m) square and 90 in (2.289 m) high. (All rough-sawn pine pieces include excess length for wastage.)*

- Pine: 4 pieces, each 10 feet (3 m) long and 2¾ in (70 mm) square (main posts)
- Pine: 4 pieces, each 8 feet (2 m) long and 2¾ in (70 mm) square (main horizontal rails)
- Ready-made pine trellis screens: 2 screens, 6 feet (1.86 m) high and 3 feet (930 mm) wide
- Pine dowel: 8 pieces of ½ in (10 mm) dowel, each 2¾ in (70 mm) long (for pegging the joints)
- Pine turned balls: 4 balls with screws to fit (post finials)
- Galvanized steel fence panel U-clips: 12 with screws to fit
- Galvanized steel large butt door hinges: 2 with screws to fit
- Clear preservative

Tools

- Pencil, ruler, tape measure, marking gauge, and square
- Portable workbench
- Mallet
- Bevel-edged chisel, 1¼ in (30 mm) wide
- Crosscut saw
- Small axe
- Claw hammer
- Electric drill with a ½ in (10 mm) flat bit
- Cordless electric drill with a Phillips screwdriver bit
- Drill bits to match the screw sizes
- Electric sander with a pack of medium-grade sandpaper
- Paintbrush: 1½ in (40 mm)

EXPLODED VIEW OF THE FOLDING SCREEN

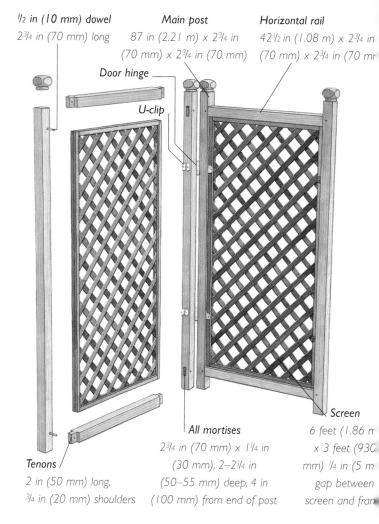

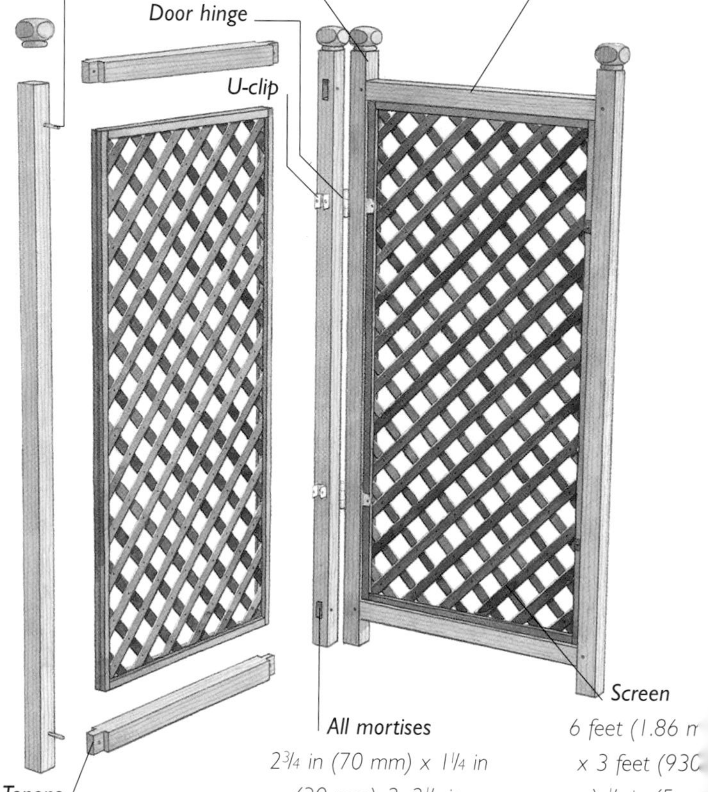

½ in (10 mm) dowel
2¾ in (70 mm) long
Main post
87 in (2.21 m) x 2¾ in (70 mm) x 2¾ in (70 mm)
Horizontal rail
42½ in (1.08 m) x 2¾ in (70 mm) x 2¾ in (70 mr
Door hinge
U-clip
Screen
6 feet (1.86 m x 3 feet (930 mm) ¼ in (5 m gap between screen and fran
All mortises
2¾ in (70 mm) x 1¼ in (30 mm), 2–2¼ in (50–55 mm) deep, 4 in (100 mm) from end of post
Tenons
2 in (50 mm) long, ¾ in (20 mm) shoulders

A COZY, QUIET CORNER

The folding screen is portable, but it is not terribly easy to move, so the idea is that it is installed in the garden in the spring, and stored away in the winter. The way it folds allows you to set it up at an angle that is greater than 90°.

You may decide to use the screen as a permanent feature, for example as a backdrop for a wall mask fountain, with the lattice being employed to disguise the workings of the fountain. Alternatively, it could become a support for a vine or other climbing plant. In either case, the feet need to be held secure in spiked post supports for safety. The frame is held together with tenons on the ends of the rails and mortises in the posts. The ready-made trellis screens are fitted with panel U-clips. The ball finials are simply screwed into the tops of the posts.

Because we chose to use contrasting materials for this project – brown-stained trellis screens and natural finish posts – we decided to protect the wood with a clear preservative to retain the freshness of the color contrast.

Step-by-step: **Making the folding screen**

Mallet size
Choose a solid mallet with a square-faced head

Chisel grip
Hold the chisel firmly and keep it upright

1 Lay out the blind mortises on all four main posts – 4 inches (100 mm) along from the ends, 1¼ inches (30 mm) wide and 2¾ inches (70 mm) long – and chop them out with the mallet and chisel. Aim to cut the mortises slightly over 2 inches (50 mm) deep.

On target
Make sure the mallet hits the axe head and not the handle

Grain
If the wood is not straight-grained, use a saw rather than the axe

2 Set out the tenons on the ends of all four main horizontal rails, making them 2 inches (50 mm) long and 1¼ inches (30 mm) wide, with ¾-inch-wide (20 mm) shoulders to the sides. Next, saw down to the waste side of the shoulder-line, then clear the waste wood using the axe and chisel.

Hole alignment
Align the holes and gently tap the dowel into place (avoid hitting it too hard, which may damage the dowel or the frame)

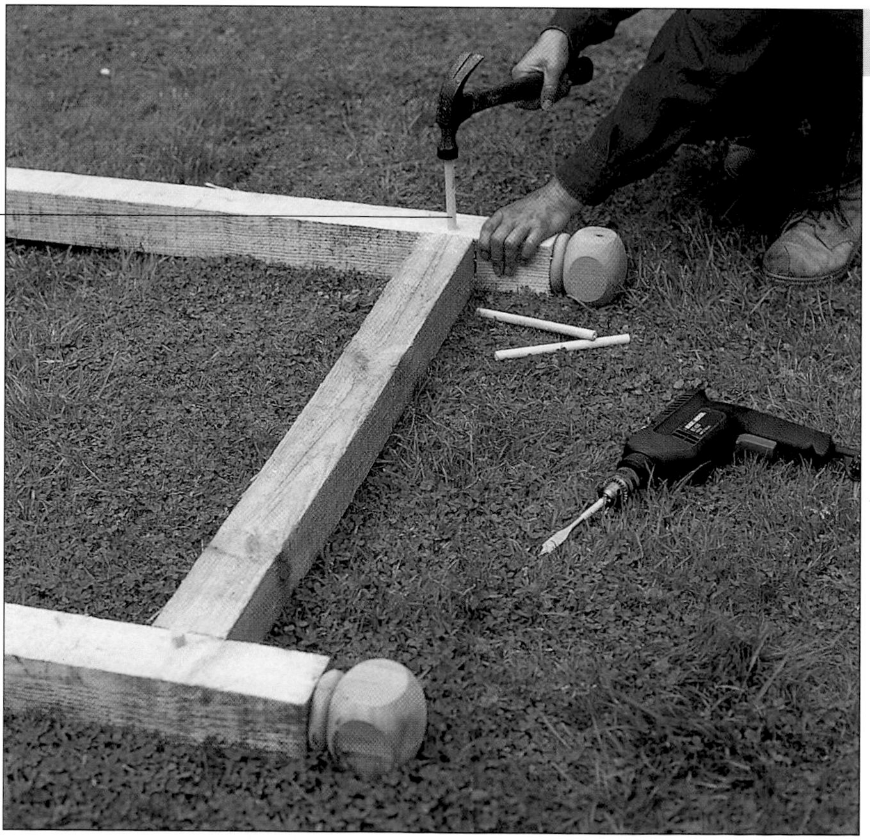

3 Knock the joint together, then drill a ½ inch (10 mm) hole right through the joint and peg it with a length of dowel. Screw the finial balls in place.

Helpful hint

If you damage a dowel while knocking it into the hole – or the dowel breaks off – use a hammer with a screwdriver to drive the dowel through the joint and out the other side. Check that the drilled hole is big enough for the dowel before trying again.

Equal gap
Maintain a ¼ in (5 mm) gap between trellis and frame all the way round

Trellis
The best trellis is either stapled or nailed at the intersections

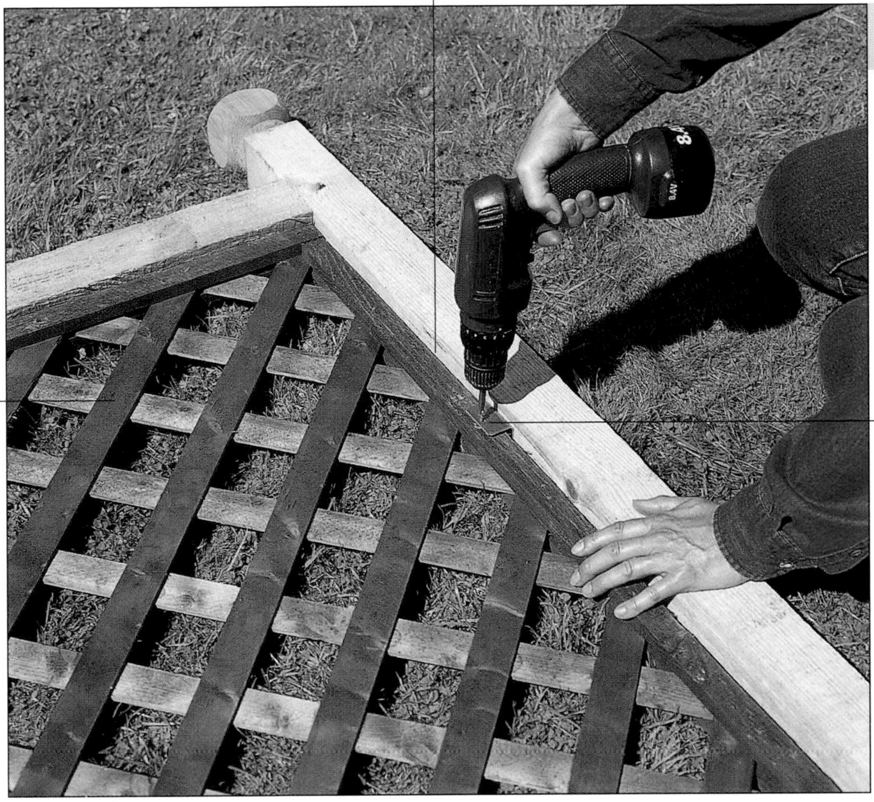

U-clips
Choose galvanized clips made from thin metal, which is easy to bend

4 Screw six U-clips on each frame, bending the tabs out and fitting the trellis in place, then bending the tabs back and screwing the clips to the frame.

Alignment
Make sure that the two frames are perfectly aligned before you screw the hinges on

Hinge position
Position the hinges to avoid knots

5 Position the two frames side by side and on edge so that the posts are uppermost. Screw the hinges in place (you can either recess the hinges or surface-mount them). Finally, rub down the screen with sandpaper and lay on a coat of clear preservative.

Picket fence

White-painted picket fences conjure up images of country cottages and flower-filled gardens. If you are fed up with your mass-produced garden fence – whether it is ungainly chicken wire or ugly concrete blocks – a picket fence is an attractive solution. (See also the Picket Gate project on page 46.)

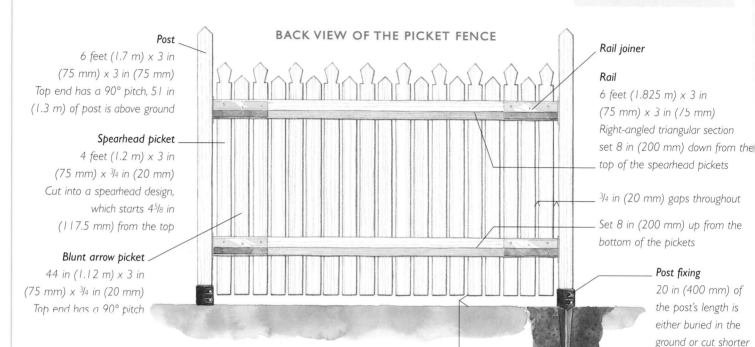

TIME

A day for every 6 feet (2 meters) of fence.

USEFUL TIP

If you can't find triangular section, use rectilinear section wood and right angle brackets for the rails.

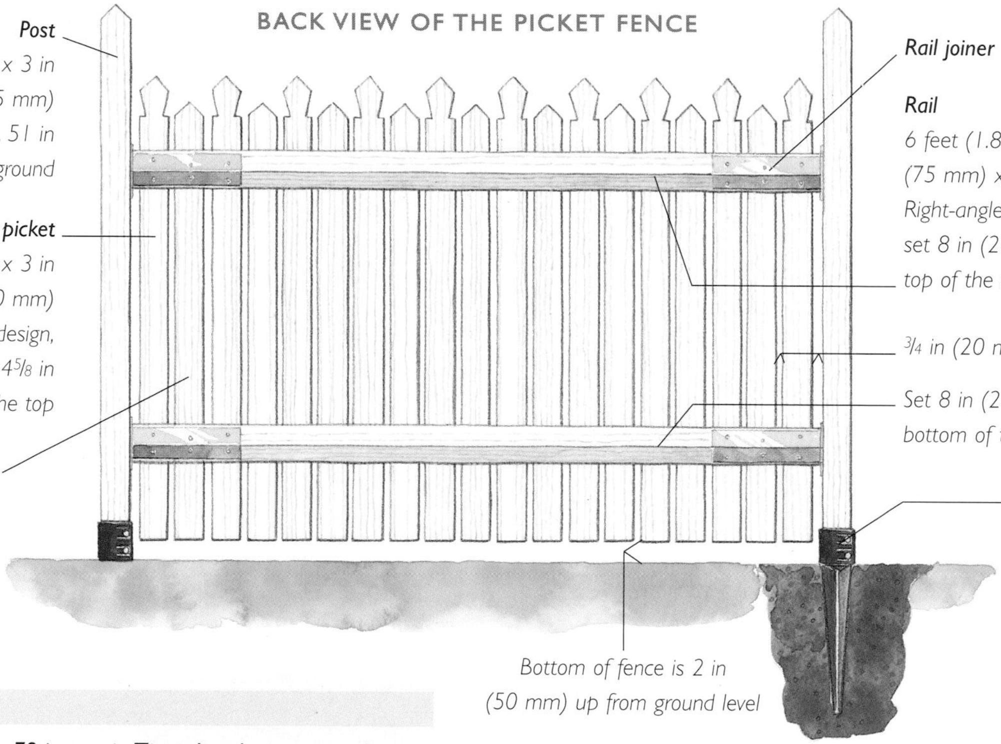
BACK VIEW OF THE PICKET FENCE
Post
6 feet (1.7 m) x 3 in (75 mm) x 3 in (75 mm) Top end has a 90° pitch, 51 in (1.3 m) of post is above ground
Spearhead picket
4 feet (1.2 m) x 3 in (75 mm) x ¾ in (20 mm) Cut into a spearhead design, which starts 4⅝ in (117.5 mm) from the top
Blunt arrow picket
44 in (1.12 m) x 3 in (75 mm) x ¾ in (20 mm) Top end has a 90° pitch
Rail joiner
Rail
6 feet (1.825 m) x 3 in (75 mm) x 3 in (75 mm) Right-angled triangular section set 8 in (200 mm) down from the top of the spearhead pickets
¾ in (20 mm) gaps throughout
Set 8 in (200 mm) up from the bottom of the pickets
Post fixing
20 in (400 mm) of the post's length is either buried in the ground or cut shorter to suit a metal post support spike
Bottom of fence is 2 in (50 mm) up from ground level

Materials *for a fence 78 in (1.975 m) long and 51¼ in (1.3 m) high. (All rough-sawn pine pieces include excess length for wastage.)*

- Pine: 10 pieces, each 10 feet (3 m) long, 3 in (75 mm) wide, and ¾ in (20 mm) thick (pickets)
- Pine: 2 pieces 3 x 3 in (75 x 75 mm) right-angled triangular section, each 79 in (2 m) long (rails)
- Pine: 1 piece, 79 in (2 m) long, 1¼ in (30 mm) wide, and ¾ in (20 mm) thick (temporary batten)
- Pine: 2 pieces, each 79 in (2 m) long and 3 in (75 mm) square (posts)
- Zinc-plated, countersunk Phillips screws: 200 x 1½ in (38 mm) no. 8
- Galvanized steel rail joiners: 4 to suit rail size and section
- Matt white exterior-quality paint

Tools

- Pencil, ruler, tape measure, bevel gauge, and square
- Crosscut saw
- Two portable workbenches
- Cordless electric drill with a Phillips screwdriver bit
- Drill bit to match the screw
- Electric sander with a pack of medium-grade sandpaper
- Paintbrush: 1½ in (40 mm)

A COUNTRY COTTAGE FENCE

The fence is made up from two picket designs: the blunt arrows have a finished length of 44 inches (1.12 m) and the spearheads reach 48 inches (1.2 m). The posts are 6 feet (1.7 m) long, with 20 inches (400 mm) of this set in the ground. The bottom of the fence is positioned about 2 inches (50 mm) up from ground level. The top rail is set 8 inches (200 mm) down from the top of the spearheads, while the bottom rail is set 8 inches (200 mm) up from the bottom of the pickets. We have allowed 2 inches (50 mm) on the length of each picket for cutting waste.

In many ways, this is a kit fence, with the rail and the rail joiners as standard; however the design of the pickets is certainly something that you can chop and change to suit your own needs. The rails are triangular in cross-section, with the short sides measuring about 3 x 3 inches (75 x 75 mm) and the hypotenuse 4 inches (100 mm). When you come to putting the fence together, the pickets are screwed to the 4 inch (100 mm) face of the rails, the galvanized joiner plates are screwed to the ends of the rails, and the flaps of the joiners are screwed to the posts. Finally, the fence is sanded to remove splinters and painted white.

Step-by-step: **Making the picket fence**

First picket

Screw the first picket 3/4 in (20 mm) from the end of the rails

Triangular jig

Use scraps of triangular section to make a cradle for each rail

1 Cut the pickets as described on page 48. Lay the two triangular rails on the workbenches (so that they are parallel and 2 feet (600 mm) apart) and screw a spearhead picket in position 3/4 inch (20 mm) along from each end of the rail. Screw the temporary batten to the bottom ends of the pickets.

Spacer

Set a picket on edge as a spacer

2 Using a picket as a spacer, screw the pickets in place so that their ends butt up against the temporary batten. Continue until you have used up all the pickets. Saw the rails to length.

Helpful hint

Stagger the positioning of the screws on each picket – one towards the top of the rail, the other towards the bottom. This avoids splitting the wood. Remember that the rails are triangular, so do not screw near their edges, otherwise the screw will break out of the wood.

Pilot holes
Run pilot holes through the plate holes and into the wood

Drill angle
Hold the drill so that the bit is at 90° to the plate

Alignment
Align the face of the flaps with the end of the rail

3 Screw the galvanized joiner plates in position on the triangular rails so that the flaps are flush with the cut ends. Be careful, because the edges of the plates are sharp.

Angled top
Make two 45° cuts to create the 90° pitched top

Saw cut
Start the saw cut with several strokes pulling towards you

4 Take the two posts and set out the top ends with a 90° pitch. Saw off the waste and use the sander to give the sawn faces a quick rub-down – just enough to remove the splinters and rough edges.

Picket pattern
The shoulders of the spearhead pickets should align with the corners of the blunt arrow pickets

Screw angle
Run the screw in at a slight angle so that it avoids the edge of the post

Rail joiner
The joiner becomes stronger when all the screws are in position

5 Align the fence with the posts (so that the joiner plate flaps are aligned with the back edge of the post) and screw it into position. Fasten the posts as described on page 49. Finally, sand off the splinters and paint the whole fence white.

Picket gate

Of all the projects in the book, the picket gate is one of the prettiest, easiest to build, and most eye-catching. If you are looking to create a yard with the appeal of a traditional cottage plot, complemented by a little gate that invites opening, this is the project for you. The gate can, of course, be incorporated into the Picket Fence project on page 42.

TIME

A weekend (a long day for building the gate and a day to get it into position).

USEFUL TIP

Don't be tempted to cut costs on the hinges: they need to be heavy-duty and galvanized.

YOU WILL NEED

Materials *for a gate 40 in (995 mm) wide and 52 in (1.3 m) high. (All rough-sawn pine pieces include excess length for wastage.)*

- Pine: 9 pieces, each 4 feet (1.185 m) long, 3 in (75 mm) wide, and ¾ in (20 mm) thick (spearhead pickets)
- Pine: 1 piece, 10 feet (3 m) long, 4 in (100 mm) wide, and ¾ in (20 mm) thick (diagonal brace and horizontal rails)
- Pine: 2 pieces, each 6 feet (2 m) long and 3 in (75 mm) square (gateposts)
- Pine: 1 piece, 4 feet (2 m) long, 1¼ in (30 mm) square (gate stop)
- Painted steel post support spikes: 2 complete with bolts (to support the gateposts)
- Galvanized steel reversible strap hinges: 2 with screws and carriage bolts to fit
- Galvanized steel latch: 1 with screws to fit
- Zinc-plated, countersunk Phillips screws: 100 x 1½ in (38 mm) no. 8, 50 x 2 in (50 mm) no. 8
- Matt exterior-quality paint

Tools

- Pencil, ruler, tape measure, bevel gauge, and square
- Portable workbench
- Plywood workboard about 4 feet (1.5 m) square
- Jigsaw
- Cordless electric drill with a Phillips screwdriver bit
- Drill bits to match the screw sizes
- Crosscut saw
- Sledgehammer
- Wrench to fit carriage bolts
- Electric sander with a pack of medium-grade sandpaper
- Paintbrush 1½ in (40 mm)

BACK VIEW OF THE PICKET GATE

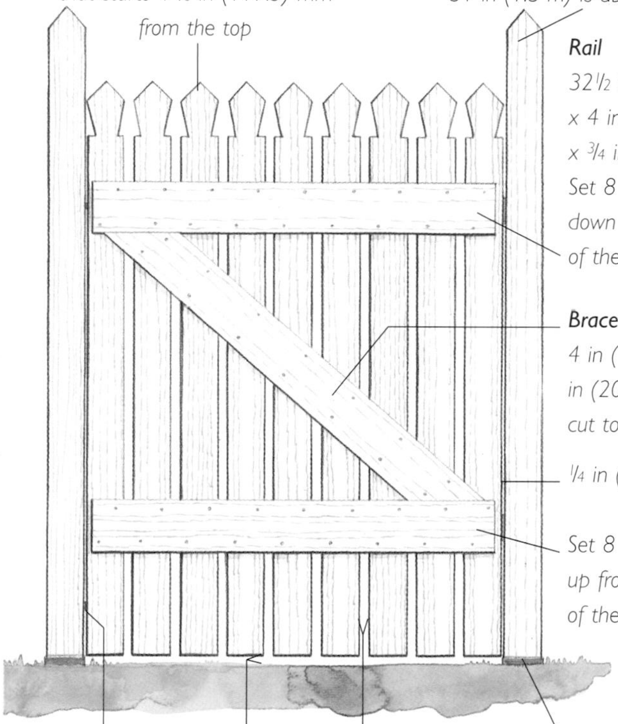
Spearhead picket
4 feet (1.185 m) x 3 in (75 mm) x ¾ in (20 mm)
Cut into a spearhead design that starts 4⅝ in (117.5) mm from the top
Post
69 in (1.7 m) x 3 in (75 mm) x 3 in (75 mm)
Top end has a 90° pitch, 51 in (1.3 m) is above ground
Rail
32½ in (825 mm) x 4 in (100 mm) x ¾ in (20 mm)
Set 8 in (200 mm) down from the top of the pickets
Brace
4 in (100 mm) x ¾ in (20 mm) Section cut to fit between rai
¼ in (5 mm) gap
Set 8 in (200 mm) up from the bottom of the pickets
¼ in (5 mm) gap
¾ in (20 mm) gap
Post fixing
16 in (400 mm) of the length is buried in the ground or cut to suit a metal post support spike
Bottom of gate is ¾–2½ in (20–65 mm) up from ground level

PICTUREBOOK PICKET GATE

Although the gate is designed to complement the picket fence, we have varied the design slightly by using spearhead pickets throughout. You do not have to follow suit, but this shows that it is possible to change the emphasis of the design simply by opting for one arrangement of pickets rather than another.

The 3-inch-wide (75 mm) pickets are spaced ¾ inches (20 mm) apart and screwed to the 4 inch (100 mm)-wide horizontal rails, and then the arrangement is braced with a single diagonal. Note how the brace – with this gate or any gate – is always fitted so that the bottom end is on the hinge side, and also how the rails are cut slightly shorter than the total width of the gate. We opted for using the post support spikes for three good reasons. Not only are they wonderfully easy to fit – you just pound them in and the job is done, but they instantly make the posts firm, and the whole operation can be managed without the need to mess up the site by digging holes. The gate is naturally quite strong, but the galvanized strap hinges greatly increase its strength, because the screws and carriage bolts clamp the layers together tightly.

Step-by-step: **Making the picket gate**

First cut
Cut inwards from the side first

Clamp
Secure the workpiece with a clamp

Jigsaw
Cut to the waste side of the drawn line

1 Take the 4-foot-long (1.185 m) pickets and set out the spearheads with 90° tops. Position the shoulders 4⅝ inches (117.5 mm) down. Saw out the shape with the jigsaw.

Right angles
Make sure that the rails cross the pickets at right angles

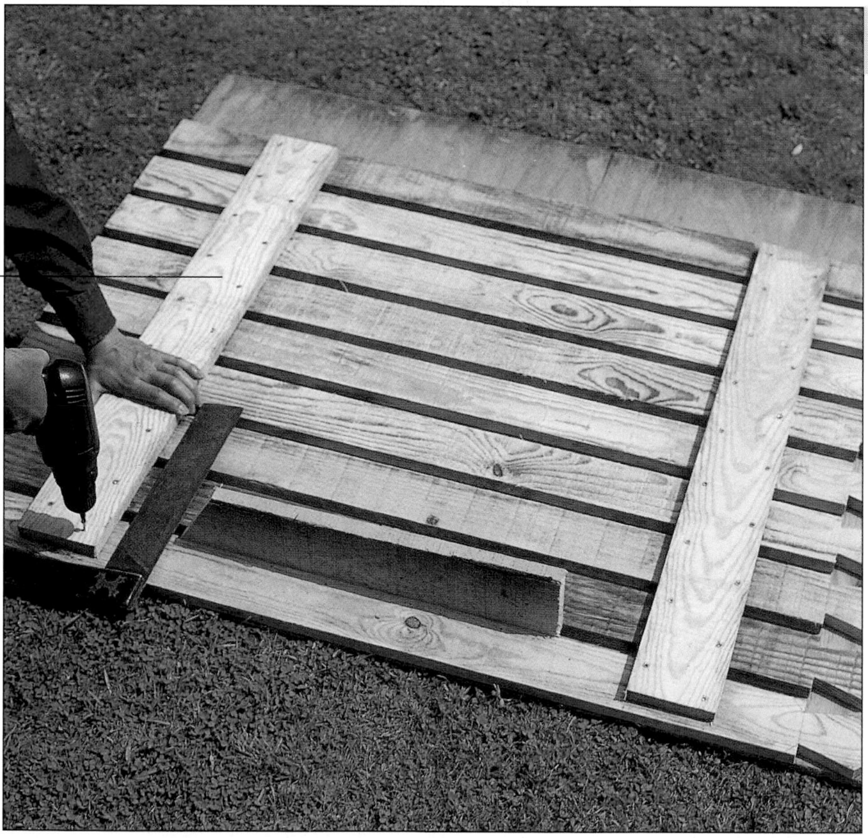

2 Place the spearhead pickets on the workboard, cross them with the horizontal rails, check the alignment and spacing, and fasten with two 1½ inch (38 mm) screws at each intersection.

Helpful hint

To double-check that the gate is square, you can use the workboard (which should be square) as a guide. First drive in one screw at each joint, align the gate with a corner of the workboard (pushing it into a square shape if needed) and then drive in the remaining screws.

Angled joint
Butt the diagonal up against the rail

Adjustments
You may need to make adjustments to the angle on the ends of the diagonal brace

3 Using the crosscut saw, cut the diagonal brace to length so that it fits the diagonal. Trim the ends to fit the angles, and then butt in place and fasten with $1^1/_2$ inch (38 mm) screws. Use two screws for each intersection.

Screwing
Use two screws to fasten each picket to the diagonal brace

Post offcut
Put a post offcut in the post support spike while you are pounding it into the ground

Bolt position
Position the spike so that you will be able to reach the bolt

4 Cut the two gateposts to shape as shown on page 45. Use the sledgehammer to pound the two post support spikes into place so that they are flush with the ground. Trim the bottom of the posts to fit and bolt them in position.

Hinge type
Use heavyweight galvanized hinges

Carriage bolt
The square shank of the bolt should be a tight fit in the square hinge hole

Gate height
Use a scrap of wood to prop up the gate at the correct height

5 Rub down the gate and gateposts with the sander and paint them white. Hang the gate in position, complete with strap hinges and latch. Using 2 inch (50 mm) screws, fasten the gate stop to the catch post and paint it white.

Inspirations: **Decorative gates**

Garden gates hint at what lies beyond them. A gate needs to be functional, but it should also express a message. It might say, "Please come in", "Welcome", or perhaps "This part of the garden is a haven, the perfect place to sit and ponder". The design can be straightforward and inexpensive to realize, or you may prefer to embellish your garden with a customized design that makes use of more expensive varieties of wood and carefully crafted details.

ABOVE A beautiful oak gate complete with finials, lapped and pegged joints, chamfered details and forged iron strap hinges. Its artistic appearance complements the formal clipped hedges that border it and suggests an interesting garden beyond.

LEFT A simple picket gate is the perfect partner for this pretty country garden. It is low in height, strong enough to keep children and pets in, and above all it is welcoming. If you want to make an inexpensive gate, this is a good type to choose.

ABOVE A beautifully constructed gate, with vertical square-section staves contained within a simple frame. Each rail is made from two components that have been cut, stepped, and bolted together to sandwich the staves.

Multi-shaped decking

If your garden is the focus for an ever-changing program of activities – an area for the children to play in and a place for hosting family barbecues or entertaining friends, all of which would benefit from a firm footing – our super modular decking is a good option. The decking can be shaped to suit your needs.

TIME

A weekend (about a day to make the three frames and the rest of the time for fastening the decking).

USEFUL TIP

You can use either grooved decking or regular decking for this project. Both work well.

YOU WILL NEED

Materials *for 3 decking shapes 3 feet (1 m) wide and 6 feet (2 m) long. (All rough-sawn pine pieces include excess length for wastage.)*

- Pine: 6 pieces, each 6 feet (2 m) long, 6 in (150 mm) wide, and ¾ in (20 mm) thick (long side frame boards)
- Pine: 5 pieces, each 10 feet (3 m) long, 6 in (150 mm) wide, and ¾ in (20 mm) thick (short end frame boards and dividing support planks)
- Pine: 24 pieces, each 10 feet (3 m) long, 3¾ in (95 mm) wide, and ¾ in (18 mm) thick (decking)
- Pine: 4 pieces, each 6 feet (2 m) long and 4 in (100 mm) square (legs)
- Zinc-plated, countersunk Phillips screws: 200 x 1½ in (38 mm) no. 8, 100 x 2 in (50 mm) no. 10
- Green acrylic paint
- Clear preservative

Tools

- Pencil, ruler, tape measure, compass, and bevel gauge and square
- Two portable workbenches
- Crosscut saw
- Electric drill with a 2-in-diameter (50 mm) hole saw to fit
- Electric jigsaw
- Cordless electric drill and Phillips screwdriver bit
- Drill bits to match screws
- Electric compound miter saw
- Electric sander with a pack of medium-grade sandpaper
- Paintbrush 1½ in (40 mm)

HIGH AND DRY AND SITTING COMFORTABLY

This is, without doubt, one of the simplest projects in the book. In essence, it is no more than three frames (each the size of a single bed), which are covered with decking boards. Each frame is made up from six 8-inch-long (200 mm) legs, with the four side boards and three dividing boards all put together in such a way that the finished frame makes a module precisely 3 feet (1 m) wide and 6 feet (2 m) long. The idea of the decking is that the three frames can variously be fitted end to end, side by side, end to side, or in any combination to create a surface that always measures a number of whole yards (meters) in width and depth. The handle holes make the decking easy to lift.

The middle legs are centered on the long side frame board; the middle dividing support plank is screwed to one side of the middle leg, with the other two dividing planks set to quarter the total length. We painted the side and end frame boards green, but you might prefer a natural finish or perhaps a more startling color.

EXPLODED VIEW OF THE MULTI-SHAPED DECKING

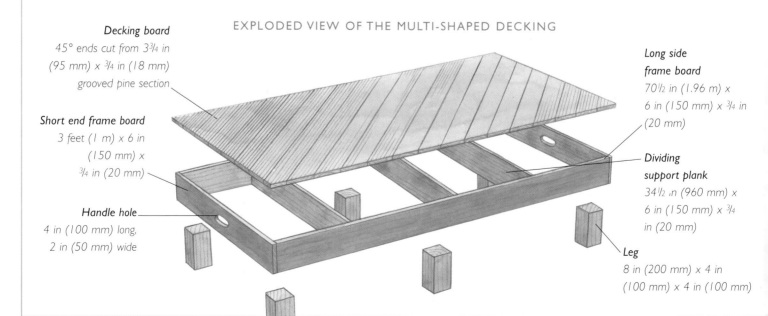

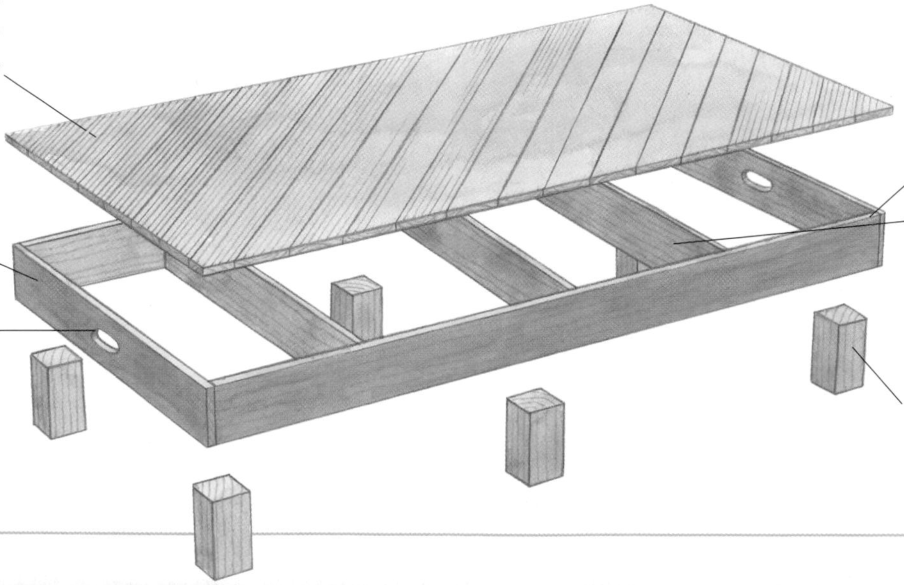

Decking board
45° ends cut from 3¾ in (95 mm) x ¾ in (18 mm) grooved pine section
Short end frame board
3 feet (1 m) x 6 in (150 mm) x ¾ in (20 mm)
Handle hole
4 in (100 mm) long, 2 in (50 mm) wide
Long side frame board
70½ in (1.96 m) x 6 in (150 mm) x ¾ in (20 mm)
Dividing support plank
34½ in (960 mm) x 6 in (150 mm) x ¾ in (20 mm)
Leg
8 in (200 mm) x 4 in (100 mm) x 4 in (100 mm)

Step-by-step: Making the multi-shaped decking

Hole saw
Hold the drill perfectly upright

Waste board
Put a piece of waste board under the hole to be drilled

1 Use the crosscut saw to cut the short end frame boards to size 3 feet (1 m long). Draw out the handle holes, making them 4 inches (100 mm) long and 2 inches (50 mm) wide, and clear the waste with the electric drill and hole saw, and the jigsaw.

Clamping
You may want to use a clamp to hold the board still

Spacer
Use a spare piece of 3/4-in-thick (20 mm) board as a spacer to help you position the leg

Flush fit
Slide the leg down until the top is flush with the board

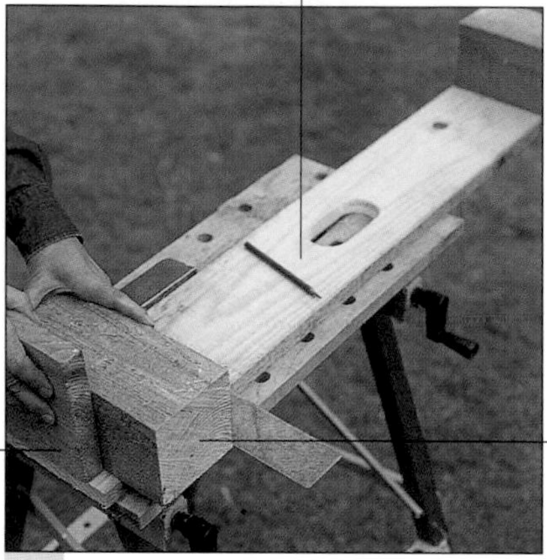

2 Cut the 4-inch-square (100 mm) wood for the legs into eighteen 8 inch (200 mm) lengths – one for each leg. Set two legs 3/4 inch (20 mm) in from the ends of the short end frame boards, check that they are square and fasten them with 2 inch (50 mm) screws.

Middle leg
Position the leg halfway along the board

3 Cut the long side frame boards to a length of 70½ inches (1.96m) and fix the middle leg in position with 2 inch (50 mm) screws. Butt the end of each board in place on the side of the corner legs and up against the inside face of the short end frame board, and fasten with 2 inch (50 mm) screws.

Helpful hint

Search out a level area of lawn to work on. Ask a friend to help hold the frame upright while you work, or clamp the frame to a workbench.

Clamping
Clamp the end of the frame in the jaws of the vise

Divider position
Screw the middle divider to one side of the leg

4 Bridge the frame across the two workbenches and fasten the three $34^1/_2$-inch-long (960 mm) dividing support planks in place. Screw the middle divider to the legs with $1^1/_2$ inch (38 mm) screws, and fasten the quarter dividers with 2 inch (50 mm) screws running through the long side board.

Screw fastening
Locate the divider by screwing through the long side frame boards and into the end of the divider

Screws
Use two $1^1/_2$ in (38 mm) screws at each end of the lengths of decking

5 Set the electric compound miter saw to an angle of 45° and set to work cutting the decking to length. Cut the longest boards first and fill in the corners with the various offcuts. Sand all the boards. Paint the long side frame and short end frame boards green. Seal the completed decking module with a coat of clear preservative.

Screws
Use one or two $1^1/_2$ in (38 mm) screws at the points where the decking crosses the dividing support

Decorative picnic table

There is something really enjoyable about eating outdoors. There are fewer worries about etiquette or spillages when you gather to eat around a picnic table, guaranteeing that any meal is a relaxed affair. The beauty of this table is that it can live outside all year and doesn't have to be dragged out and assembled to make the most of a sunny day in spring, summer, or winter.

TIME

A long day's work (about six hours for the woodwork, and the rest of the time for putting together and finishing).

USEFUL TIP

Avoid wood that has been pressure-treated with strong-smelling, toxic preserving fluid. Go for a low-odor, water-based finish.

YOU WILL NEED

Materials *for a picnic table 64 in (1.625 m) wide, 6 feet (1.826 m) deep, and 28 in (720 mm) high. (All rough-sawn pine pieces include excess length for wastage.)*

- Pine: 12 pieces, each 6 feet (2 m) long, 6 in (150 mm) wide, and 7/8 in (22 mm) thick (tabletop and seat boards; cross supports)
- Pine: 2 pieces, 6 feet (2 m) long, 4 in (100 mm) wide, and 2 in (50 mm) thick (legs)
- Pine: 4 pieces, 6 feet (2 m) long, 3 in (75 mm) wide, and 3/4 in (20 mm) thick (diagonal braces and cross tie boards)
- Galvanized carriage bolts: 16 bolts, 3½ in (85 mm) long, with nuts and washers to fit
- Zinc-plated, countersunk screws:
  100 x 1½ in (38 mm) no. 8
  100 x 2 in (50 mm) no. 8
- Clear preservative

Tools

- Pencil, ruler, tape measure, compass, and bevel gauge and square
- Two portable workbenches
- Crosscut saw
- Large clamp
- Electric jigsaw
- Plywood workboard about 4 feet (1 m) square
- Wrench to fit the nuts
- Cordless electric drill with a Phillips screwdriver bit
- Drill bits to match the screw sizes, bolt holes, and decorative holes
- Electric sander with a pack of medium-grade sandpaper
- Paintbrush 1½ in (40 mm)

PICNIC TIME

This table is strong, sturdy, decorative, and can seat up to eight. It's longer and wider than most tables, with a central hole for a sun umbrella, and lots of curves and curlicues to make it attractive and user-friendly. We have rounded off all the corners so people will not scrape their shins. The frame is fastened with lots of carriage bolts, so it stands absolutely firm. We went out of our way to use boards pre-treated with a water-based, non-toxic preservative: this is vital for a surface where food will be served. We chose to use sawn timber, because we like the texture, but rubbed down all edges and surfaces to a smooth, non-splintering finish.

EXPLODED DETAIL OF THE DECORATIVE PICNIC TABLE

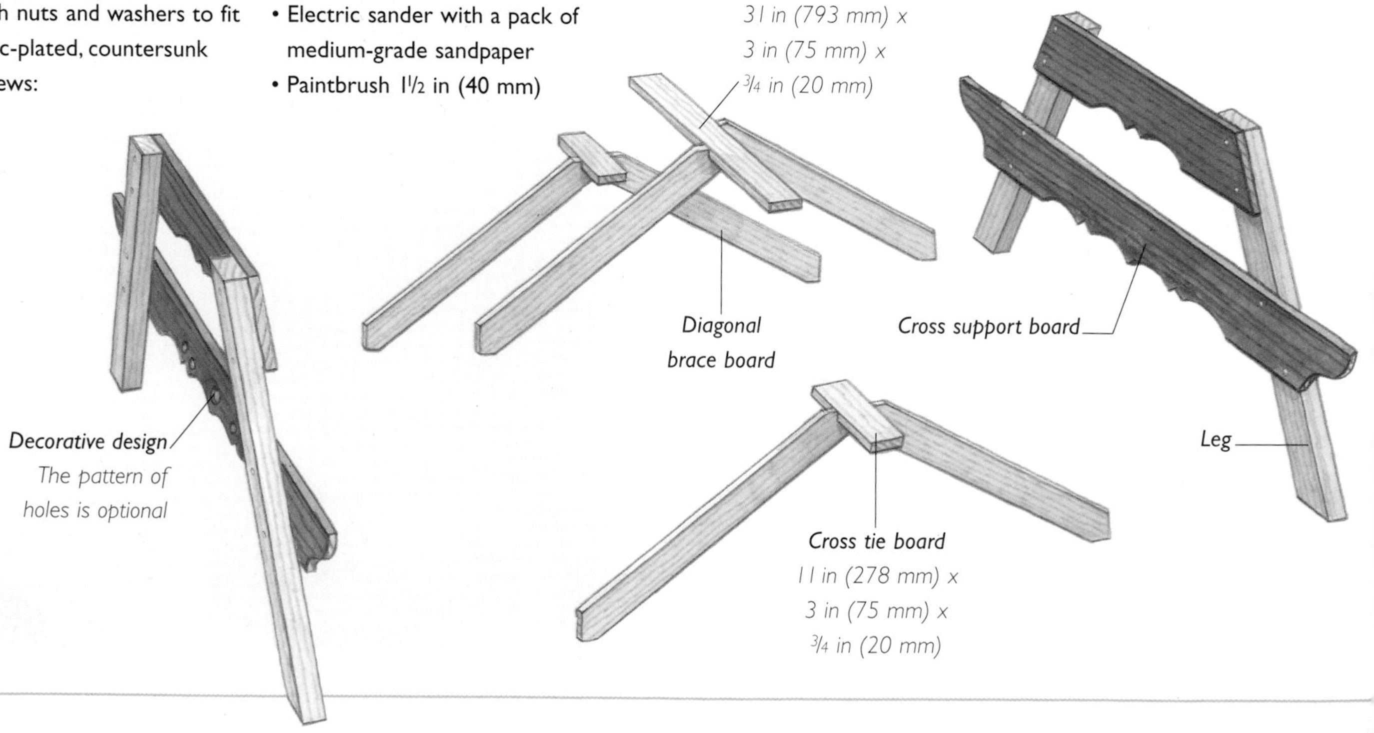
Cross tie board
31 in (793 mm) x
3 in (75 mm) x
3/4 in (20 mm)
Diagonal brace board
Cross support board
Decorative design
The pattern of holes is optional
Leg
Cross tie board
11 in (278 mm) x
3 in (75 mm) x
3/4 in (20 mm)

Decorative picnic table

END VIEW OF THE DECORATIVE PICNIC TABLE

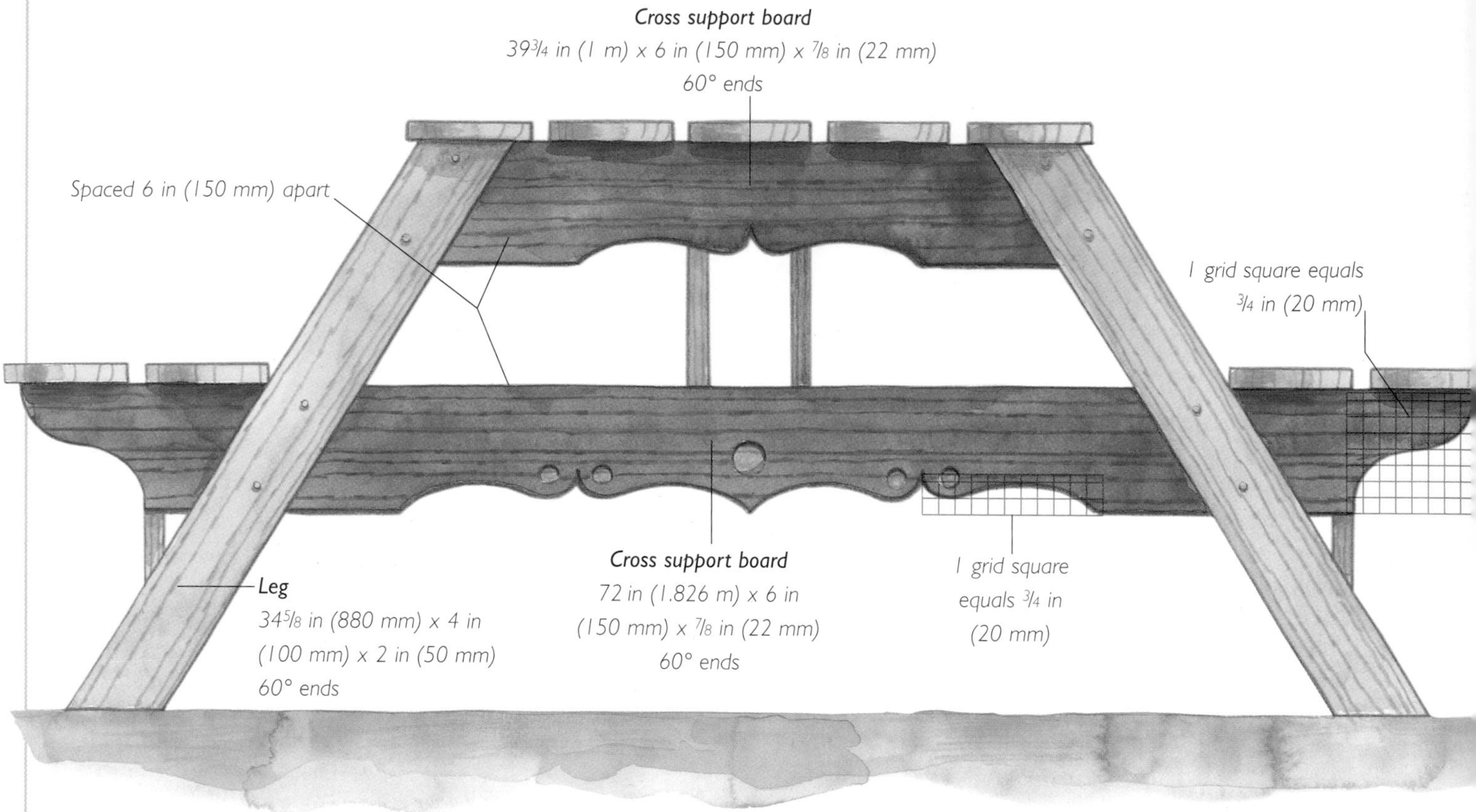
Cross support board
39¾ in (1 m) x 6 in (150 mm) x ⅞ in (22 mm)
60° ends
Spaced 6 in (150 mm) apart
1 grid square equals
¾ in (20 mm)
Leg
34⅝ in (880 mm) x 4 in
(100 mm) x 2 in (50 mm)
60° ends
Cross support board
72 in (1.826 m) x 6 in
(150 mm) x ⅞ in (22 mm)
60° ends
1 grid square
equals ¾ in
(20 mm)

FRONT VIEW OF THE DECORATIVE PICNIC TABLE

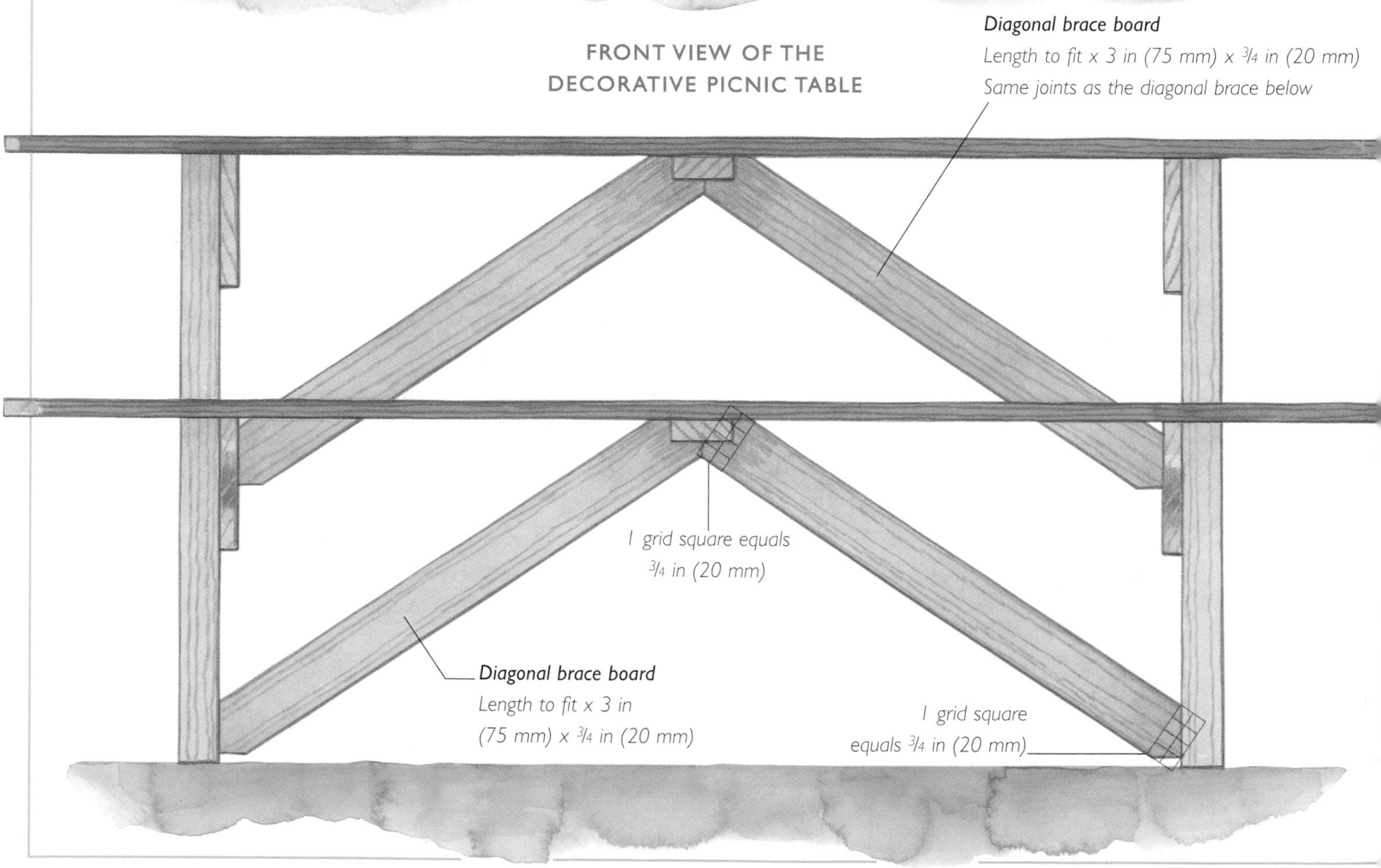
Diagonal brace board
Length to fit x 3 in (75 mm) x ¾ in (20 mm)
Same joints as the diagonal brace below
1 grid square equals
¾ in (20 mm)
Diagonal brace board
Length to fit x 3 in
(75 mm) x ¾ in (20 mm)
1 grid square
equals ¾ in (20 mm)

PLAN VIEW OF THE DECORATIVE PICNIC TABLE

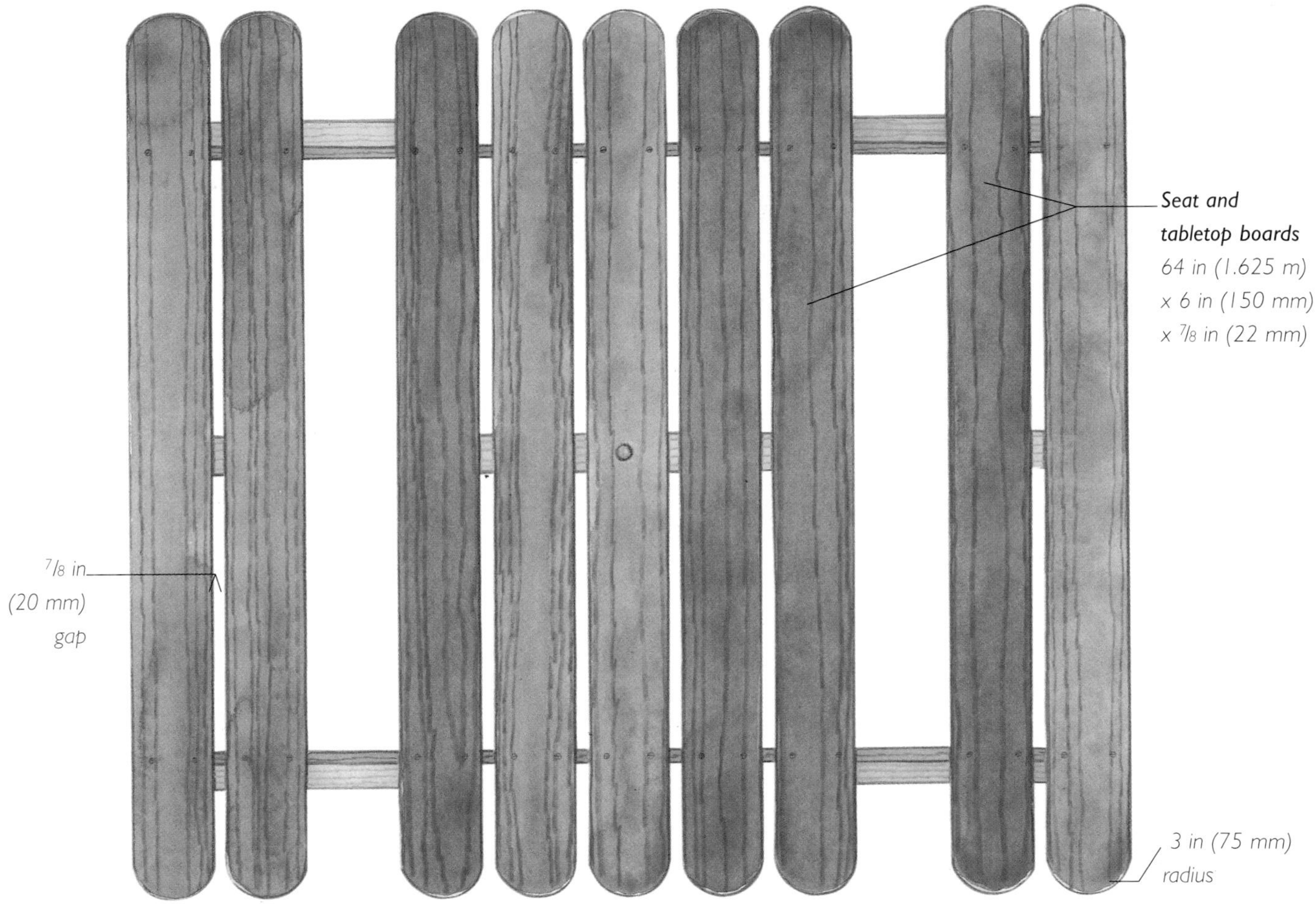
Seat and tabletop boards
64 in (1.625 m) x 6 in (150 mm) x 7/8 in (22 mm)
7/8 in (20 mm) gap
3 in (75 mm) radius

DETAIL OF HOW THE BRACES ARE FIXED UNDER THE TABLETOP

Tabletop board
Cross tie board
Notched joint
1½ in (37.5 mm) x ¾ in (20 mm)
Diagonal brace board

Step-by-step: **Making the decorative picnic table**

Cutting the curves
Rotate the saw in the direction of the cut, rather than forcing it sideways

Clamp position
Put the handle of the clamp under the bench so that it does not get in your way

Board position
Set up the board so that the area to be cut hangs over the bench

1 Cut the boards to length with the crosscut saw and draw out the imagery. Clamp each workpiece to the workbench and saw out the curves with the jigsaw. Work from side to center in order to achieve a crisp central cleft.

Hole size
Check that the hole is large enough for the bolt to pass through easily

Board spacer
Use an offcut of 6-in-wide (150 mm) board as a spacer

2 Set the plywood workboard flat on the ground to support the components, and carefully bolt the legs and the cross supports together. Check the arrangement with a square. Note how the components have been spaced with the aid of a 6-inch-wide (150 mm) board.

Diagonals
If the diagonal measurements are identical, the table is square

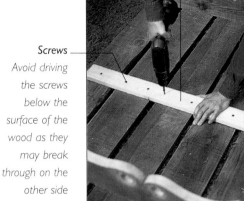

Seat board
Butt the seat board against the side of the angled leg

3 Link the legs by screwing the two outer seat boards in place with a single 2 inch (50 mm) screw at each joint. Ease the frame until its squareness is confirmed by identical diagonal measurements, and then drive in the other 2 inch (50 mm) screws. Screw all the other seat and tabletop boards in place with 2 inch (50 mm) screws.

Central hole position
Keep all the screws well away from the center

Screws
Avoid driving the screws below the surface of the wood as they may break through on the other side

Cross tie board
The cross tie board needs to be positioned centrally and squarely

4 Screw a cross tie board in place across the underside of the tabletop, using $1\frac{1}{2}$ inch (38 mm) screws, with the screws positioned well clear of the actual center-point, and then bore out a hole for the sun umbrella. Screw the diagonal braces in place with 2 inch (50 mm) screws.

Notched braces
All the braces align with the edge of a plank

5 With $1\frac{1}{2}$ inch (38 mm) screws, fasten the cross tie boards under the seat boards, and then cut and notch the two diagonal braces so that they butt join at the center. Screw the brace boards in place with 2 inch (50 mm) screws. Sand the table and brush on the preservative.

Helpful hint

If you are having trouble fitting the notched braces accurately – maybe the ones you have cut are too long – keep trimming the end of one until it fits perfectly, and then use this as a template for cutting the opposite brace.

Classic arbor

An arbor is not only a practical idea (a perfect way of providing a sheltered seat), but a beautiful and decorative structure in its own right. With climbing plants grown up its sides, particularly scented varieties such as jasmine and honeysuckle, you can create a delightful nook to escape to. Use it as a quiet place to read a book, or make it a corner for a romantic rendezvous – it's up to you.

TIME

Two weekends (four hours to prepare the site, and the rest of the time for the woodwork).

USEFUL TIP

Start by buying the lattice screens and then modify the design as necessary.

YOU WILL NEED

Materials *for an arbor 58¾ in (1.492 m) wide, 43⅞ in (1.114 m) deep, and 9 feet (2.738 m) high. (All rough-sawn pine pieces include excess length for wastage.)*

- Lattice screens: 4 screens, 6 feet (1.83 m) x 12 in (303 mm) (sides)
- Pine: 4 pieces, 6 feet (2 m) long, 3 x 3 in (75 x 75 mm) square section (main posts)
- Pine: 15 pieces, each 10 feet (3 m) long, 2 in (50 mm) wide, and 1¼ in (32 mm) thick (roof and back panels, seat supports and A-brace)
- Pine: 6 pieces, each 10 feet (3 m) long, 6 in (150 mm) wide and ⅞ in (22 mm) thick (top and bottom side boards, seat, decorative barge boards)
- Pine bevel-edged board: 20 pieces, each 10 feet (3 m) long, 4 in (100 mm) wide, and ⅜ in (10 mm) thick (back panel and roof)
- Zinc-plated countersunk Phillips screws: 100 x 2 in (50 mm) no. 8, 100 x 2¼ in (60 mm) no. 10, 20 x 3½ in (89 mm) no. 10
- Galvanized wire nails: 2 lb (1 kg) 4d (40 mm x 2.65 mm)
- Clear preservative

Tools

- Pencil, ruler, tape measure, compass, bevel gauge, and square
- Two portable workbenches
- Cordless electric drill with a Phillips screwdriver bit
- Drill bits to match screws
- Crosscut saw
- Hammer
- Four large clamps
- Electric jigsaw
- Electric sander with a pack of medium-grade sandpaper
- Paintbrush 1½ in (40 mm)

SIDE VIEW OF THE CLASSIC ARBOR

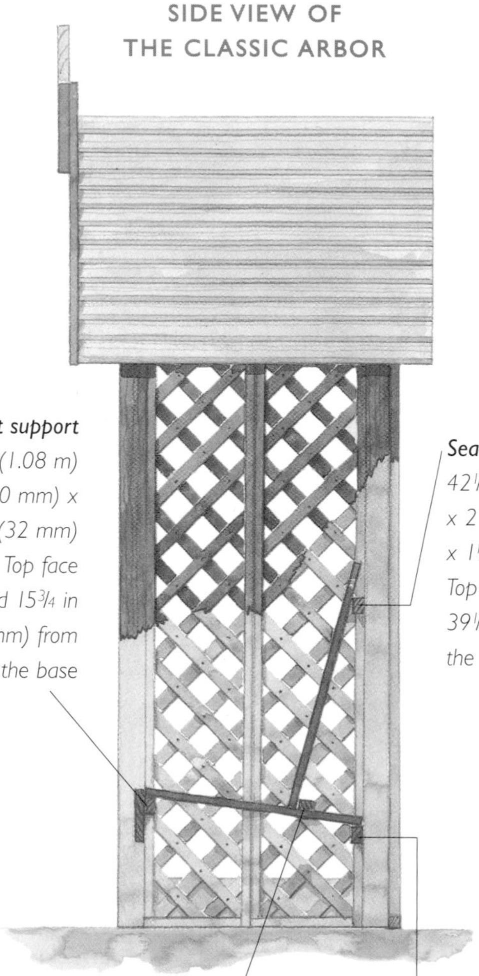

Seat support
42½ in (1.08 m) x 2 in (50 mm) x 1¼ in (32 mm)
Top face positioned 15¾ in (400 mm) from the base
Seat support
42½ in (1.08 m) x 2 in (50 mm) x 1¼ in (32 mm)
Top face positioned 39½ in (1 m) from the base
Seat support
42½ in (1.08 m) x 2 in (50 mm) x 1¼ in (32 mm)
Front face positioned 7⅞ in (200 mm) from back of the seat planks
Seat support
42½ in (1.08 m) x 2 in (50 mm) x 1¼ in (32 mm)
Top face positioned 11⅞ in (300 mm) from the base

CONTEMPLATIVE SEAT FOR TWO

This project is built around four slender lattice screens. Buy the screens first, as you may only be able to obtain them in a slightly different size to that we have quoted, and make adjustments to other materials if necessary. Basically, the arbor is a seat for two enclosed on three sides, with a roof over the top. We have designed the project so that it can be made as six knockdown units – the two lattice sides, the back panel, the two roof panels and the seat – with various other pieces used to support and decorate. The bevel-edged boards are lapped in such a way that they channel rain off the roof and back panel. The strength and stability of the overall structure are guaranteed by diagonal braces fastened to both the back panel and the roof. When we went to purchase the materials, the only available lattice screens and 6 inch (150 mm) boards were pre-treated with rather heavy brown wood preservative, so we decided to lighten the design by leaving all the other components in their natural color.

Classic arbor

EXPLODED VIEW OF THE CLASSIC ARBOR

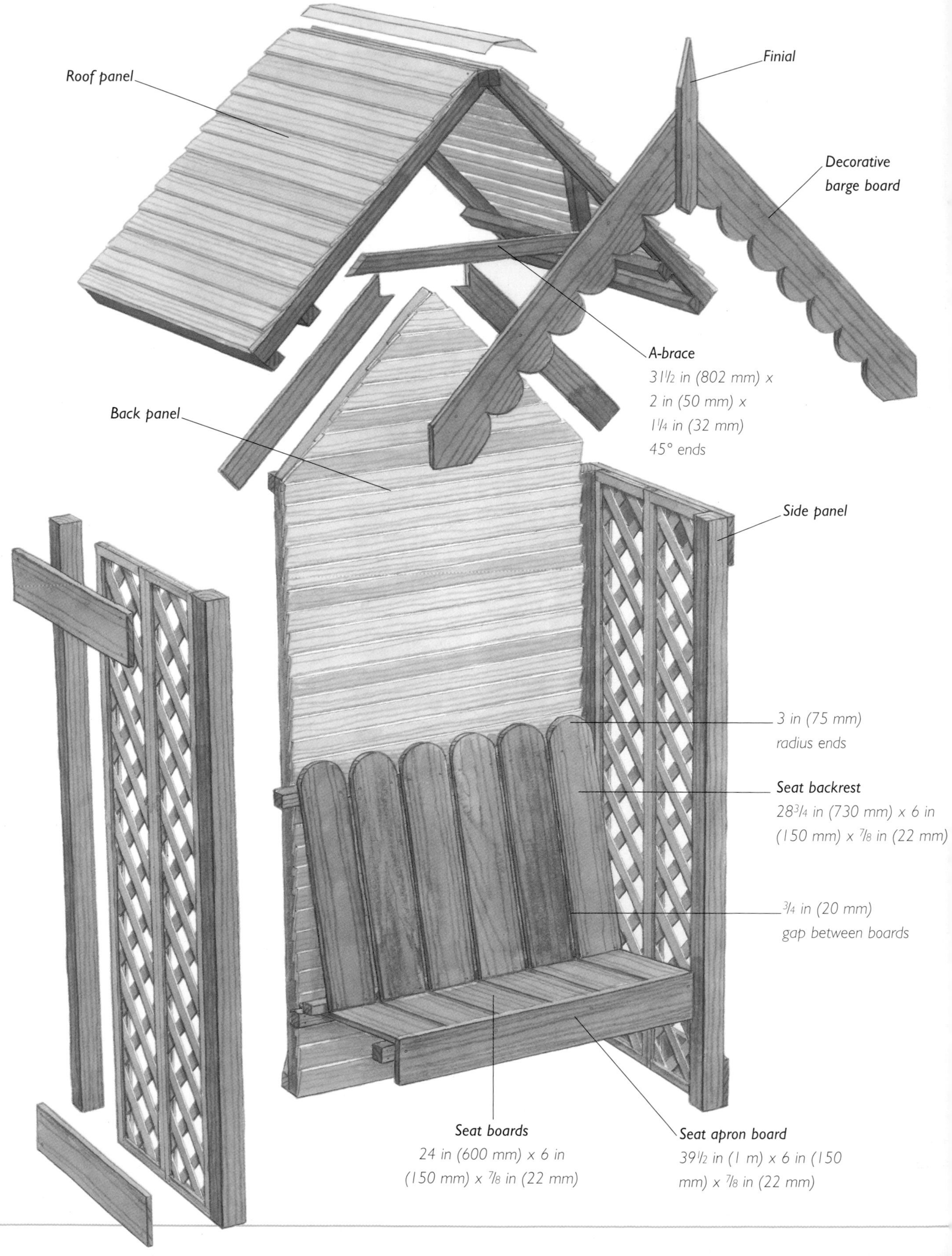
Roof panel
Finial
Decorative barge board
A-brace
31½ in (802 mm) x 2 in (50 mm) x 1¼ in (32 mm) 45° ends
Back panel
Side panel
3 in (75 mm) radius ends
Seat backrest
28¾ in (730 mm) x 6 in (150 mm) x ⅞ in (22 mm)
¾ in (20 mm) gap between boards
Seat boards
24 in (600 mm) x 6 in (150 mm) x ⅞ in (22 mm)
Seat apron board
39½ in (1 m) x 6 in (150 mm) x ⅞ in (22 mm)

SIDE VIEW
OF A ROOF PANEL

Notched end set at 45°
Bevel-edged board 42 in (1.07 m) x 4 in (100 mm) x 3/8 in (10 mm)
Location brace (top) and drip batten (bottom) 42 in (1.07 m) x 2 in (50 mm) x 1¼ in (32 mm)
38 in (965 mm) x 2 in (50 mm) x 1¼ in (32 mm)

UNDERSIDE VIEW
OF A ROOF PANEL

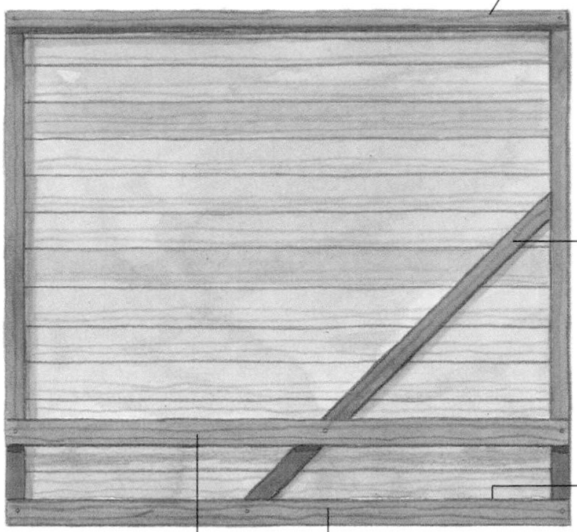
42 in (1.07 m) x 2 in (50 mm) x 1¼ in (32 mm)
Diagonal brace 33 in (846 mm) x 2 in (50 mm) x 1¼ in (32 mm) 45° ends
Location brace
Drip batten
Bottom of frame (Hidden from view) 39⅝ in (1.006 m) x 2 in (50 mm) x 1¼ in (32 mm)

FRONT VIEW
OF THE FINIAL

18 in (450 mm) x 2 in (50 mm) x 7/8 in (22 mm) 1 grid square equals 2 in (50 mm)

FRONT VIEW OF A BARGE BOARD

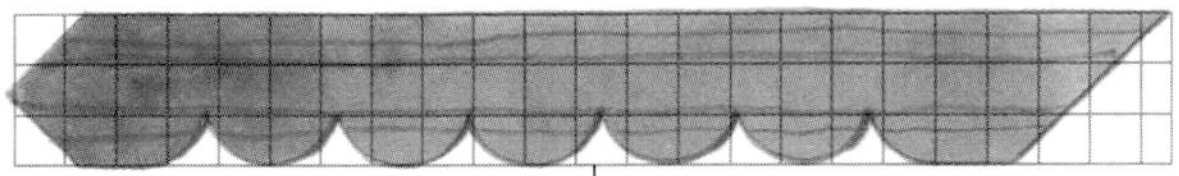
44½ in (1.131 m) x 6 in (150 mm) x 7/8 in (22 mm) 1 grid square equals 2 in (50 mm) 45° ends

BACK VIEW OF THE BACK PANEL

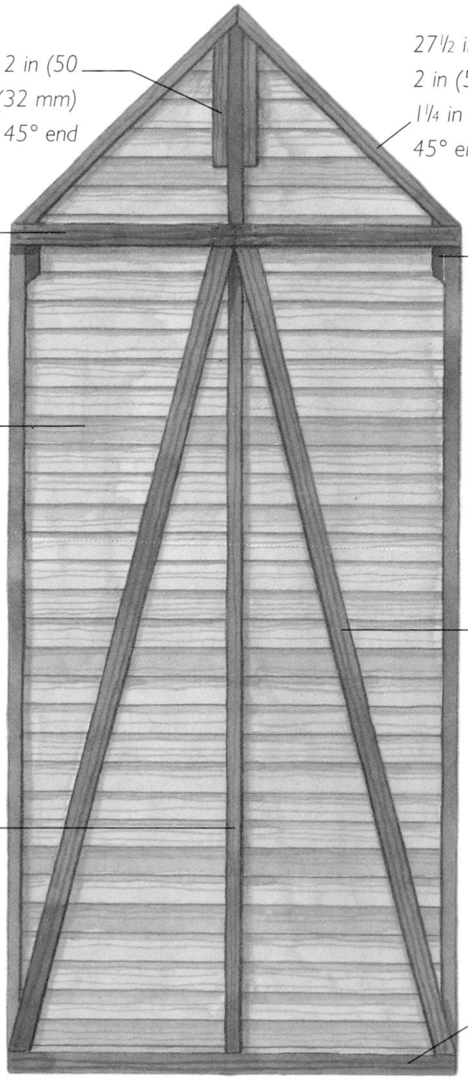
12 in (300 mm) x 2 in (50 mm) x 1¼ in (32 mm) 45° end
27½ in (697 mm) x 2 in (50 mm) x 1¼ in (32 mm) 45° ends
39½ in (1 m) x 2 in (50 mm) x 1¼ in (32 mm)
Location brace 6 in (150 mm) x 2 in (50 mm) x 1¼ in (32 mm) 45° ends
Bevel-edged board 39½ in (1 m) 4 in (100 mm) x 3/8 in (10 mm)
Diagonal brace 74½ in (1.893 m) x 2 in (50 mm) x 1¼ in (32 mm) 76° ends
93⅝ in (2.378 m) x 2 in (50 mm) x 1¼ in (32 mm) 45° pitched end
39½ in (1 m) x 2 in (50 mm) x 1¼ in (32 mm)

FRONT VIEW OF A SIDE PANEL

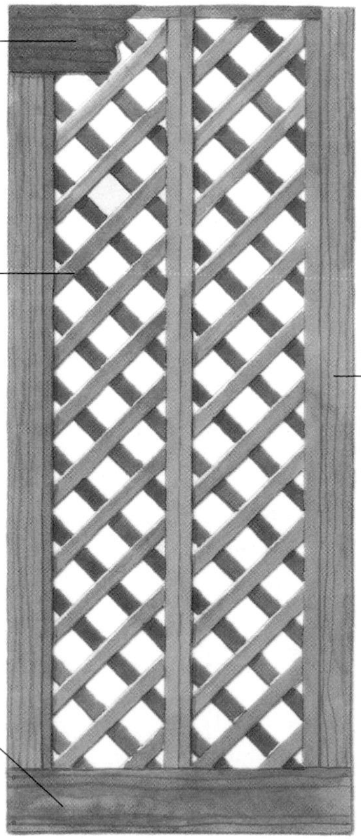
board (cut-away) 29¾ in (756 mm) x 6 in (150 mm) x 7/8 in (22 mm)
Lattice screen 6 feet (1.83 m) x 12 in (303 mm) x 1⅜ in (35 mm)
Main post 6 feet (1.83 m) x 3 in (75 mm) x 3 in (75 mm)
Side board 29¾ in (756 mm) x 6 in (150 mm) x 7/8 in (22 mm)

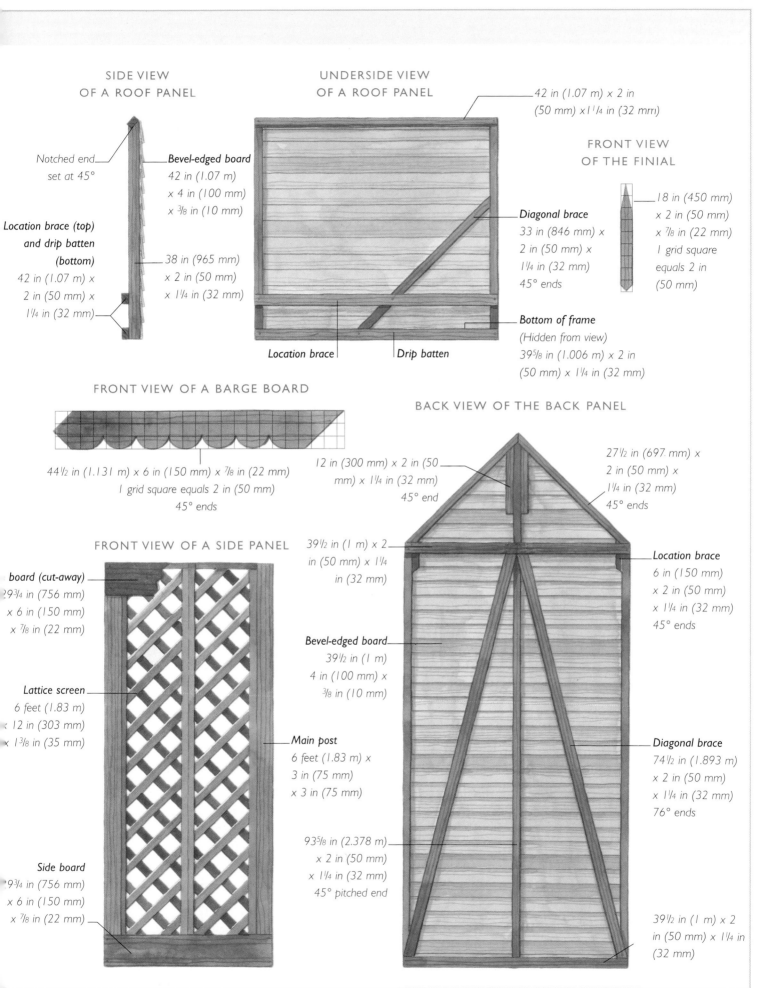

Step-by-step: **Making the classic arbor**

Screwing
Drive the screws through the side of the lattice

Lattice
Arrange the two screens side by side so that the pattern is aligned

1 Sandwich the lattice screens between the main posts and screw them in place with 2 inch (50 mm) screws. Set a 6-inch-wide (150 mm) board at top and bottom and screw these to the posts with 2 inch (50 mm) screws. Repeat this procedure so that you have two identical side panels.

Block joints
Pre-drill the blocks to prevent splitting

Strengthening
Use long offcuts to strengthen the ridge joint

2 Use the 2 inch (50 mm) x 1¼ inch (32 mm) section to make the back frame. Cut the parts to size with the crosscut saw and fasten them with 2½ inch (60 mm) screws. Screw blocks of waste at the angles to help firm up the joints.

Nailing
Use one nail at each end of the board

Overlapping
Make sure that the boards are overlapped in the correct way

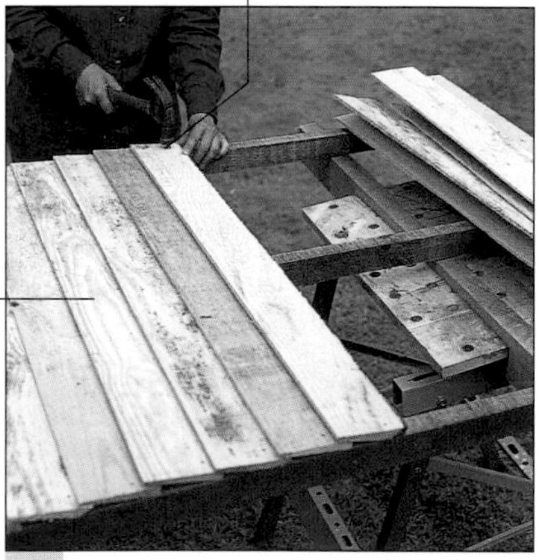

3 Cut the bevel-edged board into 39½ inch (1 m) lengths and position these on the back frame so that they lap over from top to bottom, ensuring that rain will be thrown off the back of the arbor. Drill pilot holes and then fasten the strips to the frame with the 4d (40 mm) nails.

Bevel-edged board
The boards are lapped so that water runs off the back of the arbor

Clamping
Set the clamps so that they are away from screw positions

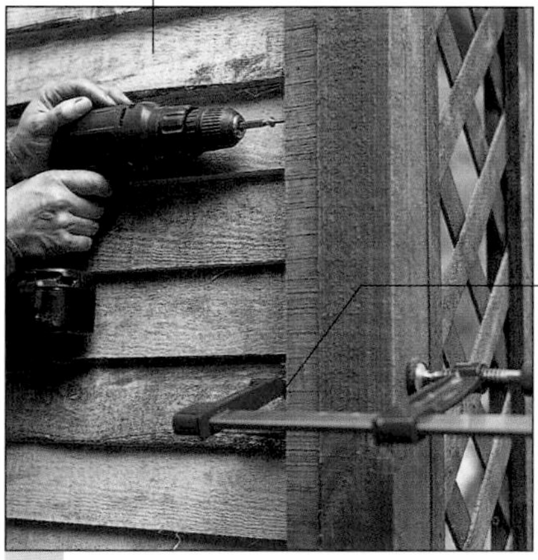

4 Clamp the two side panels to the back panel and fasten with the 2½ inch (60 mm) screws. Drive the screws through the edges of the panel and into the posts. Check that the structure is standing square and then add the additional horizontal and diagonal braces to the back panel.

Seat support
The planks that form the seat backrest are fixed to two battens

Sanding
Sand the seat boards to remove sharp corners and splinters

5 Position and fit the base for the seat, and then build off the seat to make the backrest. Fit the seat support battens with 2 inch (50 mm) screws. Use the jigsaw to cut the 3 inch (75 mm) radius curves on the top of the backrest boards. Leave a 3/4 inch (20 mm) space between the boards on both the seat and the backrest.

Location brace
The brace locates the roof on the posts and needs to be positioned accurately

Drip batten
Drill holes for the screws when you are working near the end of a piece of wood

Diagonal brace
The diagonal brace holds the roof panel square

6 Build and clad the two roof panels in much the same way as the back panel, and then fasten additional strengtheners in place with 2 1/2 inch (60 mm) screws – a diagonal brace, a drip batten, and a location brace (see the working drawing).

Location
Center the location brace on top of the post

Screwing
Angling the screw allows you to fasten the roof panel to the post

7 Set the two roof panels in place, so that the location batten is more or less centered on the post (at all four corners) and fasten with the 3 1/2 inch (89 mm) screws. Run the screws up at an angle, using at least two screws for each of the posts.

Positioning
Set the top edge of the barge board so that it is higher than the roof strips

Clamping
Use a clamp to hold the board in postion while you work

A-brace
This horizontal bar prevents the roof from spreading

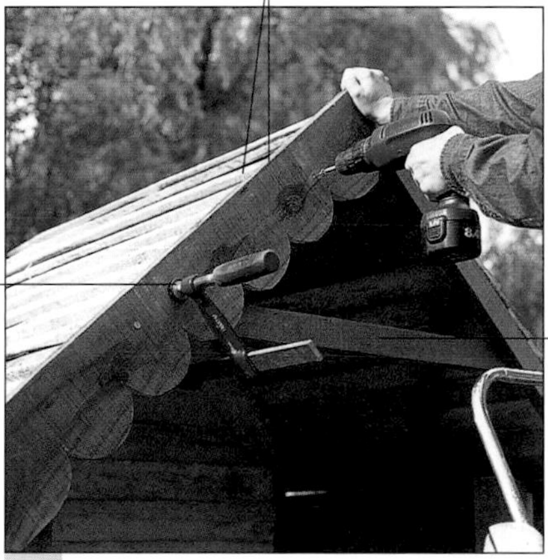

8 With 2 inch (50 mm) screws, fasten the A-brace to link the two roof panels. Draw the shape of the barge boards and saw them out with the jigsaw. Clamp the boards in place and fasten with 2 inch (50 mm) screws. Fit the finial spike to cover the joint. Finally, sand down and give the arbor a coat of preservative.

Wheeled bench

Imagine going out into the yard on a beautiful morning to sit and enjoy the sunshine. Unfortunately, as soon as the sun moves, you will be left shivering in the shade. However, if you were sitting on our beautiful wheeled bench, you would simply take hold of its handles and move it to a sunny location.

TIME

Two days' work (about a day and a half for the woodwork, and half a day for painting and finishing).

USEFUL TIP

Don't try to cut costs by using small wheels – in order to move the bench when the lawn is damp, you need large wheels.

YOU WILL NEED

Materials *for a bench 74¾ in (1.898 m) wide, 30½ in (775 mm) deep, and 34½ in (877 mm) high. (All rough-sawn pine pieces include excess length for wastage.)*

- Pine: 3 pieces, 10 feet (3 m) long, 3½ in (90 mm) wide, and 1½ in (38 mm) thick (main handle beams, legs, stretchers, axle blocks)
- Pine: 2 pieces, 8 feet (2 m) long, 6 in (150 mm) wide, and ¾ in (20 mm) thick (arms and shaped backrest boards)
- Pine: 2 pieces, 10 feet (3 m) long, 2 in (50 mm) wide, and 1¼ in (30 mm) thick (table supports, table front horizontal, back rail)
- Pine: 8 pieces, 10 feet (3 m) long, 4 in (100 mm) wide, and ¾ in (20 mm) thick (seat slats, back slats and tabletop)
- Pine: 4 pieces, 8 feet (2 m) long, 3 in (75 mm) wide, and ¾ in (20 mm) deep (seat and back supports)
- Pine: 1 piece, 8 feet (2 m) long, 1½ in (40 mm) wide, and ¾ in (20 mm) thick (underarm supports)
- Plastic wheels: 2 wheels, 8 in (200 mm) in diameter, ¾ in (20 mm) holes in centers
- Galvanized threaded rod: 3 feet (1 m) long and ¾ in (20 mm) in diameter with washers and nuts to fit
- Zinc-plated, countersunk screws: 100 x 2 in (48 mm) no. 8, 100 x 2¾ in (70 mm) no. 10
- Matt green acrylic paint
- Clear preservative

Tools

- Pencil, ruler, tape measure, and square
- Portable workbench
- Crosscut saw
- Cordless electric drill with a Phillips screwdriver bit
- Drill bits to match screw sizes
- Electric jigsaw
- Electric sander with a pack of medium-grade sandpaper
- Electric drill with a ¾ in (20 mm) flat bit and a ⅜ in (10 mm) twist bit
- Wrench to fit the nuts
- Paintbrush 1½ in (40 mm)

A SEAT IN THE SUN

This bench is built with butt joints throughout. There are no complex saw cuts to make or expensive hardware to buy – the bench is created by lots of straight cuts and put together with a generous number of screws. However, the strength of the main joints (where all the 3½ x 1½ inch (90 x 40 mm) sections come together at the corners) relies on the joints being tight. Therefore it is vital that all your measurements and saw cuts are as accurate as possible.

Note how at all the important structural intersections, for example where the legs pass through the frame, the screws are always run into strong face grain, rather than into weak end grain. While the components that make up the main frame are square to each other, the seat and back supports are, for reasons of comfort, canted back at a slight angle. The bottoms of the legs on the wheel side of the bench are reduced in height by ½ inch (15 mm) and the corners chamfered to allow the bench to be tilted up and pushed along. We painted the finished bench with a wash of green acrylic paint, and when it was dry rubbed it down to cut through the paint on edges and corners. The whole bench was then given a coat of clear preservative.

SIDE VIEW OF WHEELED BENCH

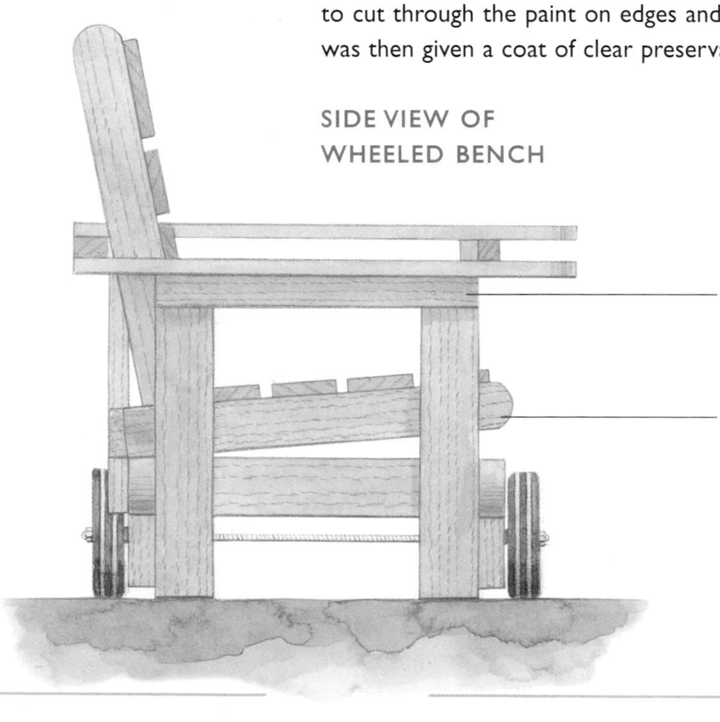

Underarm support
19¾ in (500 mm) x 1½ in (40 mm) x ¾ in (20 mm)

Seat support
Raised 1½ in (40 mm) from the top of the front beam (the back support is tilted so that the corner coincides with the top inside corner of the handle rail)

Wheeled bench

EXPLODED VIEW OF THE WHEELED BENCH

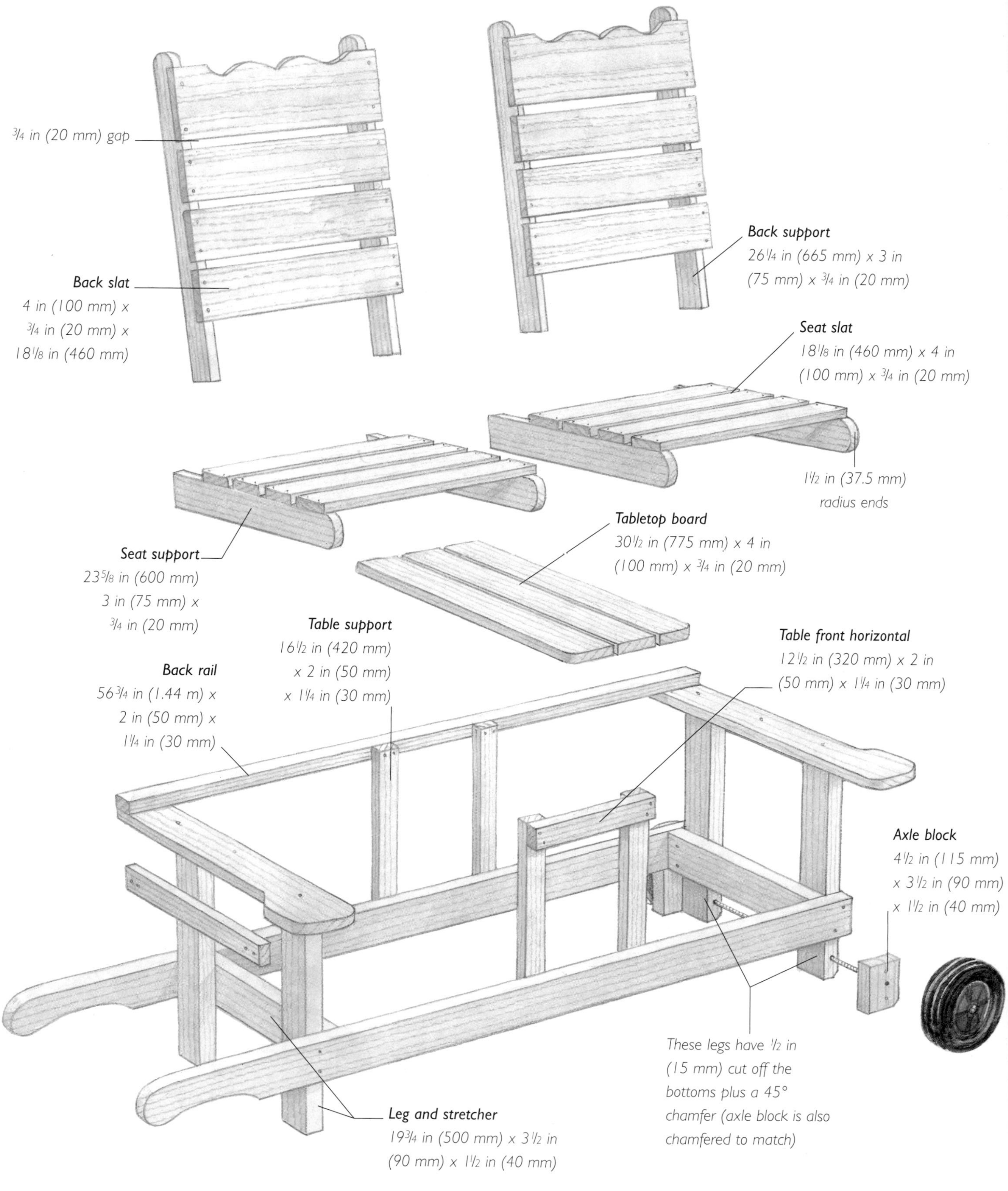
3/4 in (20 mm) gap
Back slat
4 in (100 mm) x
3/4 in (20 mm) x
18 1/8 in (460 mm)
Back support
26 1/4 in (665 mm) x 3 in
(75 mm) x 3/4 in (20 mm)
Seat slat
18 1/8 in (460 mm) x 4 in
(100 mm) x 3/4 in (20 mm)
1 1/2 in (37.5 mm)
radius ends
Tabletop board
30 1/2 in (775 mm) x 4 in
(100 mm) x 3/4 in (20 mm)
Seat support
23 5/8 in (600 mm)
3 in (75 mm) x
3/4 in (20 mm)
Table support
16 1/2 in (420 mm)
x 2 in (50 mm)
x 1 1/4 in (30 mm)
Back rail
56 3/4 in (1.44 m) x
2 in (50 mm) x
1 1/4 in (30 mm)
Table front horizontal
12 1/2 in (320 mm) x 2 in
(50 mm) x 1 1/4 in (30 mm)
Axle block
4 1/2 in (115 mm)
x 3 1/2 in (90 mm)
x 1 1/2 in (40 mm)
These legs have 1/2 in
(15 mm) cut off the
bottoms plus a 45°
chamfer (axle block is also
chamfered to match)
Leg and stretcher
19 3/4 in (500 mm) x 3 1/2 in
(90 mm) x 1 1/2 in (40 mm)

FRONT VIEW OF THE WHEELED BENCH

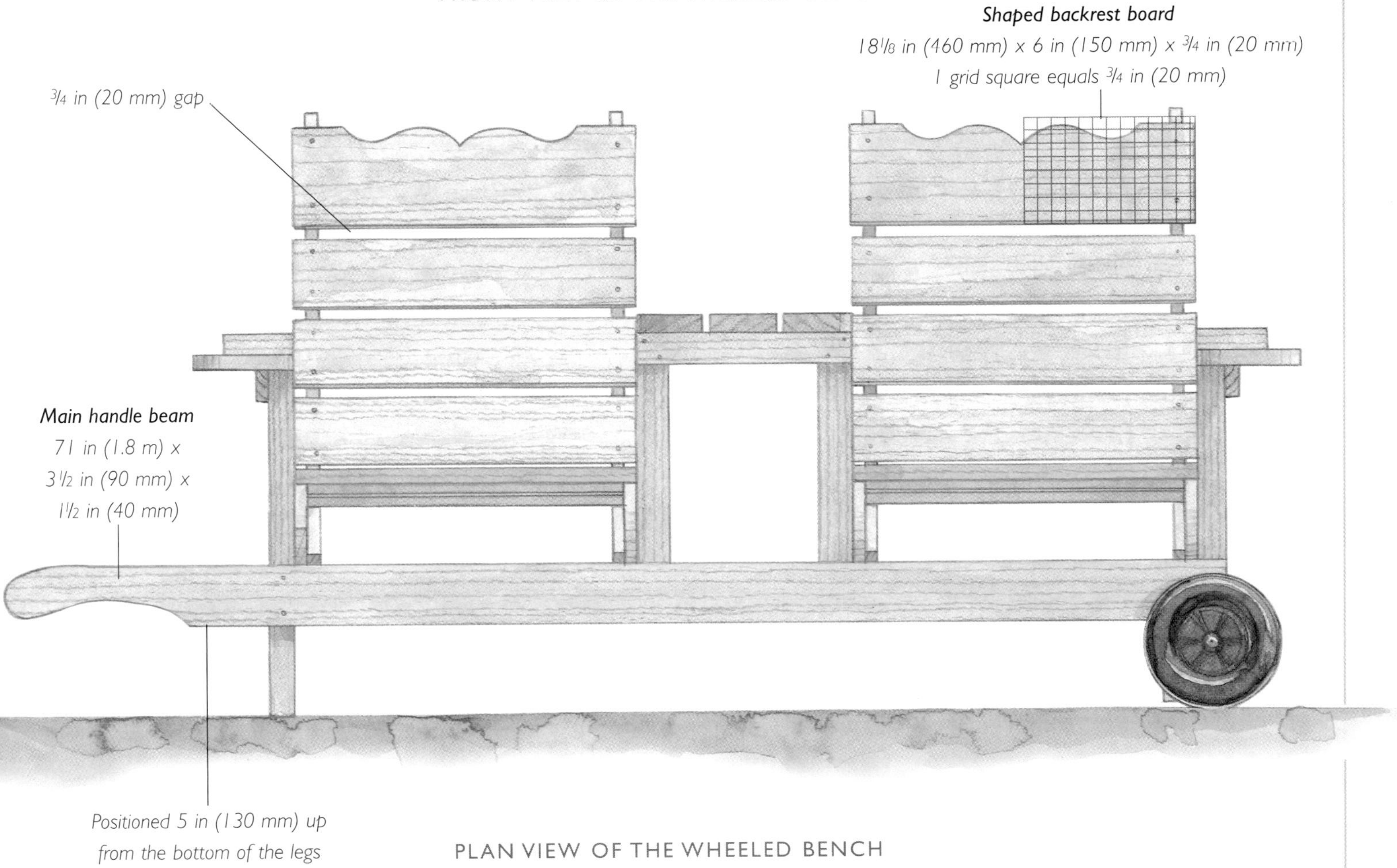
Shaped backrest board
18 1/8 in (460 mm) x 6 in (150 mm) x 3/4 in (20 mm)
1 grid square equals 3/4 in (20 mm)
3/4 in (20 mm) gap
Main handle beam
71 in (1.8 m) x
3 1/2 in (90 mm) x
1 1/2 in (40 mm)
Positioned 5 in (130 mm) up
from the bottom of the legs

PLAN VIEW OF THE WHEELED BENCH

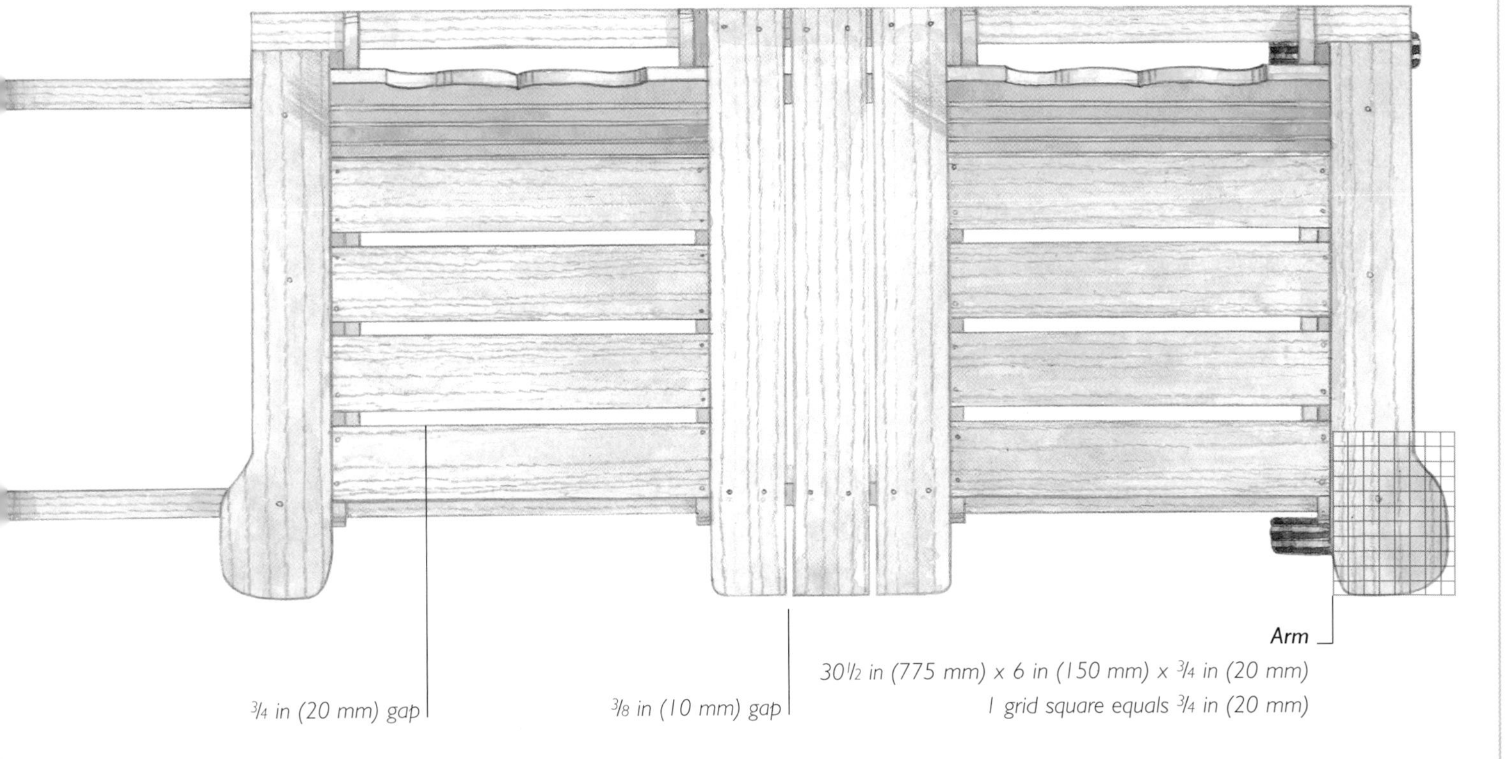
Arm
30 1/2 in (775 mm) x 6 in (150 mm) x 3/4 in (20 mm)
1 grid square equals 3/4 in (20 mm)
3/4 in (20 mm) gap
3/8 in (10 mm) gap

Step-by-step: **Making the wheeled bench**

Legs
Make sure that the legs are parallel to each other
Right angle
Check that the leg is square to the stretcher

1 With the crosscut saw, cut the legs and the stretchers to length (all at 19¾ inches (500 mm)), establish the position of the crossover, and fasten with one 2¾ inch (70 mm) screw at each joint. Check for squareness and then drive in a second 2¾ inch (70 mm) screw.

Sawing the handle
Work slowly as the wood is very thick
Beam position
Position the beam so that the line of cut is unobstructed
Sanding
Use the electric sander to soften the edges of the handle

2 Cut the handle beams to a length of 71 inches (1.8 m) with the crosscut saw. Next, draw the shape of the handle and, working slowly, saw out the profile with the jigsaw. Work in the direction of the end of the handle, to avoid cutting directly into end grain.

Tabletop position
Screw on one tabletop board to establish the middle of the table
Marking
Use a square to mark the position of the two flanking planks

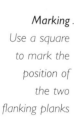

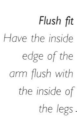

3 Link the arms with the back support and screw it in place. Using 2 inch (48 mm) screws, screw on the table supports, fasten the middle tabletop board to establish the center of the table and then flank it with another tabletop board at each side.

Screw position
Make sure that the screws are centered in the thickness of the underarm support
Flush fit
Have the inside edge of the arm flush with the inside of the legs
Underarm support
Screw the support so that it is flush with the top of the legs

4 Cut the arms to shape and sand them to a smooth finish. Using 2 inch (48 mm) screws, fasten the underarm supports to the top of the legs (so the legs are set parallel) and then screw the arms in place with screws

Back support
Ease the bottom of the board forward to make the back angle

Screw position
Drive the screws through both boards and into the legs

5 Take the two boards that go to make the seat supports, establish the correct canted angle, and fasten them with 2 inch (48 mm) screws at the front end and the intersection of the two boards. Use a 2¾ inch (70 mm) screw (recessed in a ⅜ inch (10 mm) hole by 1¼ inches (30 mm) from the back rail through into the edge of the back support.

End of cut
Run the cut to finish in the central cleft

Clamping
Position and clamp the board so that the cutting line is unobstructed

Template
Use the waste from cutting the first half of the design to mark out the other half

6 Draw half of the cyma curve at the center of the shaped backrest board and saw out with the jigsaw. Use the waste piece as a template to establish the other half of the design, and to create the total shape on the other shaped backrest board.

Back slats
Use waste pieces of board as spacers

Spacer
Use two thicknesses of waste board to bring the first board up to the correct height

7 Screw the seat and back slats in place with 2 inch (48 mm) screws. Ensure that the spacing between the slats is correct by sliding pieces of waste wood between neighboring boards.

Threaded rod
Drill a hole for the rod (it should not be a tight fit)

Leg blocks
Chamfer the corner of the blocks and legs with a saw

Fastening wheels
The order for fastening the wheels is washer, nut, washer, wheel, washer, nut and a final nut to lock

8 Cut away the lower outside corners of the legs. Drill holes, ¾ inch (20 mm) in diameter, through both the leg blocks and the legs, and then slide the axle in place. Finally, sand everything to a smooth finish, lay on a thin wash of paint, and give the bench a coat of preservative.

Inspirations: Benches and chairs

Dreams about my childhood often feature an old oak bench in a neglected, overgrown orchard, dappled sunshine, buzzing insects, and a rich carpet of fallen fruit! You may dedicate a lot of time to working on your yard and garden to create a leafy heaven, but it is important to spend time actually sitting and enjoying the changing seasons and their cast of plants and flowers. A good selection of seats is vital.

RIGHT Swinging benches are a great place to while away an afternoon. Incorporating one into an arbor makes a delightful feature that is very pleasant to sit in when it is surrounded by scented climbers.

ABOVE A grand bench and a modern push-along lounger provide a variety of seating options on this patio, to suit both mood and weather.

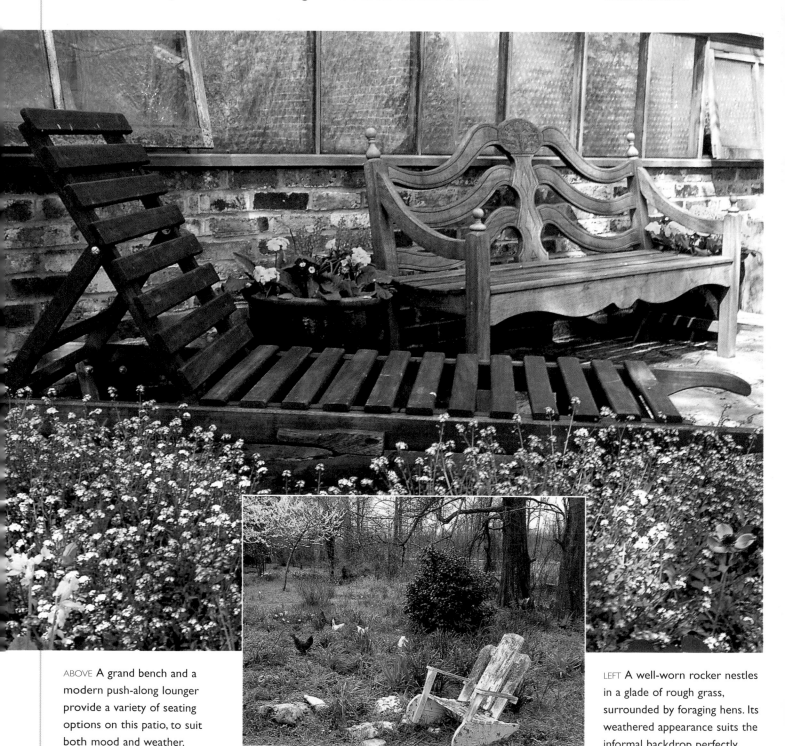

LEFT A well-worn rocker nestles in a glade of rough grass, surrounded by foraging hens. Its weathered appearance suits the informal backdrop perfectly.

Romantic arch

This project really comes into its own in summer – there is something gloriously exciting about a wooden arch heavy with clematis and honeysuckle, and it makes a really beautiful feature. Position it at the entrance to a garden area, where it will frame the vista behind it, or site it midway along a path to add a romantic touch.

TIME

A full weekend (about twelve hours for the woodwork, and four hours for putting together and finishing).

USEFUL TIP

Avoid using a wood preservative that is toxic to plants. Use a water-based finish – for example matt white paint.

YOU WILL NEED

Materials *for an arch 45 in (1.150 m) wide, 18 in (440 mm) deep, and 89 in (2.250 m) high. (All rough-sawn pine pieces include excess length for wastage.)*

- Pine: 4 pieces, 6 feet (2 m) x 3 in (75 mm) square (posts)
- Pine: 4 pieces, 8 feet (2 m) long, 2 in (50 mm) wide, 1¼ in (30 mm) thick (cross ties)
- Pine: 1 piece, 3 feet (1 m) long, 3 in (75 mm) x 3 in (75 mm) triangular section (capital cross ties)
- Pine: 4 pieces, each 8 feet (2 m) long, 6 in (150 mm) wide, and ¾ in (20 mm) thick (arch laminations)
- Spiked post supports: 4 (one for each post)
- Zinc-plated, countersunk screws: 100 x 1½ in (38 mm) no. 8, 100 x 2½ in (65 mm) no. 10
- Exterior-quality matt paint

Tools

- Pencil, ruler, tape measure, compass, protractor, bevel gauge, and square
- Two portable workbenches
- Plywood workboard, about 4 feet (1 m) square
- Electric jigsaw
- Large clamp
- Cordless electric drill with a Phillips screwdriver bit
- Drill bits to match screw sizes
- Electric sander with a pack of medium-grade sandpaper
- Crosscut saw
- Mallet
- Bevel-edged chisel: 2 in (50 mm)
- Sledgehammer
- Wrench to fit the post support nuts
- Paintbrush 1½ in (40 mm)

FRONT VIEW OF THE ROMANTIC ARCH

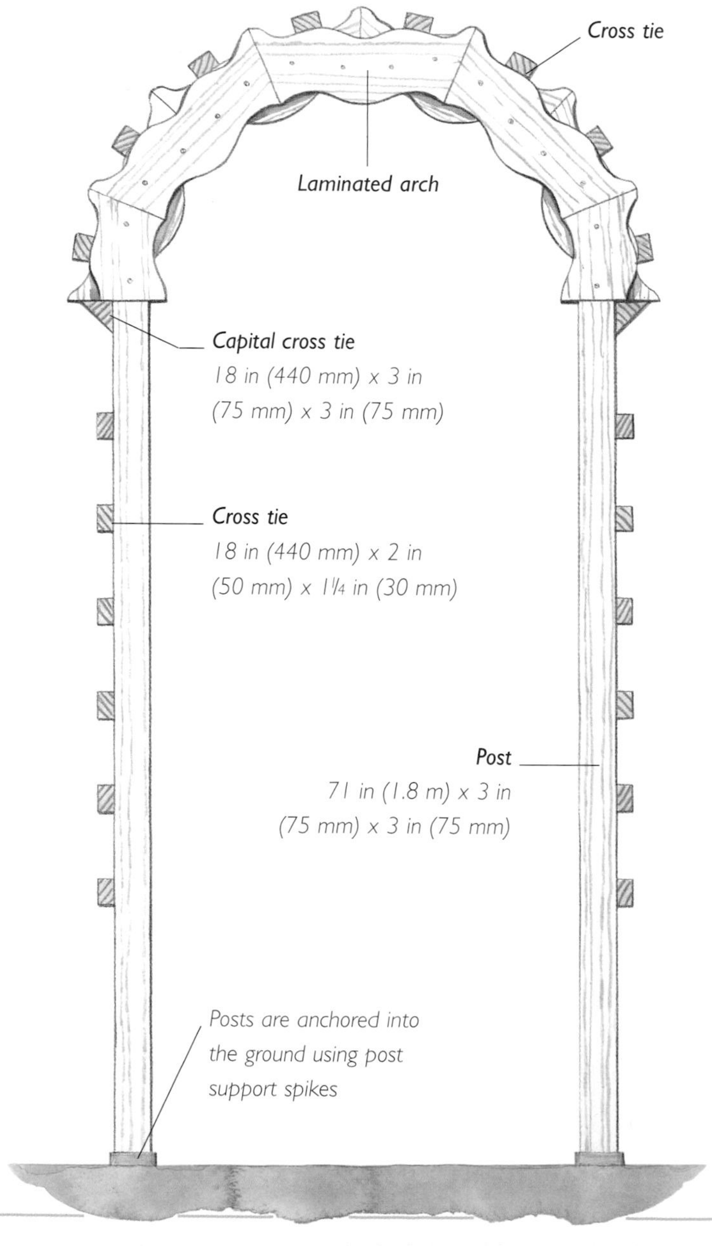
Cross tie
Laminated arch
Capital cross tie
18 in (440 mm) x 3 in (75 mm) x 3 in (75 mm)
Cross tie
18 in (440 mm) x 2 in (50 mm) x 1¼ in (30 mm)
Post
71 in (1.8 m) x 3 in (75 mm) x 3 in (75 mm)
Posts are anchored into the ground using post support spikes

UNDERNEATH THE ARCHES

The clever thing about this structure is the way that the arch tops consist of a number of identical components. Each is made up of eight curvy-shaped boards (one cut in half), which are cut from 6 inch (150 mm)-wide board and laminated together with screws. Once made, the arches are screwed into the half-laps at the top of the posts, and the whole thing is held together and braced with cross ties. We used ties 2 inches (50 mm) wide and 1¼ inches (30 mm) thick for running up the sides of the posts and over the arch, and two triangular-section ties to act as capitals at the point where the arched top joints into the posts. Finally, just to make sure that the structure stays put, the four posts are located in spiked post supports. The finished arch is an ideal structure for hanging a gate – see the Picket Gate project on page 46.

Romantic arch

THE PIECES THAT MAKE UP THE INNER LAYER OF ONE ARCH

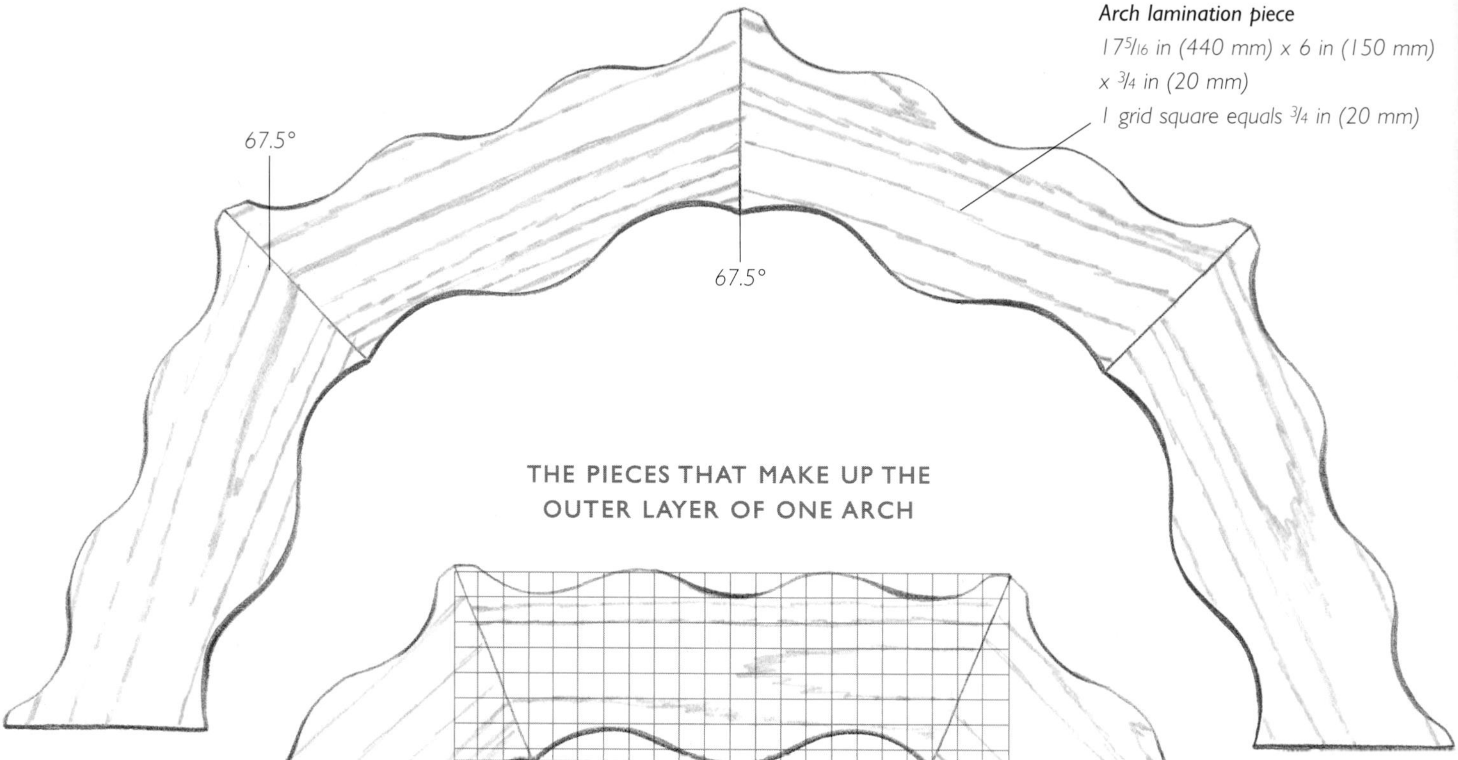
Arch lamination piece
17 5/16 in (440 mm) x 6 in (150 mm) x 3/4 in (20 mm)
1 grid square equals 3/4 in (20 mm)
67.5°
67.5°

THE PIECES THAT MAKE UP THE OUTER LAYER OF ONE ARCH

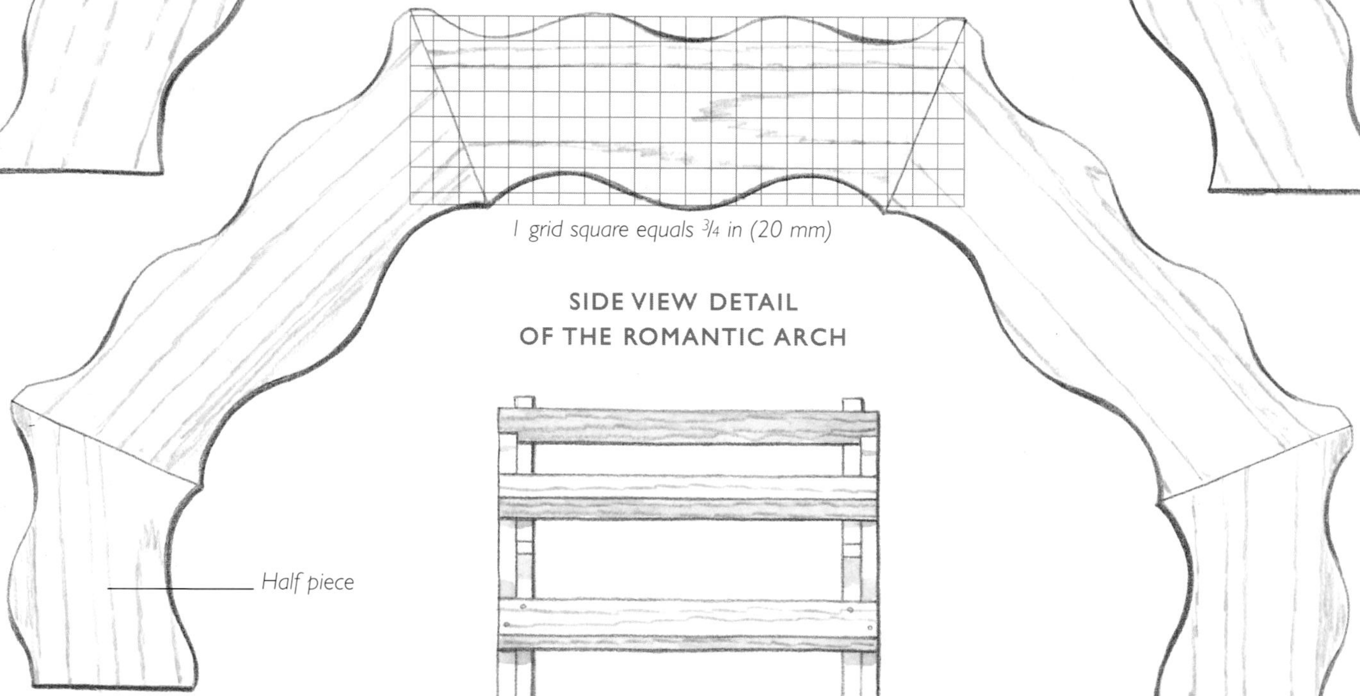
1 grid square equals 3/4 in (20 mm)
Half piece

SIDE VIEW DETAIL OF THE ROMANTIC ARCH

Cross tie
18 in (440 mm) x 2 in (50 mm) x 1 1/4 in (30 mm)
Capital cross tie
18 in (440 mm) x 3 in (75 mm) x 3 in (75 mm) right-angled triangular section

EXPLODED VIEW OF THE ROMANTIC ARCH

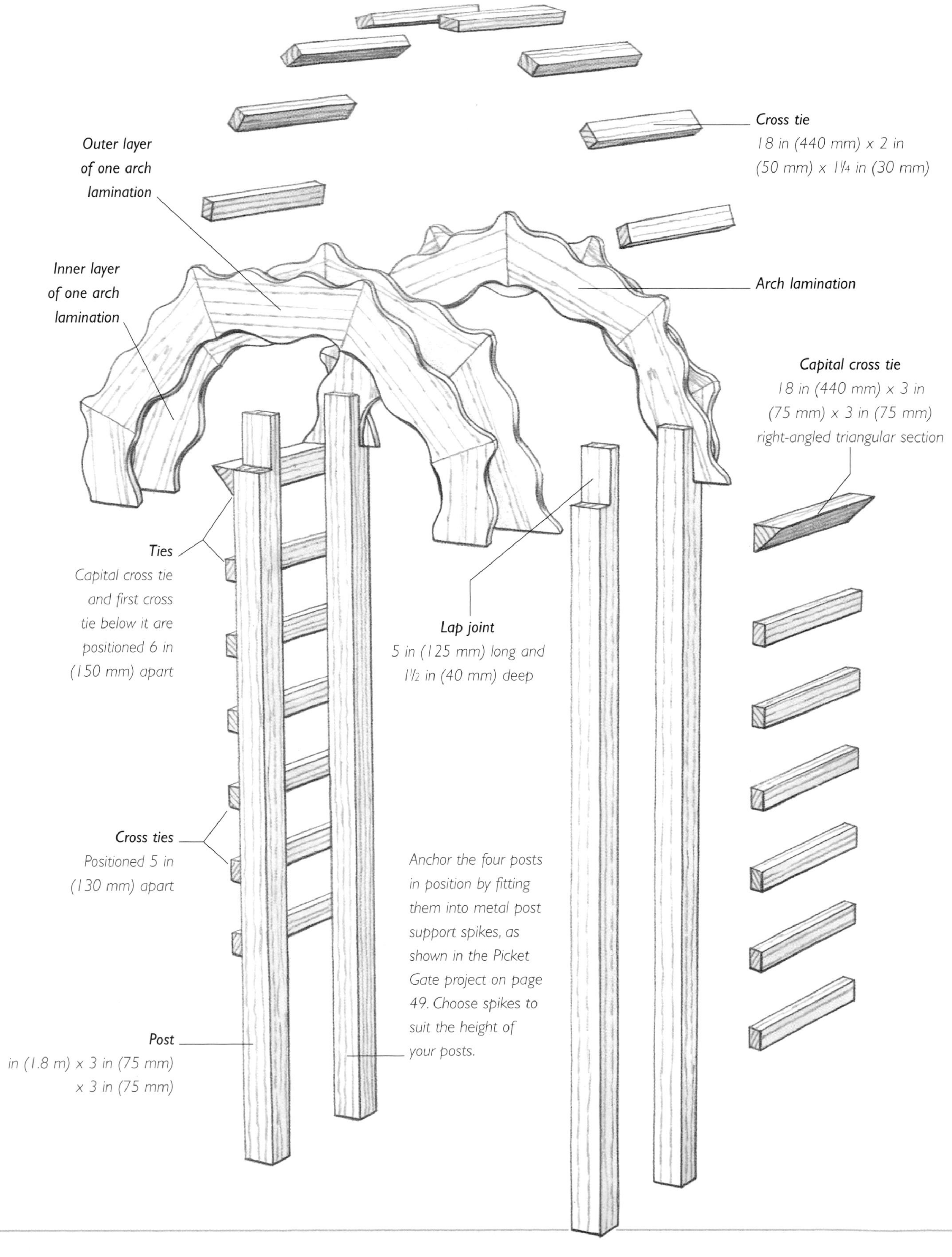
Cross tie
18 in (440 mm) x 2 in (50 mm) x 1¼ in (30 mm)
Outer layer of one arch lamination
Inner layer of one arch lamination
Arch lamination
Capital cross tie
18 in (440 mm) x 3 in (75 mm) x 3 in (75 mm) right-angled triangular section
Ties
Capital cross tie and first cross tie below it are positioned 6 in (150 mm) apart
Lap joint
5 in (125 mm) long and 1½ in (40 mm) deep
Cross ties
Positioned 5 in (130 mm) apart
Anchor the four posts in position by fitting them into metal post support spikes, as shown in the Picket Gate project on page 49. Choose spikes to suit the height of your posts.
Post
in (1.8 m) x 3 in (75 mm) x 3 in (75 mm)

Step-by-step: **Making the romantic arch**

Sawing square
Hold the saw at right angles to the wood

Cutting angle
Neighboring boards share the same 67.5° cut

1 Set the engineer's protractor to an angle of 67.5° and lay out the sixteen boards that make up the arch laminations for the top of the arch. The longest side of each board should measure 17 5/16 inches (440 mm) from point to point.

Template
Use the piece of waste as a template

Holding firm
If you can't hold the wood with your hand, use a clamp to hold it down

2 Draw the curved profile of the arch lamination on one board and use the jigsaw to saw it out. Use the waste pieces as templates to help you draw the shapes on the other fifteen boards.

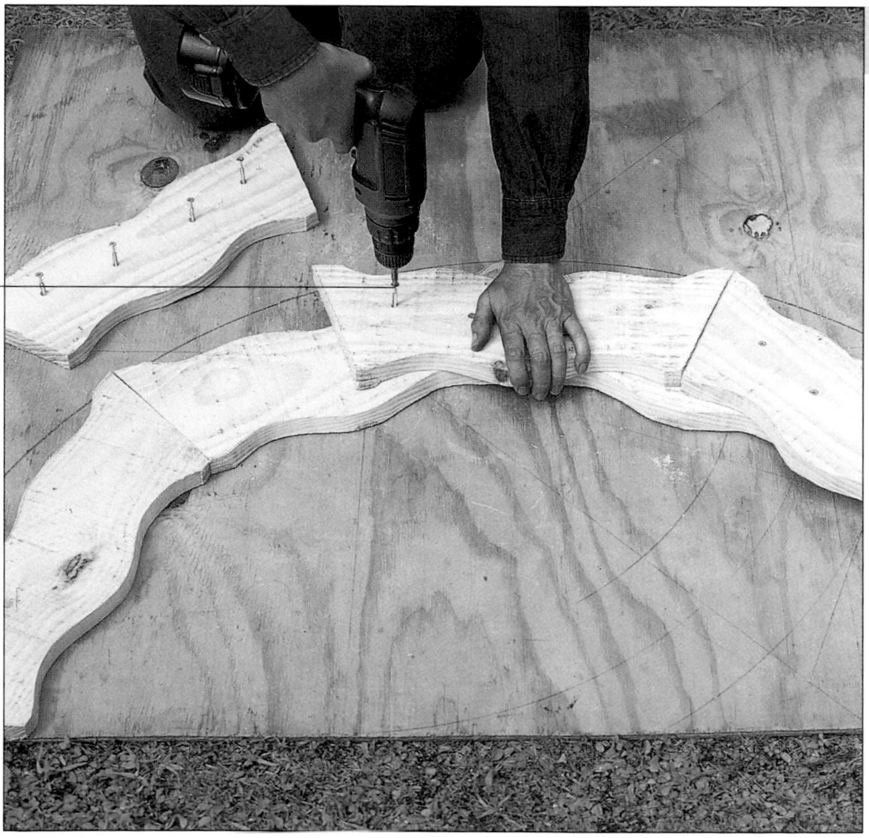

Screwing
Run four screws in from one side

3 Sandwich and clamp the boards together to make the double-thickness shape and fasten together with 1 1/2 inch (38 mm) screws. You will need two half-boards to complete each form.

Helpful hint

When you have lots of pieces to fit together, as in this design, you may find that inaccuracies in marking out and cutting are amplified. To avoid problems, arrange the pieces that make up the arch (without screwing them), check that they fit well, and make adjustments as necessary.

Lapped ends
The end of the arch fits squarely against the top of the post

Waste block
Use the lap waste to lift the arch up to the correct height

Flush fit
The face of the arch must be flush with the face of the post

4 Set out the top of the posts with laps at 5 inches (125 mm) long and $1^1/_2$ inches (40 mm) deep, and cut them out with the crosscut saw, mallet and chisel. Screw the arch in place in the lap with $2^1/_2$ inch (60 mm) screws. Repeat this sequence for the other arch.

Angled screws
Run the screws in at a slight angle

Butted fit
Butt the triangular section hard into the right angle

5 Cut the triangular section for the capital cross ties into two lengths of 18 inches (440 mm) and use $2^1/_2$ inch (65 mm) screws to fasten them in place so that they are butted hard up against the underside edge of the bottom of the laminated arch.

Tie position
Center the cross ties between humps

Screwholes
Drill holes for the screws

Parallel ties
Ensure that the cross ties are parallel to each other

6 Using $1^1/_2$ inch (38 mm) screws, fasten all the cross ties up the posts and over the arch. Rub down the arch to remove splinters, give it a generous coat of white paint, and anchor in spiked supports as shown in the Picket Gate project (see page 46).

Corner patio planter

If your patio is dotted with a colorful collection of little potted plants that are forever being knocked over by children or pets, this is the perfect project for you. Gather up your plants, arrange them in the planter, and you have an enviable patio feature that keeps the area tidy and displays the plants attractively.

TIME

A weekend (twelve hours for the woodwork and a few hours for finishing).

USEFUL TIP

The joints are slightly tricky to cut, so take your time.

YOU WILL NEED

Materials *for a planter 22 in (565 mm) high and 37½ in (950 mm) square. (All rough-sawn pine pieces include excess length for wastage.)*

- Pine: 1 piece, 6 feet (2 m) long and 3 in (75 mm) square (main posts)
- Pine: 5 pieces 8 feet (7 pieces 2 m) long, each 4 in (100 mm) wide, and 1 in (25 mm) thick (back and front pickets)
- Pine: 3 pieces 8 feet (4 pieces 2 m) long, each 6 in (150 mm) wide, and ¾ in (20 mm) thick (front rails, floorboards, post capitals)
- Pine: 2 pieces, each 6 feet (2 m) long, 2 in (50 mm), and 1½ in (35 mm) thick (back rails)
- Zinc-plated, countersunk Phillips screws: 100 x 1½ in (38 mm) no. 8
- Acrylic paint in color to suit
- Clear preservative

Tools

- Pencil, ruler, tape measure, compass, bevel gauge, and square
- Portable workbench
- Flexible metal rule
- Electric jigsaw
- Crosscut saw
- Tenon saw
- Cordless electric drill and Phillips screwdriver bit
- Drill bit, ¾ in (20 mm) wide (for boring out the mortises)
- Mallet
- Bevel-edged chisel, 1½ in (35 mm) wide
- Drill bits to match screws
- Electric sander with a pack of medium-grade sandpaper
- Paintbrush: 1¼ in (30 mm) wide

COMPLETELY CORNERED

The design brief for this project was six-fold. The planter had to be raised up off the ground, it had to fit into a right-angled corner, it had to present a curved front, it had to look good alongside a picket fence, it had be scaled and detailed so it suited a cottage garden, and it had to be strong.

In many ways, the resulting design is very straightforward – really it is just a right-angled box with pickets to the sides. However, the curved front rails and the mortise and tenon joints make it a little more complex. The front rails are slightly unusual in that the tenons run at a skewed angle into the mortises. The joints aren't particularly difficult to cut, but you do need to spend longer than usual at the laying out stage. When we came to painting the finished piece, we decided that the only way to achieve a subtle color was to water down the acrylic paint to a thin wash, and then to top this with a coat of clear preservative.

FRONT VIEW OF THE CORNER PATIO PLANTER

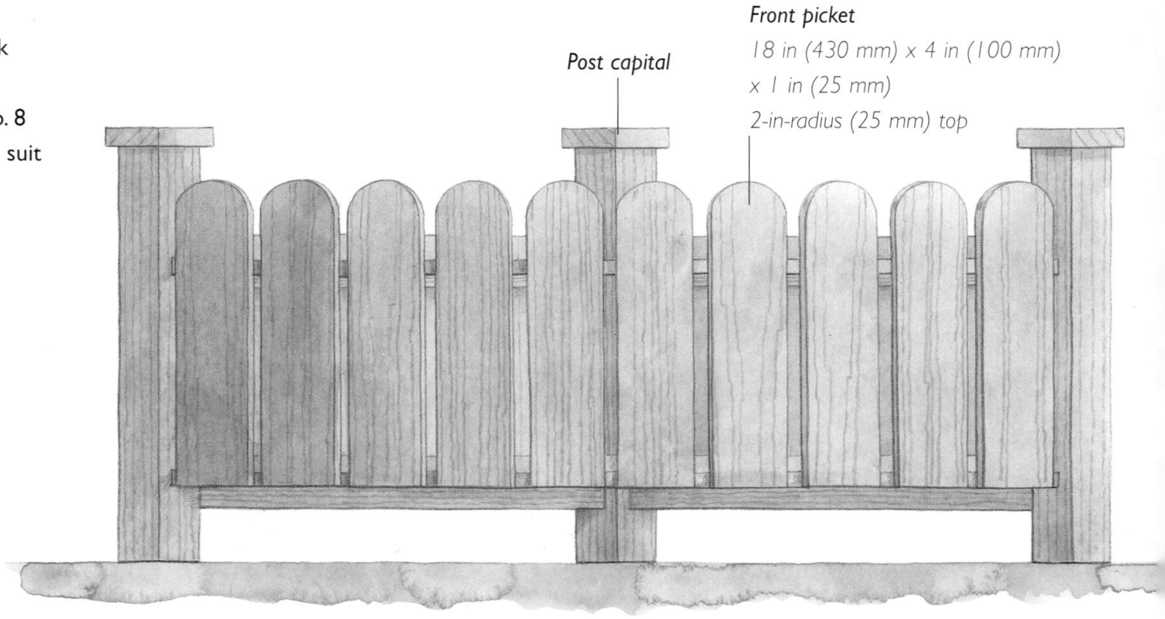
Post capital
Front picket
18 in (430 mm) x 4 in (100 mm) x 1 in (25 mm)
2-in-radius (25 mm) top

Corner patio planter

SIDE VIEW OF THE CORNER PATIO PLANTER

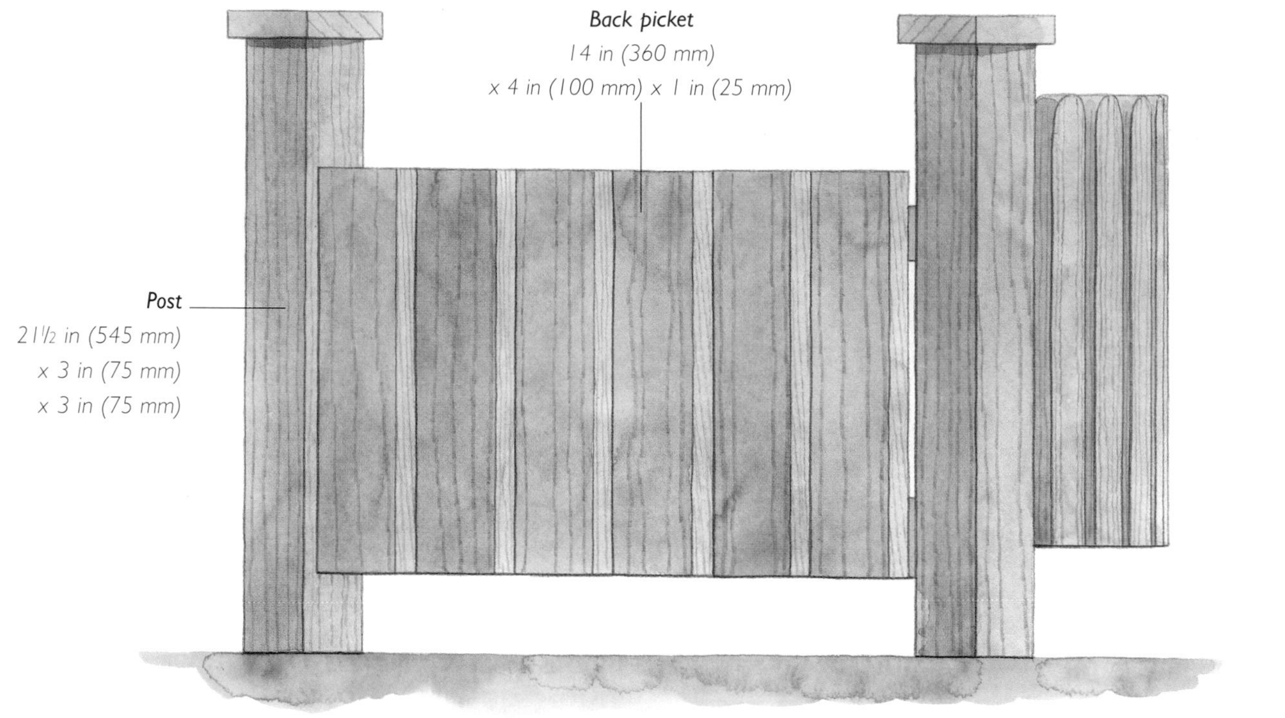
Back picket
14 in (360 mm)
x 4 in (100 mm) x 1 in (25 mm)
Post
21½ in (545 mm)
x 3 in (75 mm)
x 3 in (75 mm)

PLAN VIEW OF THE CORNER PATIO PLANTER

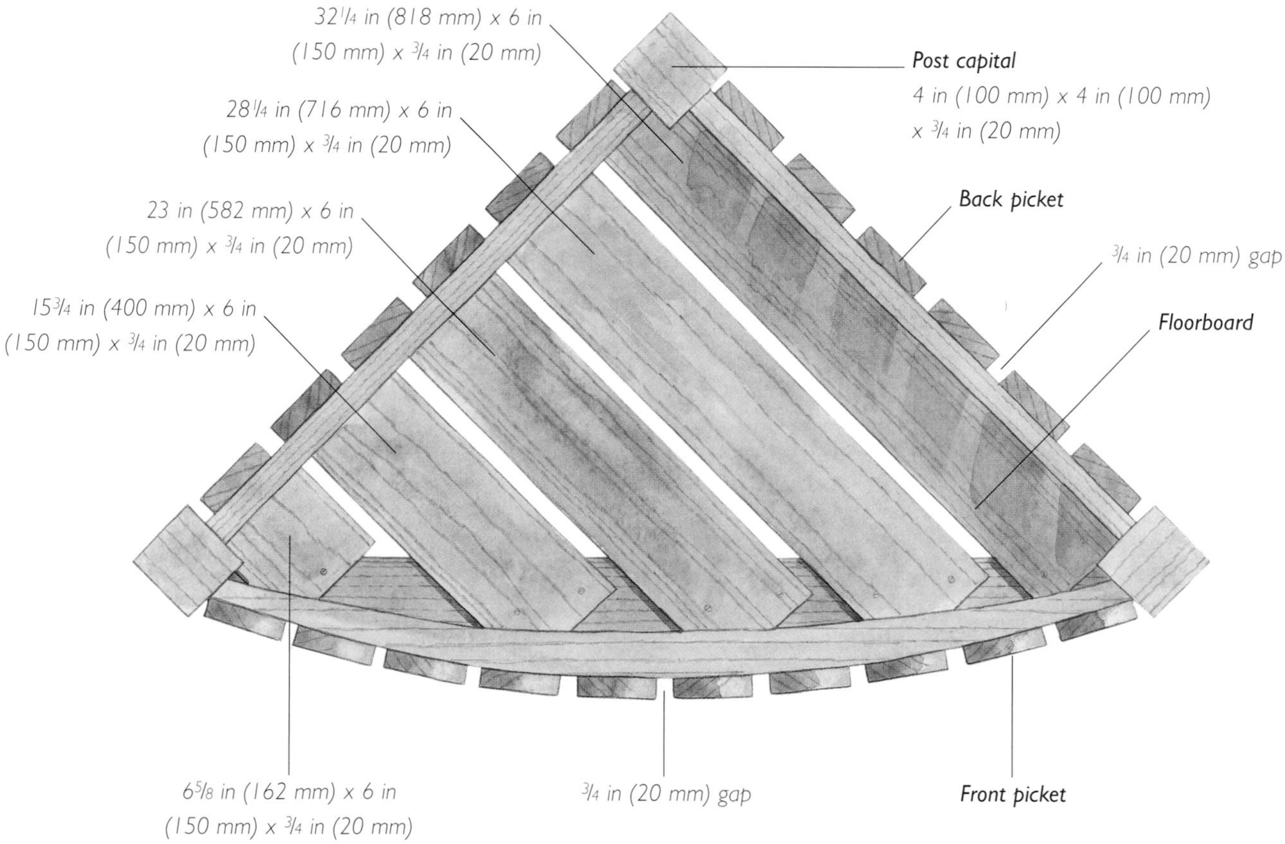
32¼ in (818 mm) x 6 in
(150 mm) x ¾ in (20 mm)
28¼ in (716 mm) x 6 in
(150 mm) x ¾ in (20 mm)
23 in (582 mm) x 6 in
(150 mm) x ¾ in (20 mm)
15¾ in (400 mm) x 6 in
(150 mm) x ¾ in (20 mm)
Post capital
4 in (100 mm) x 4 in (100 mm)
x ¾ in (20 mm)
Back picket
¾ in (20 mm) gap
Floorboard
6⅝ in (162 mm) x 6 in
(150 mm) x ¾ in (20 mm)
¾ in (20 mm) gap
Front picket

EXPLODED VIEW OF THE CORNER PATIO PLANTER

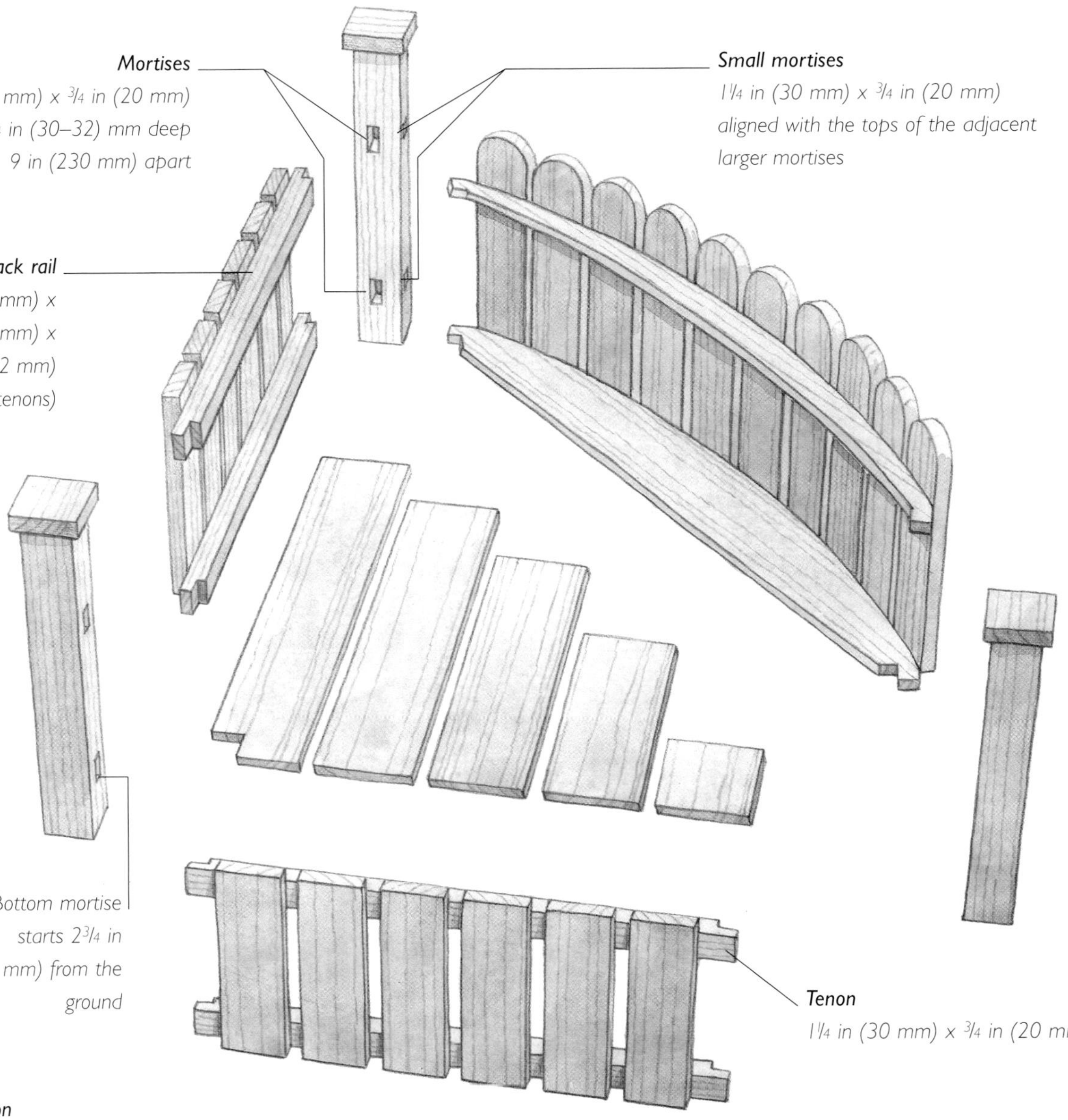

Mortises
2 in (50 mm) x ¾ in (20 mm)
1¼ in (30–32) mm deep
9 in (230 mm) apart
Small mortises
1¼ in (30 mm) x ¾ in (20 mm)
aligned with the tops of the adjacent
larger mortises
Back rail
33 in (835 mm) x
2 in (50 mm) x
1¼ in (32 mm)
(including tenons)
Bottom mortise
starts 2¾ in
(70 mm) from the
ground
Tenon
1¼ in (30 mm) x ¾ in (20 mm)

DETAIL OF THE TOP CURVED FRONT RAIL

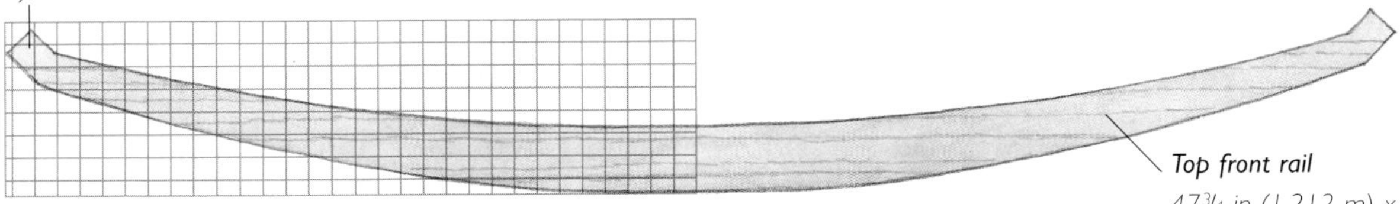

Tenon
1¼ in (30 mm)
x ¾ in (20 mm)
Top front rail
47¾ in (1.212 m) x 6 in
(150 mm) x ¾ in (20 mm)
1 grid square equals ¾ in (20 mm)

DETAIL OF THE BOTTOM CURVED FRONT RAIL

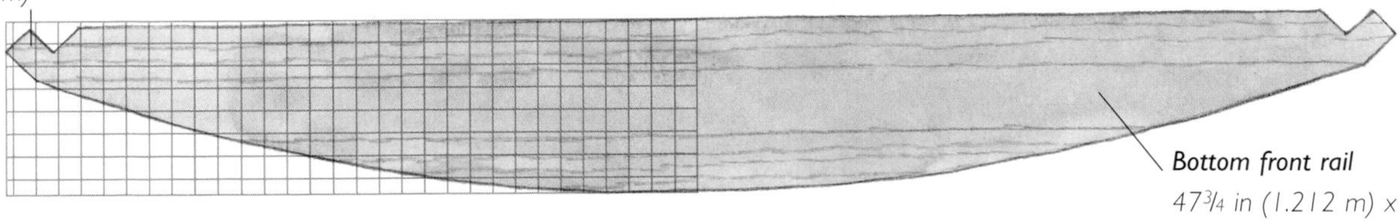

Tenon
1¼ in (30 mm)
x ¾ in (20 mm)
Bottom front rail
47¾ in (1.212 m) x 6 in
(150 mm) x ¾ in (20 mm)
1 grid square equals ¾ in (20 mm)

Step-by-step: **Making the corner patio planter**

Marking the curve
Bend the rule to mark out one half of the curve at a time

Nails
Secure the end of the rule between two nails

1 Lay out the design of the curved front rails on the 6-inch-wide (150 mm) board. Use the metal rule to achieve the shape of the curve. Saw out the profile with the jigsaw.

Cutting the tenon
Cut down the grain of the wood to the waste side of the line

Sawing
Use your forefinger to help set the angle of the saw cut

2 Lay out the ends of the straight back rails with tenons $1\frac{1}{4}$ inches (30 mm) long and $\frac{3}{4}$ inch (20 mm) wide, the waste piece measuring $1\frac{1}{4}$ inches (30 mm) long and $\frac{1}{2}$ inch (15 mm) wide. Cut the joint with the crosscut and tenon saws and tidy up with the chisel.

Chisel
Square the back of the chisel with the line

Securing
Make sure that the post is tightly clamped in the bench

3 Cut the three main posts to length and lay out the position of the mortises. Clear the bulk of the mortise waste with the drill and then cut back to the line with the mallet and chisel.

Screwing
Run a screw through the mortise and tenon joint

Bottom board
The wide board goes at the bottom

4 Assemble the frame, knock the joints home and secure them with screws. The bottom board is positioned so that the generous straight edge becomes a support for the floorboards.

Notched board
Cut the first board so that it fits around the post

Board ends
Save time by leaving the board ends square

5 Cut the waste lengths of board to make floorboards to fit inside the base, spacing them $3/4$ inch (20 mm) apart. Fasten with screws. The boards can be left square-cut where they fit the front rail, but the longest board needs to be notched to fit around the back post.

Helpful hint

If you have plenty of wood to spare and you want to make the finish of the base neater, the ends of the floorboards can be cut to fit the shape of the curved front rail piece.

Bottom of picket
The bottom of the pickets should be flush with the rail

Spacer
Use a piece of scrap wood for a spacer

6 Cut semicircular radius curves on top of the front pickets. Screw the pickets in place, so that they are spaced by the thickness of a board, and so that the bottom edge of the picket is flush with the underside of the front rail. Cut three post capitals 4 inches (100 mm) square and $3/4$ inch (20 mm) thick and screw them in place on top of the posts. Finally, sand the planter, then paint it and coat with preservative.

Potting table

A potting table is a real boon to keen gardeners. No more stooping to dip into massive bags of compost, or fumbling around looking for a level surface to work on. You simply fill the table's side tray with compost, line up flowerpots and plants, and get on with potting. Everything you need is comfortably at hand.

TIME

A weekend to have the table ready for use.

USEFUL TIP

You may wish to adjust the height of the table to suit your own needs.

YOU WILL NEED

Materials *for a potting table 51 in (1.295 m) wide, 26 in (662 mm) deep, and 62 in (1.547 m) high.*

- Pine: 2 pieces, each 8 feet (2 m) long, 3½ in (90 mm) wide, and 1½ in (35 mm) thick (front and back legs)
- Pine: 3 pieces, each 10 feet (3 m) long, 4 in (100 mm) wide, and ¾ in (20 mm) thick (end boards, top and bottom horizontal rails, tray pieces, peg board)
- Pine: 1 piece, 3 feet (1 m) long, 1¼ in (30 mm) wide, and ¾ in (20 mm) thick (tray corner support blocks)
- Pine: 3 pieces, each 10 feet (3 m) long, 6 in (150 mm) wide, and ⅞ in (22 mm) thick (tray base, table base, tabletop, decorative back board, brackets, top shelf)
- Dowel: 1 piece, 3 feet (1 m) long and ⅞ in (22 mm) in diameter (pegs)
- Waterproof glue
- Zinc-plated, countersunk Phillips screws: 100 x 1½ in (38 mm) no. 8
- Teak oil

Tools

- Pencil, ruler, tracing paper and square
- Portable workbench
- Crosscut saw
- Cordless electric drill with a Phillips screwdriver bit
- Selection of drill bits
- Electric jigsaw
- Electric sander with a pack of medium-grade sandpaper
- Paintbrush 1½ in (40 mm)

SIDE VIEW OF THE POTTING TABLE

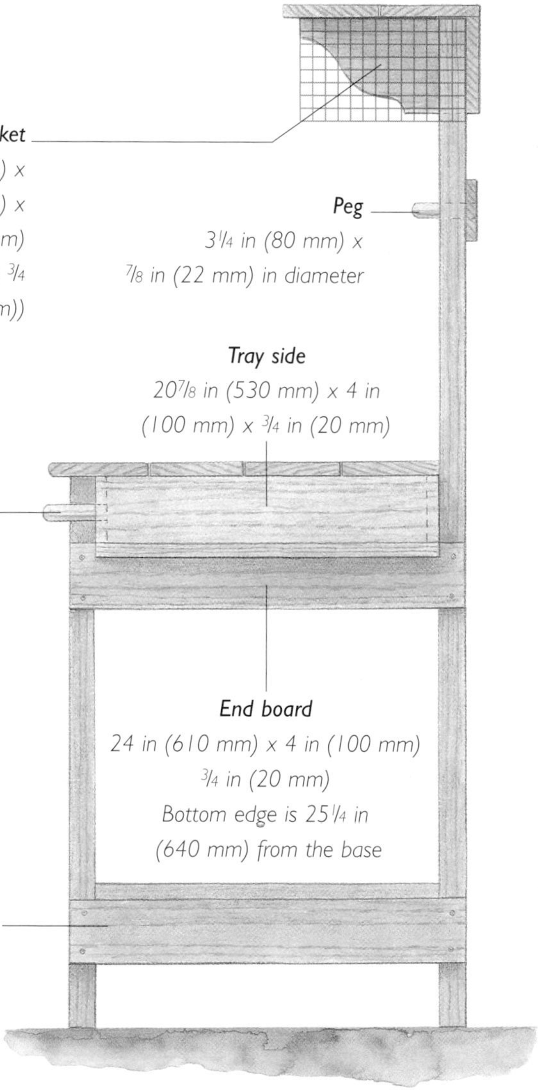
Shelf bracket
10 in (253 mm) x
6 in (150 mm) x
⅞ in (22 mm)
(1 grid square equals ¾ in (20 mm))
Peg
3¼ in (80 mm) x
⅞ in (22 mm) in diameter
Tray side
20⅞ in (530 mm) x 4 in (100 mm) x ¾ in (20 mm)
Peg
3¼ in (80 mm) x
⅞ in (22 mm) in
diameter
End board
24 in (610 mm) x
4 in (100 mm) x
¾ in (20 mm)
Bottom edge is
4 in (100 mm)
from the base
End board
24 in (610 mm) x 4 in (100 mm)
¾ in (20 mm)
Bottom edge is 25¼ in
(640 mm) from the base

A POTTING TABLE FOR ALL SEASONS

The total height of the bench is 62 inches (1.574 m), with the worksurface set at 34 inches (862 mm) high. The top horizontal rails, which link the legs and support the worksurface at back and front, also run through to the right-hand side of the worksurface to form the sides of the compost tray. If you are left-handed, all you do is modify the design so that the rails run through to the other end of the bench. The structure is simple and direct – there are no complicated joints to cut and the horizontal members are butted and screwed to the vertical posts. In use, the tray is filled with compost, small tools are hung on the pegs, seed packets and other items are stored on the top shelf, and of course the base surface is just right for stacking flowerpots and a watering can. Note how the worksurface boards are butted edge to edge, while the base surface boards are spaced to allow for easy cleaning.

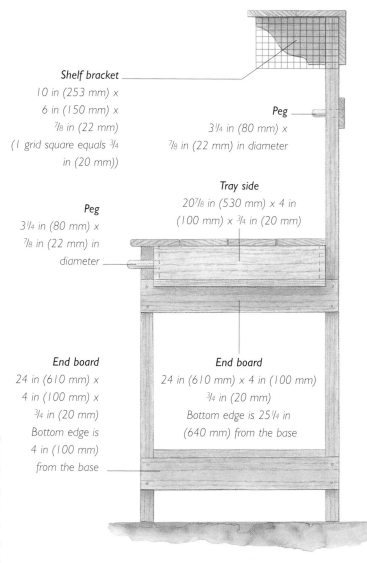

It's a perfect no-nonsense piece of garden furniture that draws inspiration from early nineteenth-century furniture designs in featuring smooth cyma curves on the back board and the brackets. If you are a keen gardener and enjoy taking cuttings and potting plants, this potting table will contribute something special to your workshop or greenhouse.

Potting table

FRONT VIEW OF THE POTTING TABLE

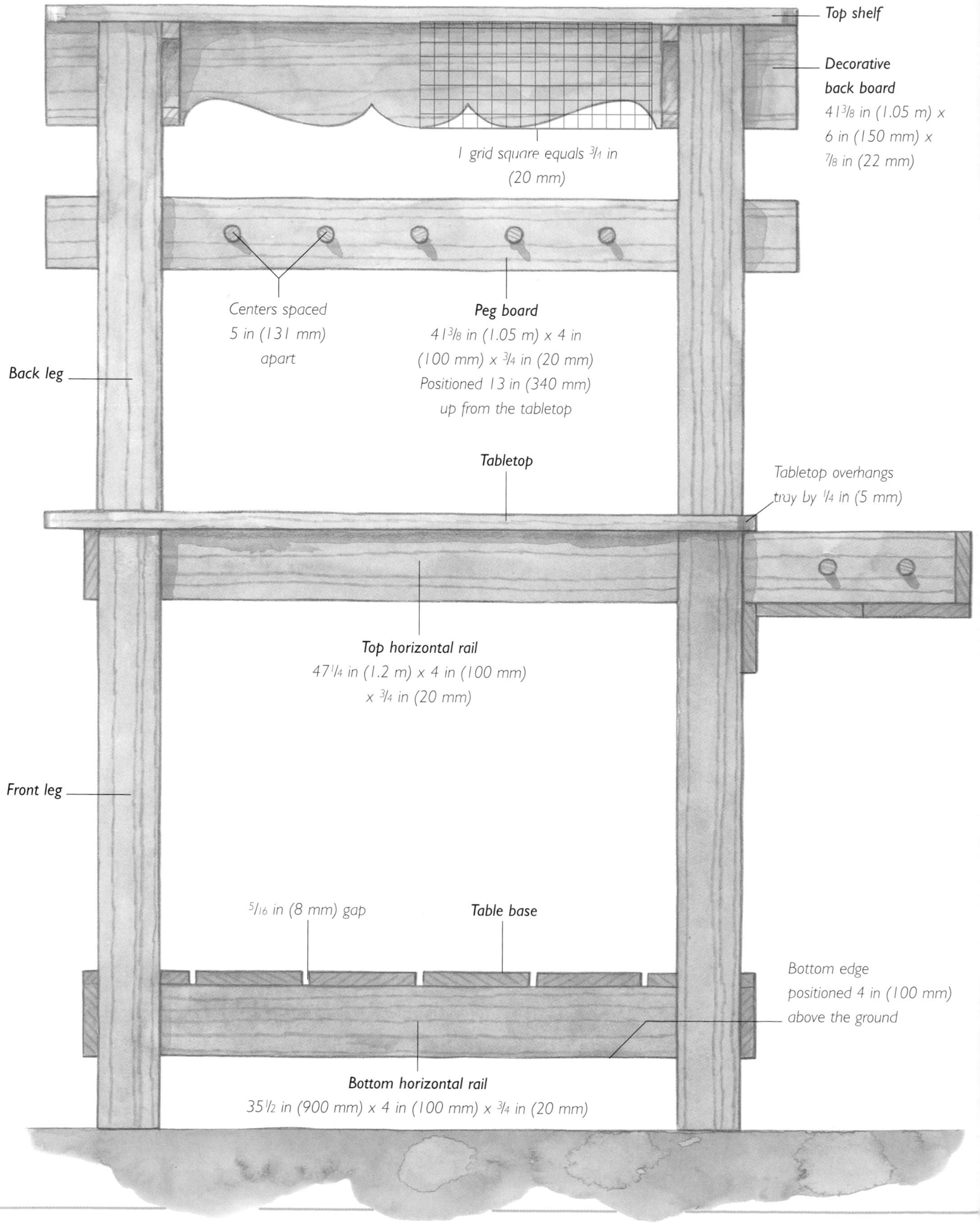

Top shelf
Decorative back board
41 3/8 in (1.05 m) x 6 in (150 mm) x 7/8 in (22 mm)
1 grid square equals 3/4 in (20 mm)
Centers spaced 5 in (131 mm) apart
Peg board
41 3/8 in (1.05 m) x 4 in (100 mm) x 3/4 in (20 mm)
Positioned 13 in (340 mm) up from the tabletop
Back leg
Tabletop
Tabletop overhangs tray by 1/4 in (5 mm)
Top horizontal rail
47 1/4 in (1.2 m) x 4 in (100 mm) x 3/4 in (20 mm)
Front leg
5/16 in (8 mm) gap
Table base
Bottom edge positioned 4 in (100 mm) above the ground
Bottom horizontal rail
35 1/2 in (900 mm) x 4 in (100 mm) x 3/4 in (20 mm)

EXPLODED VIEW OF THE POTTING TABLE

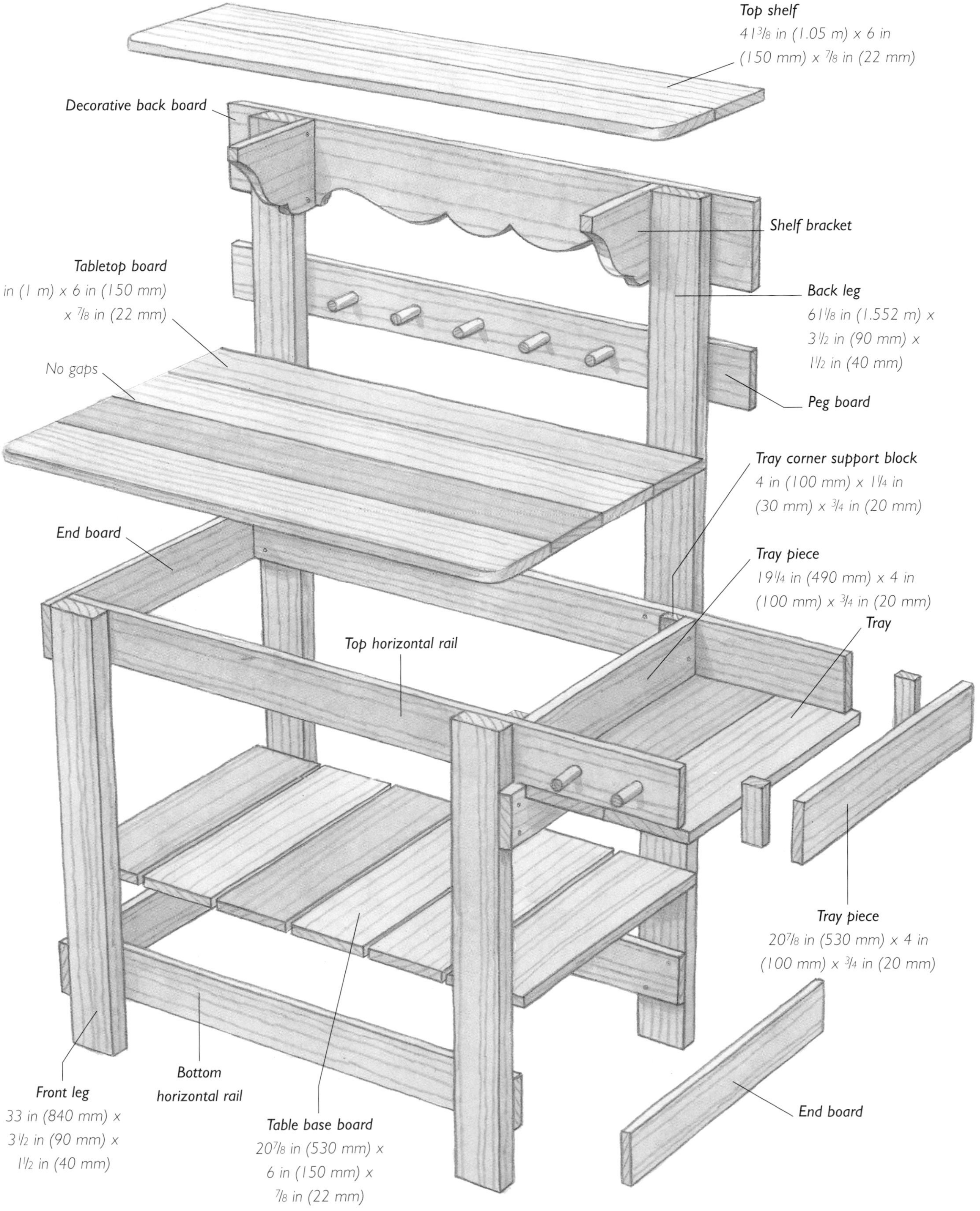
Top shelf
41³/₈ in (1.05 m) x 6 in (150 mm) x ⁷/₈ in (22 mm)
Decorative back board
Shelf bracket
Tabletop board
40 in (1 m) x 6 in (150 mm) x ⁷/₈ in (22 mm)
Back leg
61¹/₈ in (1.552 m) x 3¹/₂ in (90 mm) x 1¹/₂ in (40 mm)
No gaps
Peg board
Tray corner support block
4 in (100 mm) x 1¹/₄ in (30 mm) x ³/₄ in (20 mm)
End board
Tray piece
19¹/₄ in (490 mm) x 4 in (100 mm) x ³/₄ in (20 mm)
Tray
Top horizontal rail
Tray piece
20⁷/₈ in (530 mm) x 4 in (100 mm) x ³/₄ in (20 mm)
End board
Front leg
33 in (840 mm) x 3¹/₂ in (90 mm) x 1¹/₂ in (40 mm)
Bottom horizontal rail
Table base board
20⁷/₈ in (530 mm) x 6 in (150 mm) x ⁷/₈ in (22 mm)

Step-by-step: **Making the potting table**

Square
The horizontal rails must be square to the legs
Parallel
Make sure that the two legs are parallel to each other

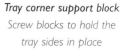

1 Use the crosscut saw to cut all the wood to size. Set out the two 61¹/₈-inch-long (1.552 m) back legs, linking them with the top and bottom horizontal boards, check for squareness, and then run pilot holes through the boards and fasten them with two screws at each intersection.

Tray corner support block
Screw blocks to hold the tray sides in place
Leg position
The leg is on the outside of the frame
Tight fit
Push the end board tight under the top horizontal rail

2 Having built both the front and back units, complete with pegholes in the tray end of the top horizontal rail, link them together with the four 24-inch-long (610 mm) end boards. Screw on the corner support blocks for fitting the two tray pieces.

Board position
Push the board tight up against the back posts

3 Set the four 40-inch-long (1 m), 6-inch-wide (150 mm) tabletop boards in position so that they are butted tight up against the two back posts. Leave a ¹/₄ inch (5 mm) overhang on the right-hand side, so that the surface hangs over the tray. Check for squareness and fasten with screws.

Helpful hint

Before you fasten the tabletop boards in place, check that the potting table is square. Use a large square or a tape measure to check that the diagonal measurements are identical.

Shelf bracket
Fit the board at right angles to the back post

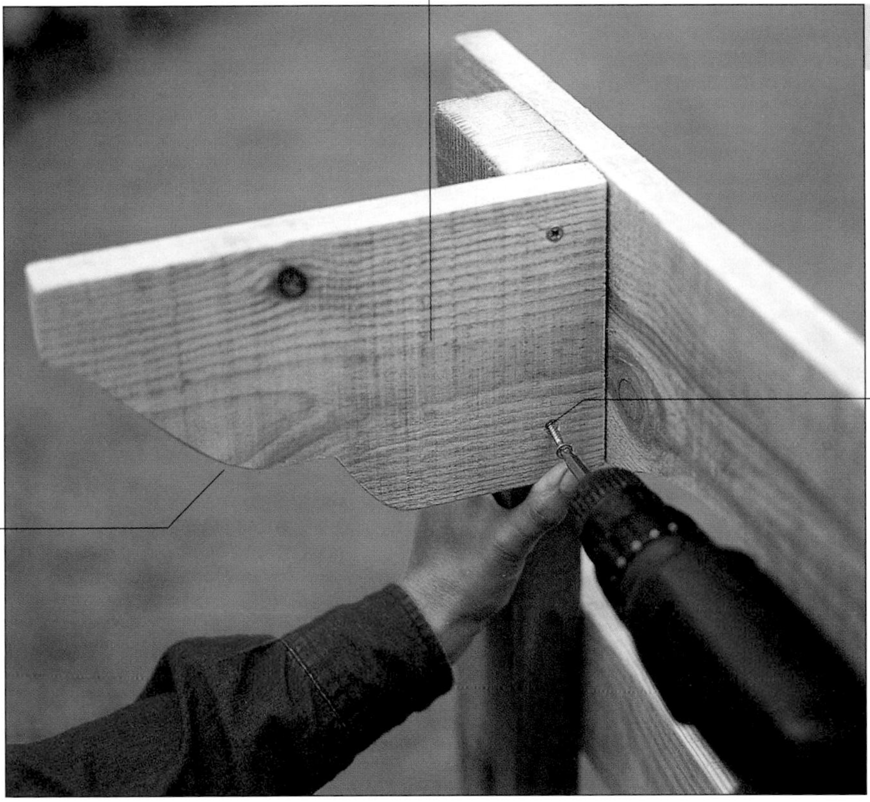

Cyma curve
Sand the curve to a smooth finish

Screwing
Run two screws through the bracket and into the back post

4 Trace off the cyma curves of the decorative back board and shelf brackets, transfer the lines through to the wood, and cut the curves with the jigsaw. Screw the back board and brackets in place so that their top edges are flush with the top of the back posts. Drill and fit the peg board.

Screwing
Fasten the planks with two screws at each end

Screwholes
Drill a hole for each screw that is near the end of a plank

5 Fasten all other members in place (the boards for the base of the table, and the boards on the underside and ends of the tray). Position the table base boards flush with the horizontal rails that link the legs, but spaced by 5/16 inch (8 mm).

Sandpaper
Make a double fold of sandpaper

Sanding
Rub the end of the peg to a rounded finish

6 Use the graded sandpapers to round over the ends of the pegs, and to generally bring all the edges and corners to a slightly rounded finish. Finally, give all the surfaces a coat of teak oil.

Rabbit hutch

Children love rabbits, so why not give them a couple of furry friends to play with? The new members of the family will need housing, and that's where our hutch comes in. It folds up for easy transport and has handles so that you can move it around the yard (position it in different locations to allow the rabbits to trim your lawn).

TIME

About sixteen hours for the woodwork, and another three hours for fastening the wire, hinges, and latches.

USEFUL TIP

Buy special rabbit wire – the rabbit cannot get its feet through the holes.

EXPLODED VIEW OF THE RABBIT HUTCH

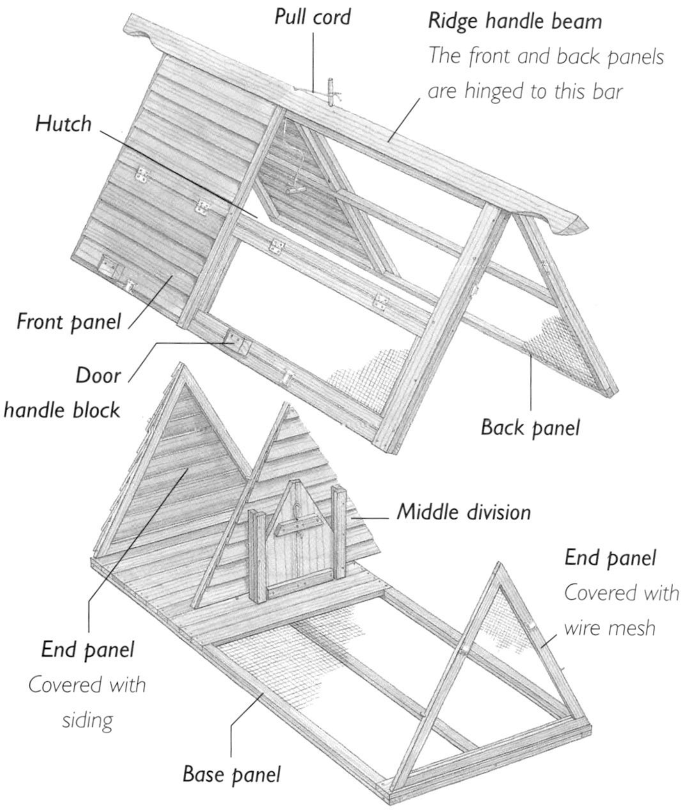
Pull cord
Ridge handle beam
The front and back panels are hinged to this bar
Hutch
Front panel
Door handle block
Back panel
Middle division
End panel
Covered with wire mesh
End panel
Covered with siding
Base panel

A-FRAME RABBIT HOME

The clever thing about this rabbit hutch is the fact that it folds up for transport and storage. While in essence the hutch is made up from seven component parts (a base, two long sides, three triangular divisions, and a carrying beam), the ingenious design means that it can be swiftly broken down into three flat-pack units. These are the two sides, which hinge to the handle beam like a book; the base, complete with the two hinged ends; and the middle division.

To put the hutch together, set the base flat on the grass, open up the two triangular ends, locate the middle division on its dowels, open the book-like sides and drop them over the ends, and then do up all the latches. When you want to move the hutch, ask a friend to help and simply lift it up by the beam handles. To shut the rabbits in for the night, wait until they are safely in the enclosed end, unhitch the pull cord and lower the sliding door.

YOU WILL NEED

Materials *for a hutch 94¾ in (2.405 m) long, 30¼ in (769 mm) high, and 32¾ in (830 mm) wide.*

- Pine: 15 pieces, each 10 feet (3 m) long, 1⅜ in (35 mm) wide, and ¾ in (20 mm) thick (for frames and corner trim)
- Pine: 4 pieces, 10 feet (3 m) long, 3 in (75 mm) wide, and ¾ in (20 mm) thick (floor)
- Pine: 1 piece, 10 feet (3 m) long, 3 in (75 mm) triangular section, 4 in (100 mm) across the base (ridge handle beam)
- Pine: 1 piece, 3 feet (1 m) long, 2 in (50 mm) wide, and 1¼ in (30 mm) thick (door handle blocks)
- Pine: 1 piece, 8 feet (2 m) long, 3 in (75 mm) wide, and ¾ in (20 mm) thick (end frame trim)
- Pine bevel-edged board: 20 pieces, 10 feet (3 m) long, 4 in (100 mm) wide, and ⅜ in (10 mm) thick (for siding the walls of the enclosed end of the hutch)
- Pine: 1 piece, 3 feet (1 m) long, 6 in (150 mm) wide, and ⅞ in (22 mm) thick (door)
- Pine dowel: 2 pieces, 12 in (300 mm) long, one ¼ in (6 mm) in diameter and the other ½ in (12 mm) (for locating the middle division and making the pull cord)
- Galvanized rabbit wire: 20 feet (6 m) roll, 3 feet (1 m) wide (cage)
- Galvanized staples: 2 lb (1 kg) x ⅜ in (10 mm)
- Galvanized butt door hinges: 14 x 2¼ in (60 mm) long, ¾ in (20 mm) wide, screws to fit
- Plated snap-fit case latches: 8 medium size, with screws
- Zinc-plated, countersunk Phillips screws: 100 x ¾ in (20 mm) no. 8, 100 x 1½ in (38 mm) no. 8, 10 x 2 in (50 mm) no. 10, 100 x 2½ in (65 mm) no. 10
- Exterior-quality PVA glue
- Nylon cord (for door pull)
- Clear preservative

Tools

- Pencil, ruler, tape measure, marking gauge, and square
- Two portable workbenches
- Crosscut saw
- Cordless electric drill with a Phillips screwdriver bit
- Drill bits to match screw sizes
- Wire snips
- Small hammer
- Electric jigsaw
- Drill bit to match dowel size
- Electric sander with a pack of medium-grade sandpaper
- Small screwdriver to fit the hinge and latch screws
- Paintbrush 1½ in (40 mm)

Rabbit hutch

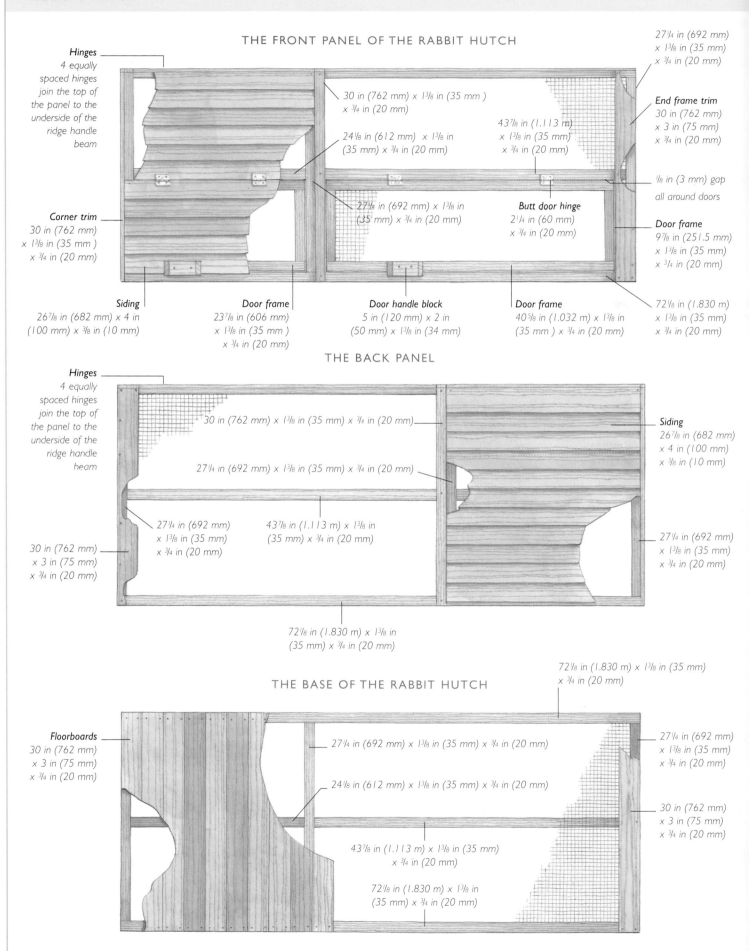

THE FRONT PANEL OF THE RABBIT HUTCH

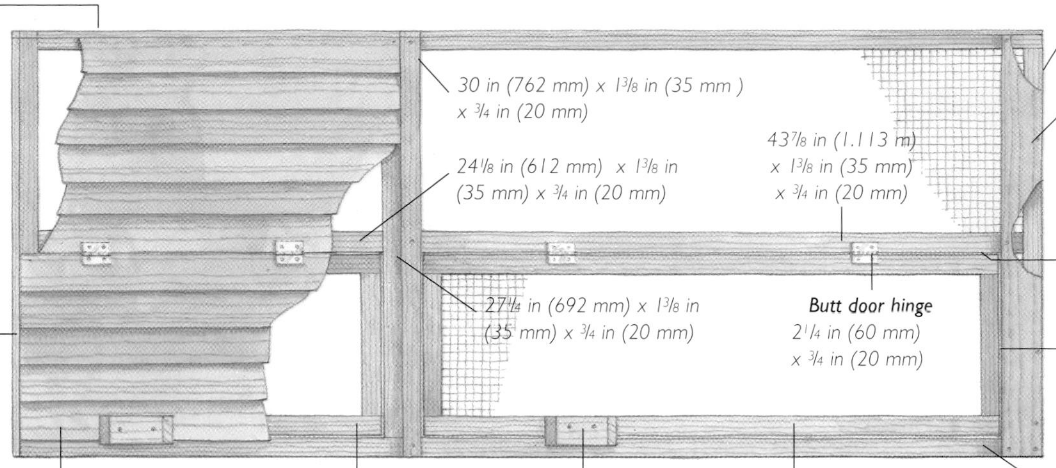
Hinges
4 equally spaced hinges join the top of the panel to the underside of the ridge handle beam
27 1/4 in (692 mm) x 1 3/8 in (35 mm) x 3/4 in (20 mm)
30 in (762 mm) x 1 3/8 in (35 mm) x 3/4 in (20 mm)
End frame trim
30 in (762 mm) x 3 in (75 mm) x 3/4 in (20 mm)
43 7/8 in (1.113 m) x 1 3/8 in (35 mm) x 3/4 in (20 mm)
24 1/8 in (612 mm) x 1 3/8 in (35 mm) x 3/4 in (20 mm)
1/8 in (3 mm) gap all around doors
27 1/4 in (692 mm) x 1 3/8 in (35 mm) x 3/4 in (20 mm)
Butt door hinge
2 1/4 in (60 mm) x 3/4 in (20 mm)
Corner trim
30 in (762 mm) x 1 3/8 in (35 mm) x 3/4 in (20 mm)
Door frame
9 7/8 in (251.5 mm) x 1 3/8 in (35 mm) x 3/4 in (20 mm)
Siding
26 7/8 in (682 mm) x 4 in (100 mm) x 3/8 in (10 mm)
Door frame
23 7/8 in (606 mm) x 1 3/8 in (35 mm) x 3/4 in (20 mm)
Door handle block
5 in (120 mm) x 2 in (50 mm) x 1 3/8 in (34 mm)
Door frame
40 5/8 in (1.032 m) x 1 3/8 in (35 mm) x 3/4 in (20 mm)
72 1/8 in (1.830 m) x 1 3/8 in (35 mm) x 3/4 in (20 mm)

THE BACK PANEL

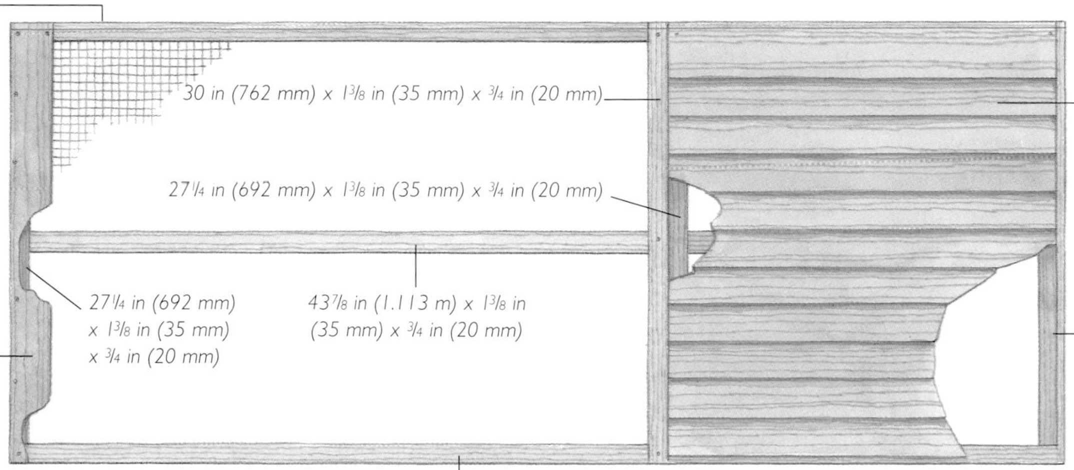
Hinges
4 equally spaced hinges join the top of the panel to the underside of the ridge handle beam
30 in (762 mm) x 1 3/8 in (35 mm) x 3/4 in (20 mm)
Siding
26 7/8 in (682 mm) x 4 in (100 mm) x 3/8 in (10 mm)
27 1/4 in (692 mm) x 1 3/8 in (35 mm) x 3/4 in (20 mm)
27 1/4 in (692 mm) x 1 3/8 in (35 mm) x 3/4 in (20 mm)
43 7/8 in (1.113 m) x 1 3/8 in (35 mm) x 3/4 in (20 mm)
30 in (762 mm) x 3 in (75 mm) x 3/4 in (20 mm)
27 1/4 in (692 mm) x 1 3/8 in (35 mm) x 3/4 in (20 mm)
72 1/8 in (1.830 m) x 1 3/8 in (35 mm) x 3/4 in (20 mm)

THE BASE OF THE RABBIT HUTCH

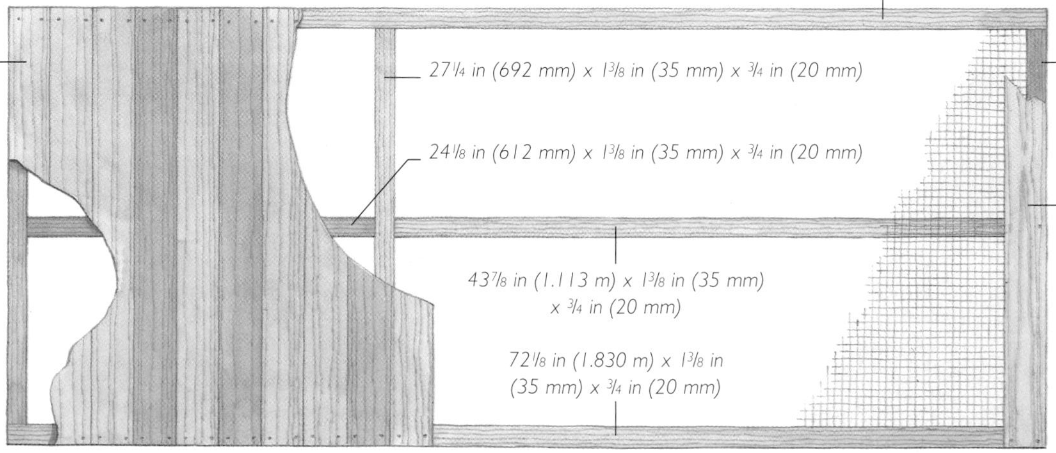
72 1/8 in (1.830 m) x 1 3/8 in (35 mm) x 3/4 in (20 mm)
Floorboards
30 in (762 mm) x 3 in (75 mm) x 3/4 in (20 mm)
27 1/4 in (692 mm) x 1 3/8 in (35 mm) x 3/4 in (20 mm)
27 1/4 in (692 mm) x 1 3/8 in (35 mm) x 3/4 in (20 mm)
24 1/8 in (612 mm) x 1 3/8 in (35 mm) x 3/4 in (20 mm)
30 in (762 mm) x 3 in (75 mm) x 3/4 in (20 mm)
43 7/8 in (1.113 m) x 1 3/8 in (35 mm) x 3/4 in (20 mm)
72 1/8 in (1.830 m) x 1 3/8 in (35 mm) x 3/4 in (20 mm)

A TRIANGULAR FRAME (USED FOR THE END PANELS AND THE MIDDLE DIVISION)

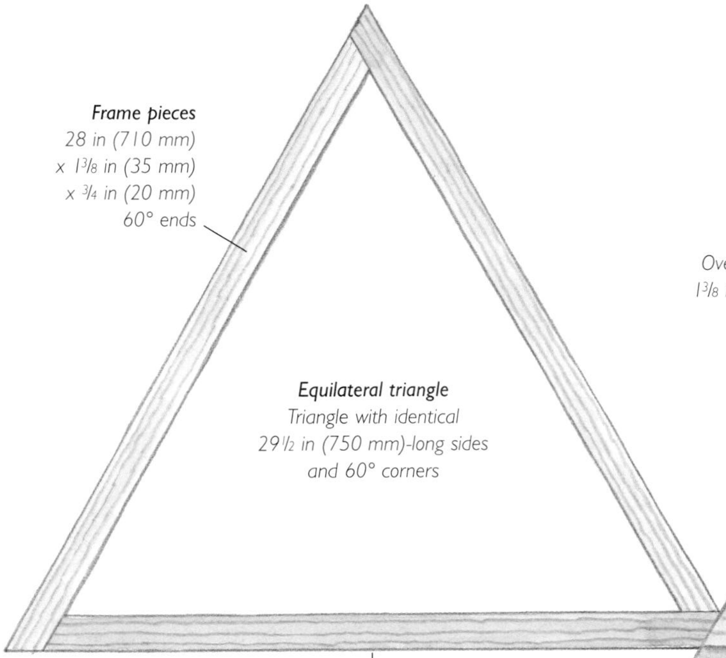
Frame pieces
28 in (710 mm)
x 1 3/8 in (35 mm)
x 3/4 in (20 mm)
60° ends
Equilateral triangle
Triangle with identical
29 1/2 in (750 mm)-long sides
and 60° corners
Hinges
2 equally spaced hinges join the bottom
of the panel to the edge of the base

AN END PANEL WITH SIDING

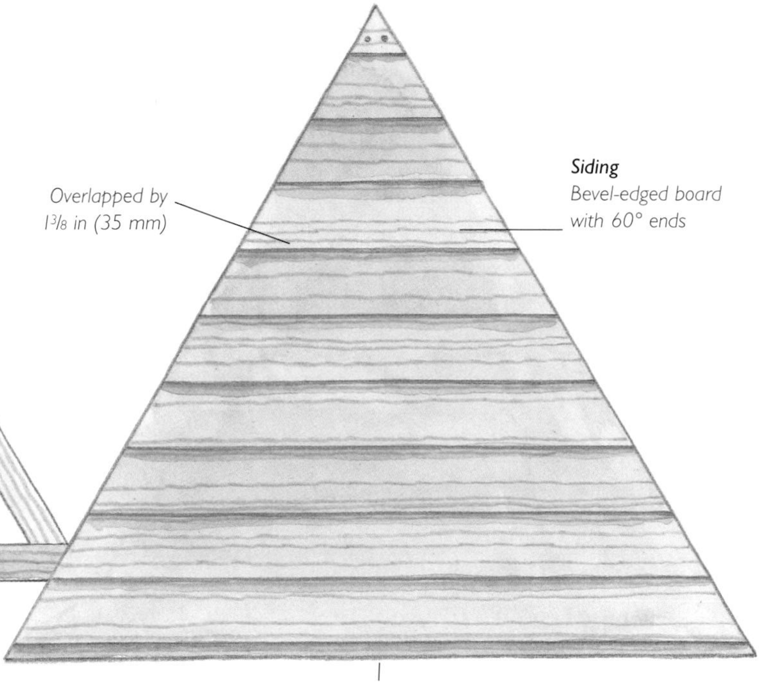
Overlapped by
1 3/8 in (35 mm)
Siding
Bevel-edged board
with 60° ends
Hinges
2 equally spaced hinges join the bottom
of the panel to the edge of the base

MIDDLE DIVISION

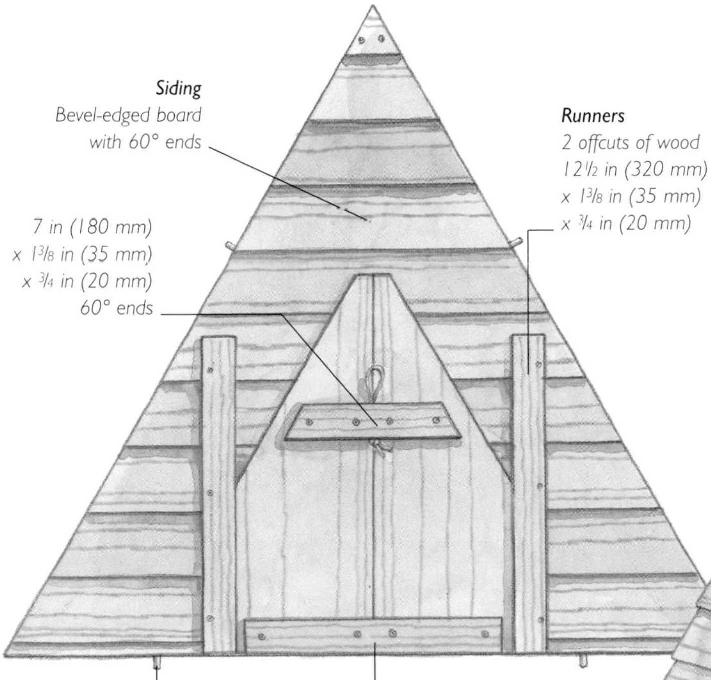
Siding
Bevel-edged board
with 60° ends
7 in (180 mm)
x 1 3/8 in (35 mm)
x 3/4 in (20 mm)
60° ends
Runners
2 offcuts of wood
12 1/2 in (320 mm)
x 1 3/8 in (35 mm)
x 3/4 in (20 mm)
10 1/4 in (260 mm) x 1 3/8 in (35 mm)
x 3/4 in (20 mm)
Location dowel

MIDDLE DIVISION (WITH THE DOOR RAISED)

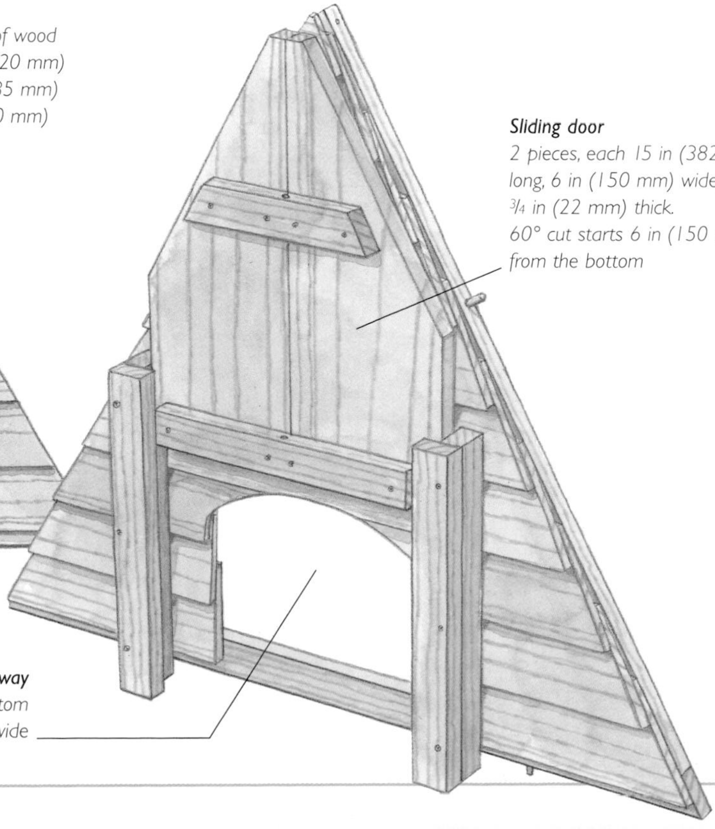
Sliding door
2 pieces, each 15 in (382 mm)
long, 6 in (150 mm) wide, and
3/4 in (22 mm) thick.
60° cut starts 6 in (150 mm)
from the bottom
Arched doorway
8 1/2 in (215 mm) high (from bottom
of panel) and 10 in (226 mm) wide

Step-by-step: **Making the rabbit hutch**

Screwing
Fasten each joint with two screws

Support boards
Clamp boards in the workbench to support the frame

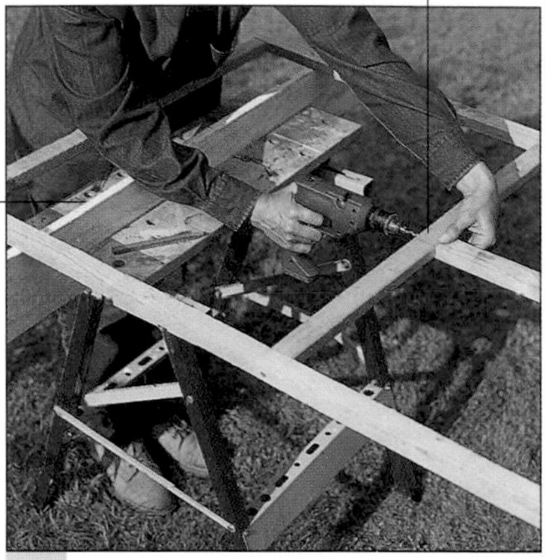

1 Cut the lengths of wood that make up the frame, butt joint them together and fasten with 2½ inch (60 mm) screws. Build all eight frames: the base, the front panel, the back panel, the two doors in the front panel, and the three triangles that make up the end panels and middle division. Screw the door handle blocks in place on the doors with 2 inch (50 mm) screws.

Rabbit wire
Cut the wire about ¼ in (10 mm) smaller than the frame all around

Cutting
It may help to bend the wire out of the way of the snips as you cut

Supports
Rest the frame on a couple of spare boards

2 Set the base down flat on a couple of spare pieces of wood, and use the wire snips to cut the rabbit wire to fit. Cut the large pieces first. Hammer in staples at about 2 inch (50 mm) intervals. Screw the corner trim in place on the front panel using 1½ inch (38 mm) screws (see working drawing).

Screwholes
Drill holes through the bevel-edged board to take the screws

Jig
Use a simple jig to help you space the boards equally

3 Side the frames with bevel-edged board. When you are doing this, use a little scrap of wood, marked off at 2⅝ inches (65 mm), to ensure that the board overlap is always constant at about 1⅜ inches (35 mm). Screw the boards in place with ¾ inch (20 mm) screws.

Cord loop
Tie a loop for attaching the pull cord

Door runners
The door should be a loose fit within the runners

Bevel
Saw a bevel on the underside of the top of the door

4 Cut out the door hole in the middle division with the jigsaw and build the two door-slide runners from lengths of 1⅜-inch-wide (35 mm), ¾-inch-thick (20 mm) offcuts. Make the door from two lengths of 6-inch-wide (150 mm) board and trim it to fit.

Door pull cord
The door pull cord, complete with the $\frac{1}{2}$ in (12 mm) dowel handle, runs down through a hole in the ridge handle beam to link up with a looped cord on the top of the sliding door

Location dowels
Spread glue inside the hole and then tap the dowel in place

Alignment
Double-check that the dowels locate in the holes in the floor panel

5 Drill and glue-fit two lengths of $\frac{1}{4}$ inch (6 mm) dowel into the underside edge of the middle division. Set the partition upright on the floor to establish its position, and drill matching location holes in the floor beam.

Helpful hint

If you make a mistake while positioning the location holes for the dowels, leave the location dowel where it is and plug the location hole with a piece of dowel. Wait for the glue to dry, then sand the plugged dowel flush. Drill another hole.

Fastening hinges
Screw the hinges to the frame first and then to the handle beam

Prop the sides
Ask a friend to hold the side panels at the angle shown here

6 Saw and sand the ends of the triangular-section ridge handle beam to make comfortable handles, and screw hinges in place, centering the two sides on the beam's 4 inch (100 mm) hypotenuse.

Alignment
Before you fit the latches, ensure the end panel is flush with the sides

Latches
Have a trial run for fitting a latch so that you know how far apart the two pieces should be

Screwing
Drill pilot holes for the screws and use the correct size of screwdriver

7 Use $1\frac{1}{2}$ inch (38 mm) screws to fit the two 3-inch-wide (75 mm) pieces of end frame trim, and then screw the snap-fit latches in place at a point about two-thirds of the way up the sides of the triangle. Thread and fit the door-pull cord. Paint with preservative.

Classic pergola

If you want to create a feature that instantly establishes a focal point and invites visitors to wander under it, consider the merits of a pergola. It provides a place to sit in the shade, a spot for children to play in, somewhere to snooze on a summer's day, and a structure that will host a vine or flowering climbers.

TIME

A weekend (twelve hours for the woodwork and four hours for putting the pergola together).

USEFUL TIP

You will need assistance when putting the structure together – ideally two helpers.

YOU WILL NEED

Materials *for a pergola 8 feet 4 in (2.55 m) high and 12 feet (3.59 m) square. (All rough-sawn pine pieces include excess length for wastage.)*

- Pine: 5 pieces, each 10 feet (3 m) long and 3 in (75 mm) square (main posts, and the 12 short linking posts that laminate and link the boat beams and top boards)
- Pine: 14 pieces, each 12 feet (4 m) long, 6 in (150 mm) wide, and 3/4 in (20 mm) thick (top boards, boat beams, support boards)
- Pine: 2 pieces, each 10 feet (3 m) long, 2 in (50 mm) wide, and 1 1/4 in (30 mm) thick (brackets)
- Pine: 6 pieces, each 14 feet (4 m) long, 2 in (30 mm) wide and 3/4 in (20 mm) thick (various temporary battens)
- Zinc-plated, countersunk Phillips screws: 100 x 1 3/4 in (38 mm) no. 8, 10 x 2 1/2 in (65 mm) no. 10
- Brown preservative

Tools

- Pencil, ruler, tape measure, compass, bevel gauge, and square
- Two portable workbenches
- Crosscut saw
- Electric jigsaw
- Large clamps: 4 clamps
- Cordless electric drill and Phillips screwdriver bit
- Drill bits to match screws
- Carpenter's level
- Electric sander with a pack of medium-grade sandpaper
- Paintbrush 1 1/2 in (40 mm)

COOL CANOPY

This project is made up from four posts set square to each other, with the top of the posts linked by two laminated "boat" beams on paired support boards, and six top boards crossing the boat beams at right angles. The boat beams are made by sandwiching the 12-inch-long (300 mm) linking posts between boards in such a way that the posts protrude at the top of the beam by 6 inches (150 mm), providing link-up points for the topmost boards.

The structure is held square and prevented from wracking by eight brackets. We have allowed a good amount of extra length for the bracket pieces so that you can miter the ends at 45° without worrying about cutting them too short. The ends of all the top boards are decorated with a classic cyma curve (an S-shaped detail), which can be cut easily with the jigsaw. The crossover of the boards at the corner posts, plus the addition of the top boards, results in a generous, bold structure which is really eye-catching. We purchased the wood ready-treated, and used the preservative to touch up the cut edges.

CORNER DETAIL OF THE CLASSIC PERGOLA

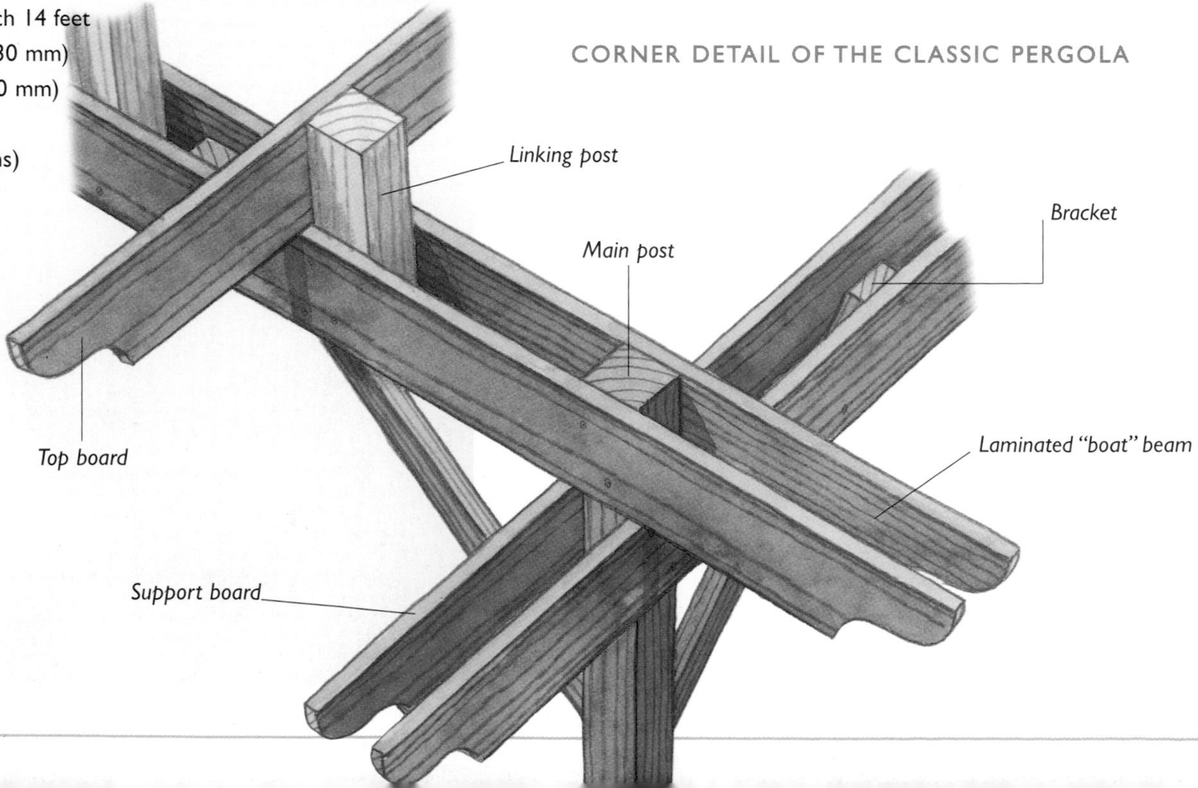
Linking post
Bracket
Main post
Top board
Laminated "boat" beam
Support board

Classic pergola

FRONT VIEW OF THE CLASSIC PERGOLA

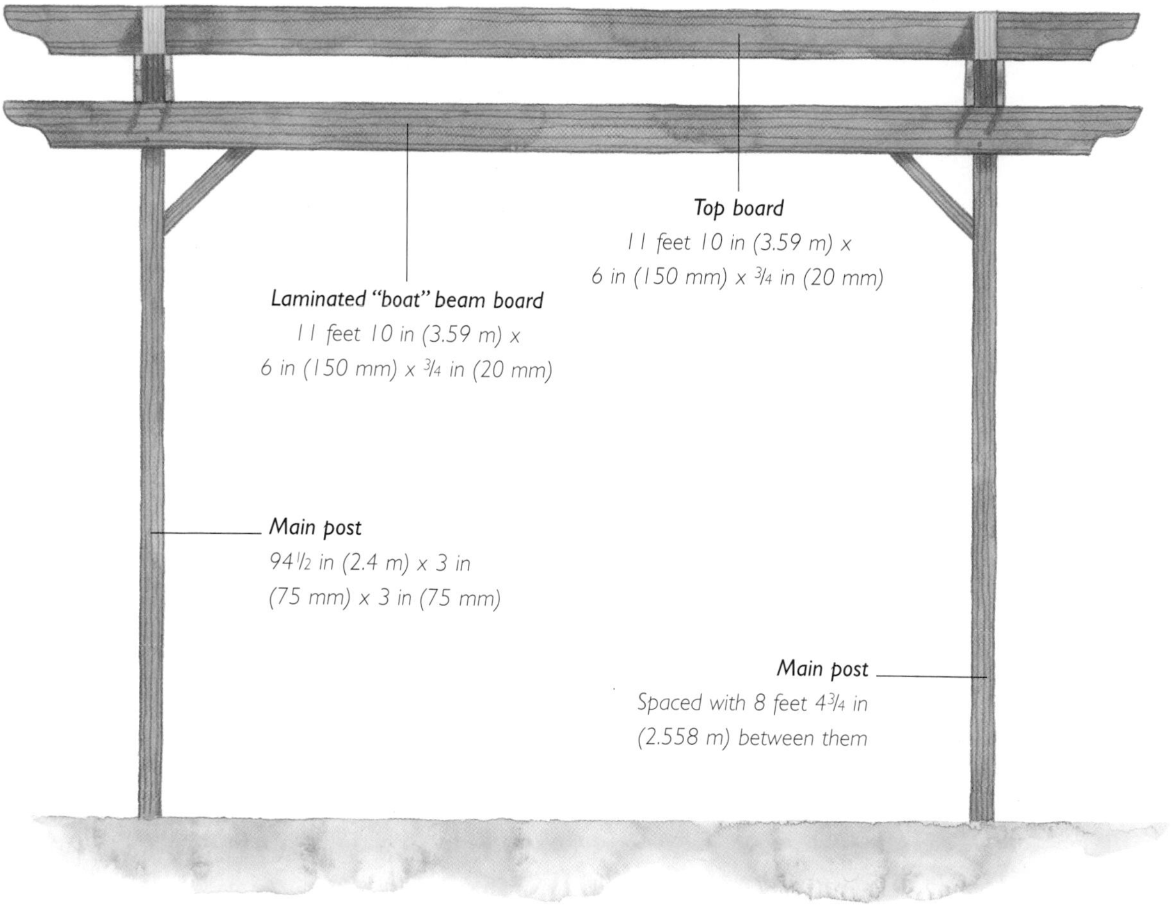
Top board
11 feet 10 in (3.59 m) x
6 in (150 mm) x 3/4 in (20 mm)
Laminated "boat" beam board
11 feet 10 in (3.59 m) x
6 in (150 mm) x 3/4 in (20 mm)
Main post
94 1/2 in (2.4 m) x 3 in
(75 mm) x 3 in (75 mm)
Main post
Spaced with 8 feet 4 3/4 in
(2.558 m) between them

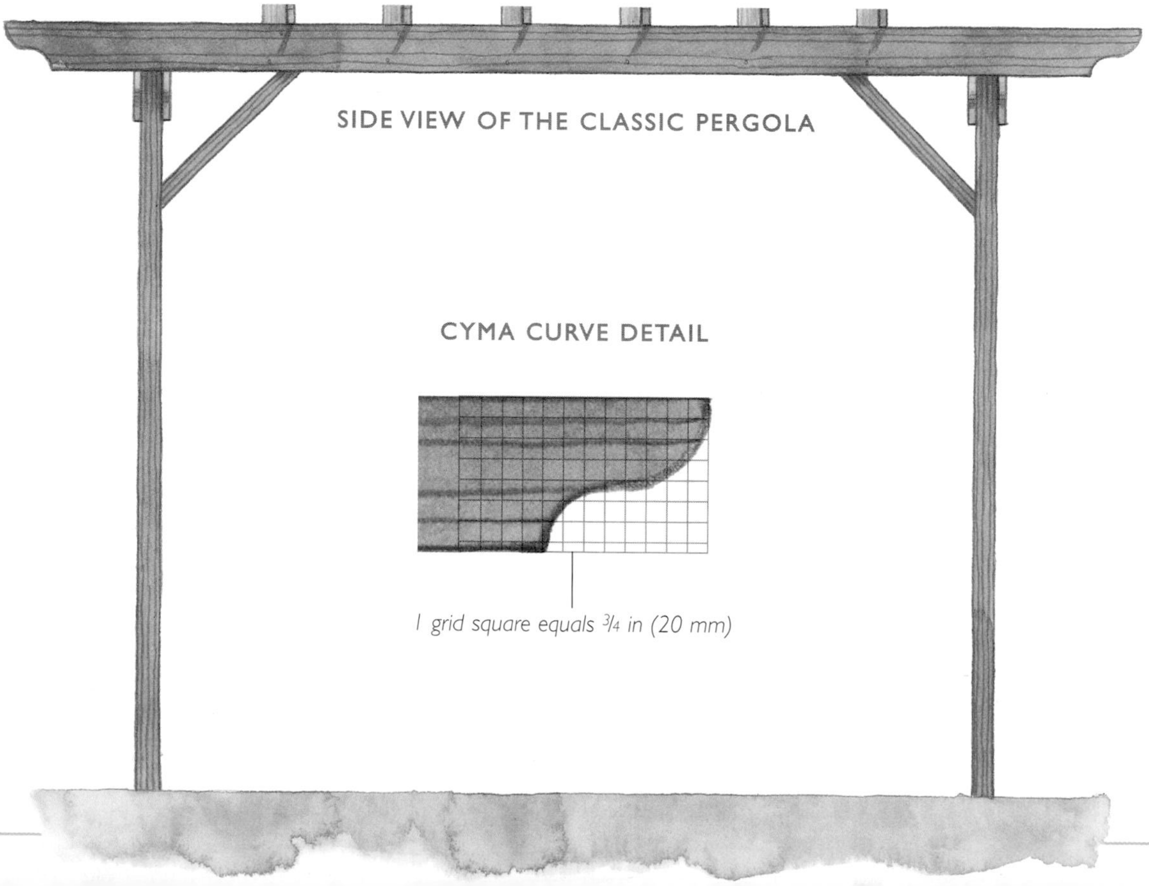
SIDE VIEW OF THE CLASSIC PERGOLA
CYMA CURVE DETAIL
1 grid square equals 3/4 in (20 mm)

EXPLODED VIEW OF THE CLASSIC PERGOLA

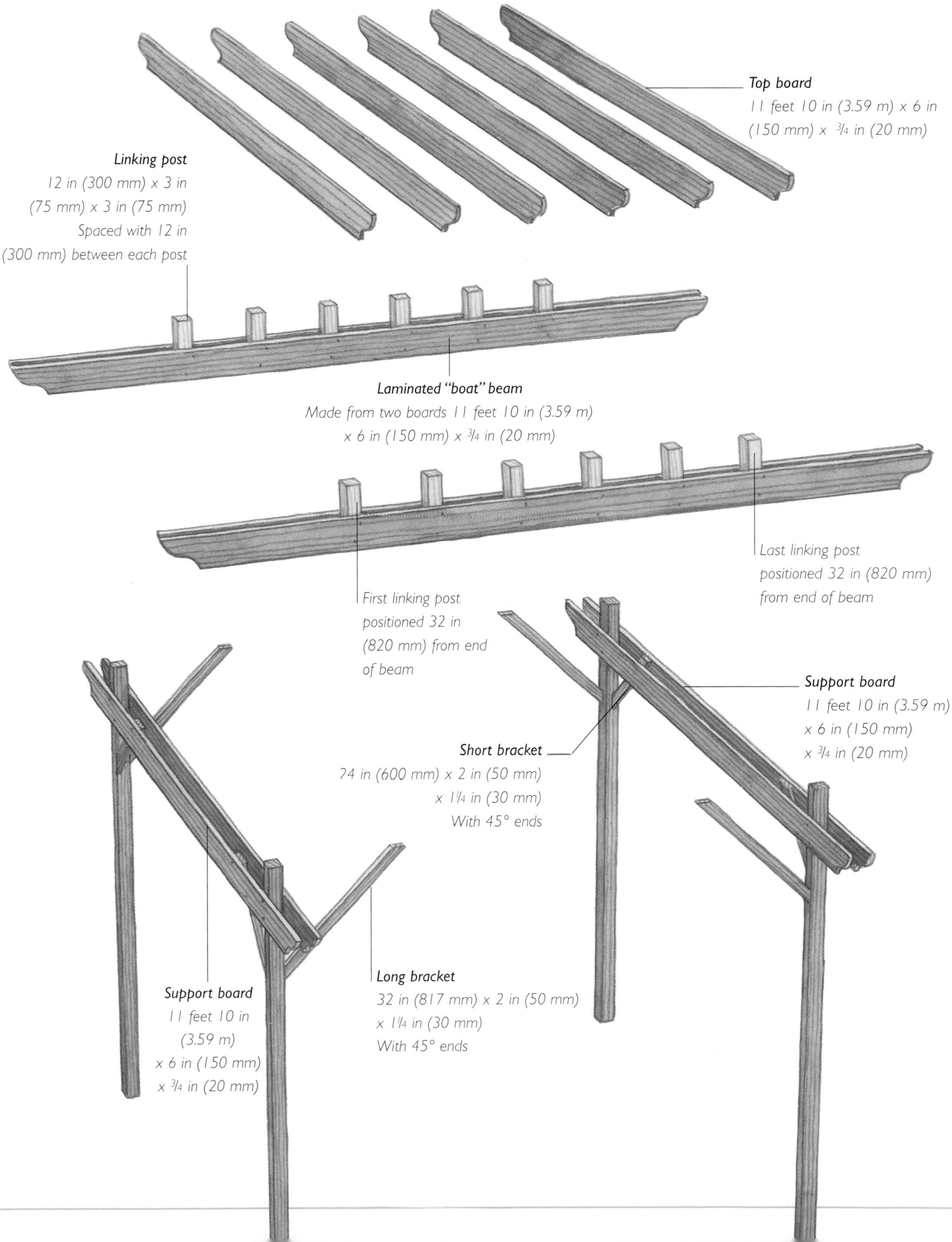
Top board
11 feet 10 in (3.59 m) x 6 in (150 mm) x 3/4 in (20 mm)
Linking post
12 in (300 mm) x 3 in (75 mm) x 3 in (75 mm) Spaced with 12 in (300 mm) between each post
Laminated "boat" beam
Made from two boards 11 feet 10 in (3.59 m) x 6 in (150 mm) x 3/4 in (20 mm)
Last linking post positioned 32 in (820 mm) from end of beam
First linking post positioned 32 in (820 mm) from end of beam
Support board
11 feet 10 in (3.59 m) x 6 in (150 mm) x 3/4 in (20 mm)
Short bracket
24 in (600 mm) x 2 in (50 mm) x 1 1/4 in (30 mm) With 45° ends
Long bracket
32 in (817 mm) x 2 in (50 mm) x 1 1/4 in (30 mm) With 45° ends
Support board
11 feet 10 in (3.59 m) x 6 in (150 mm) x 3/4 in (20 mm)

Step-by-step: **Making the classic pergola**

Jigsaw
Fit the jigsaw with a new blade

Template
Use the waste bit as a template for drawing the other shapes

1 Use the crosscut saw to cut all the wood to size. Draw the cyma curve on the end of one of the fourteen top, boat and support boards, and saw out with the jigsaw. Use the waste as a pattern for the shape of all the other board ends.

Fastening
Run screws through from both boards

Workboard
Use a spare piece of 6-in-wide (150 mm) wood as a workboard

Clamp
Secure the post with a clamp and then screw it into position

2 Sandwich six of the 12-inch-long (300 mm) linking posts between two shaped boards to make a boat beam. Establish the position of the linking posts and clamp them in place. Run 2 inch (48 mm) screws through the boards and into the posts. Repeat the procedure to build the other boat beam.

Temporary battens
The battens hold the arrangement square during construction

3 Set the boat beam on the ground and screw the two main posts in place, using one 2 inch (48 mm) screw for each post. Link the bottom of the posts with a batten. Set a batten across the diagonal, make adjustments until the two diagonal measurements are identical, and screw it in position with 2 inch (48 mm) screws.

Helpful hint

Don't remove the temporary supporting battens until the main posts are securely in the ground and the beams are braced with the brackets.

Assistance
You may need one or two people to help you at this stage

Batten supports
Use battens to create tripod-like supports

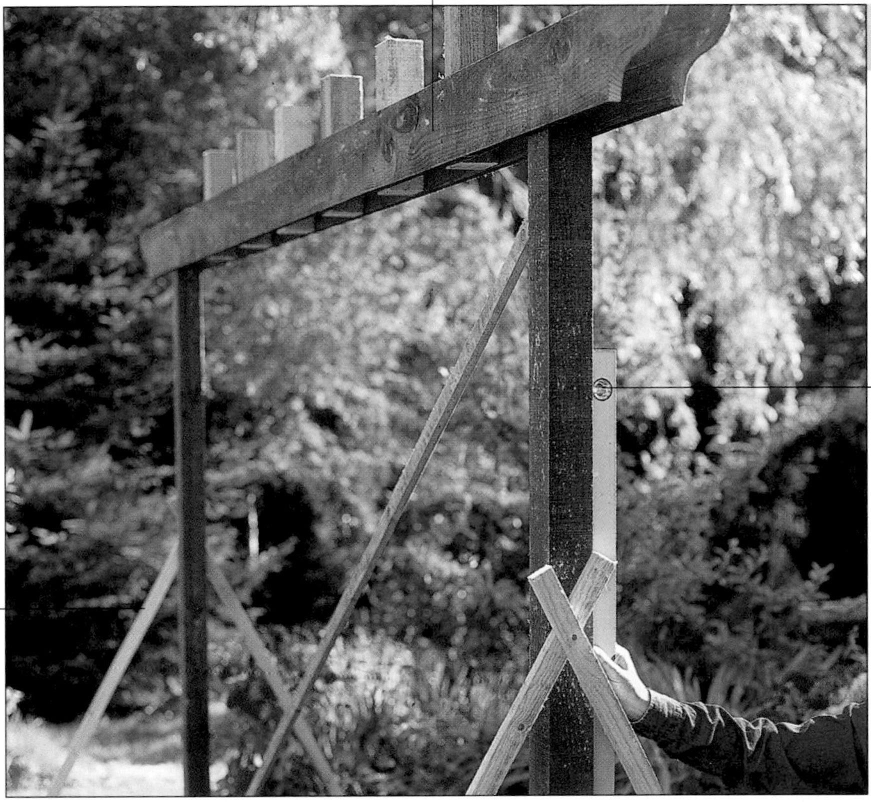

Carpenter's level
Check the frame to ensure that it is upright and square

4 Set the two-post boat-beam structure upright and use battens to brace it in place. Check the vertical with a carpenter's level. Make adjustments by altering the position of the struts.

Clamp
Clamp the boards in place if you have trouble holding them

5 When you have mounted both boat-beam structures square with each other, so they are well placed and upright, link them with the two pairs of support boards that run underneath the boat beams. Screw the four support boards to the main posts with 2 inch (48 mm) screws.

Support boards
The paired boards provide extra support

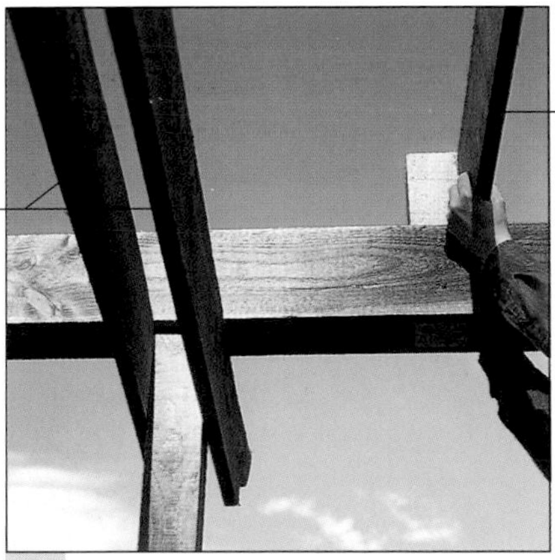

Top boards
Butt each board tightly against the linking post

6 Fasten the six top boards with 2 inch (48 mm) screws. Cut the brackets to shape and fasten between the posts and cross beams. Use 2½ inch (65 mm) screws to join to the posts and 2 inch (48 mm) screws to join to the beams. Sand and paint it with preservative.

Inspirations: **Pergolas**

The visual impact of a structure clothed in flowers can be absolutely stunning. Perennials such as wisteria, roses, honeysuckle, clematis, passion flower, jasmine, and climbing hydrangeas can be relied on to delight you every year. Annuals such as morning glory, sweet peas, and nasturtiums can be grown to provide extra color, or used to create a pergola that changes its coat each season.

ABOVE A pergola can be a frame for climbing plants, a focal point in a rose garden, or a place for a swing. This rustic green wood pergola, with its decorative balustrades, makes an attractive addition to any garden.

RIGHT As well as supporting flowers, a pergola is perfect for grapevines or for creating a tapestry of exciting leaf effects, weaving the blazing reds of Virginia creeper, or various colors and shapes of ivy.

FAR RIGHT A pergola with brick pillars creates a traditional walkway, hosting plants such as wisteria, which has blooms that droop attractively through the beams. Scented roses make for an equally pleasant experience.

Victorian tool shed

This beautiful shed draws inspiration from a Victorian earth closet that I loved when I was a child. The proportions of the design make a shed that is just right for storing your lawnmower and tools. If you would like to build an attractive and practical tool shed that will impress your neighbors, give this one a try.

TIME

A weekend (about twelve hours for the woodwork, and another four hours or so for fastening the hinges and latch, and getting it painted).

USEFUL TIP

We recommend that you buy a strong padlock for the door: tool sheds are a target for burglars.

YOU WILL NEED

Materials *for a shed 8 feet 4 in (2.546 m) high, 49½ in (1.259 m) wide, and 48½ in (1.230 m) deep.*

- Pine: 35 pieces, 10 feet (3 m) long, 1½ in (35 mm) wide, and ¾ in (20 mm) thick (frames for front, side, back, door and roof; braces for side and back panels; corner trim; doorway battens; roof support blocks; roof ridge boards; roof location bar)
- Pine: 6 pieces, 10 feet (3 m) long, 6 in (150 mm) wide, and ¾ in (20 mm) thick (barge boards, front feature boards, finial, and floorboards)
- Pine: 2 pieces, 8 feet (2 m) long, 2 in (50 mm) wide, and 1¼ in (30 mm) thick (floor joists)
- Pine: 2 pieces, 10 feet (3 m) long, 2½ in (65 mm) wide, and ¾ in (20 mm) thick (ledge and brace details for the door)
- Pine bevel-edged board: 60 pieces, each 10 feet (3 m) long, 4 in (100 mm) wide, and ⅜ in (13 mm) thick (for siding frames)
- Galvanized T-strap hinges: 3 hinges, about 10 in (250 mm) long
- Galvanized sliding gate latch, with screws and carriage bolts to fit
- Zinc-plated, countersunk Phillips screws: 200 x 1½ in (38 mm) no. 8, 100 x 2 in (50 mm) no. 8
- Galvanized nails: 4 lb (2 kg) x 4d (40 mm x 2.65 mm)
- Roof felt: 4 feet (1.2 m) x 1 foot (300 mm)
- Acrylic paint, colors to suit
- Clear preservative

Tools

- Pencil, ruler, tape measure, marking gauge, and square
- Two portable workbenches
- Crosscut saw
- Cordless electric drill with a Phillips screwdriver bit
- A selection of drill bits
- Small hammer
- Coping saw
- Electric jigsaw
- Small screwdriver
- Electric sander and sandpaper
- Paintbrush 1½ in (40 mm)

FRONT VIEW OF THE VICTORIAN TOOL SHED

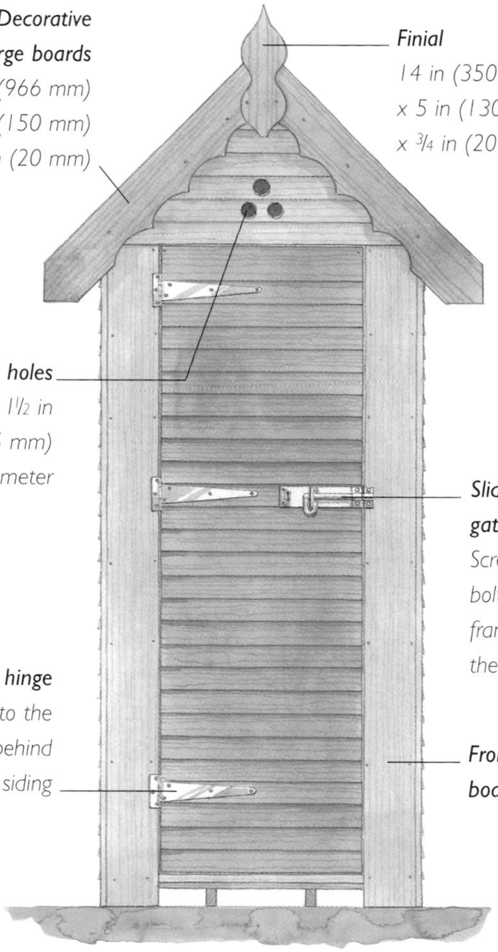
Decorative barge boards
38 in (966 mm) x 6 in (150 mm) x ¾ in (20 mm)
Finial
14 in (350 mm) x 5 in (130 mm) x ¾ in (20 mm)
Vent holes
1½ in (35 mm) in diameter
Sliding gate latch
Screwed and bolted to the frame behind the siding
T-strap hinge
Screwed to the frame behind the siding
Front feature board

PRETTY AND PRACTICAL

The tool shed comprises four primary frames (the front, back and two sides), which are all made from 1½ inch (35 mm) x ¾ inch (20 mm) sections covered in bevel-edged board. It has a steeply pitched roof sloping down at each side, a narrow door and airholes in the gable. The decorative details are made from 6-inch-wide (150 mm) boards. The floor is built directly on small-section joists, so you can mount on blocks, a concrete base, or slabs. Two people can easily move the component parts to the site. The interior has been left plain, so that you can customize it to suit your own requirements. We are planning to fit a 6-inch-wide (150 mm) board for screwhooks and pegs to store the spade, fork, rake and so on. There will be an extra-strong hook for the mower, and a shelf at gable level for small items.

Victorian tool shed

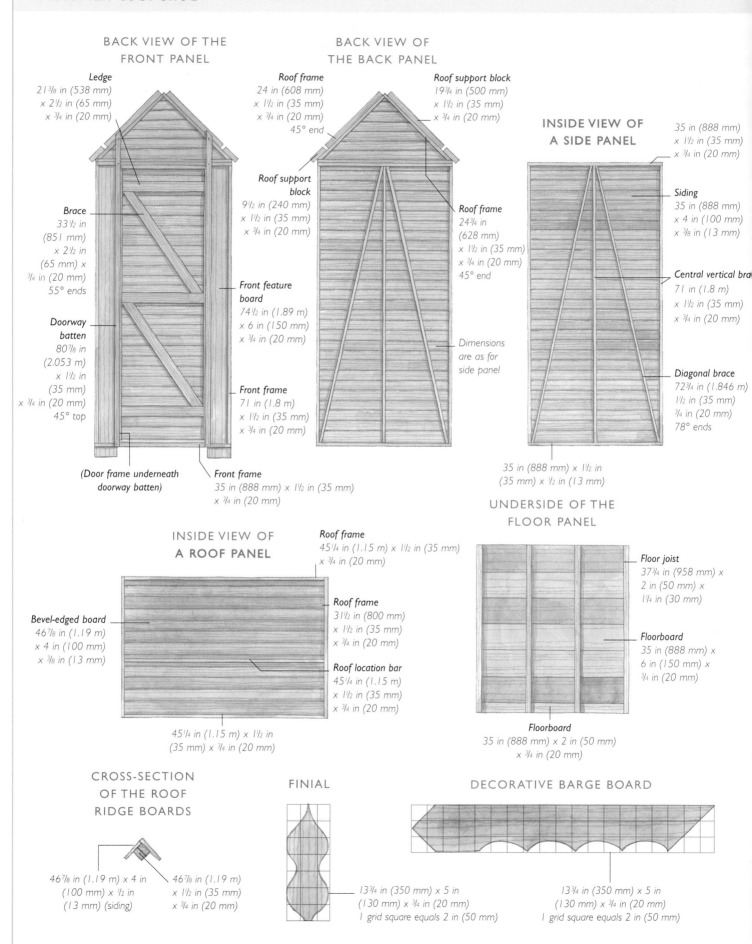

BACK VIEW OF THE FRONT PANEL

Ledge
21 3/8 in (538 mm)
x 2 1/2 in (65 mm)
x 3/4 in (20 mm)
Brace
33 1/2 in
(851 mm)
x 2 1/2 in
(65 mm) x
3/4 in (20 mm)
55° ends
Doorway batten
80 7/8 in
(2.053 m)
x 1 1/2 in
(35 mm)
x 3/4 in (20 mm)
45° top
Front feature board
74 1/2 in (1.89 m)
x 6 in (150 mm)
x 3/4 in (20 mm)
Front frame
71 in (1.8 m)
x 1 1/2 in (35 mm)
x 3/4 in (20 mm)
(Door frame underneath doorway batten)
Front frame
35 in (888 mm) x 1 1/2 in (35 mm)
x 3/4 in (20 mm)

BACK VIEW OF THE BACK PANEL

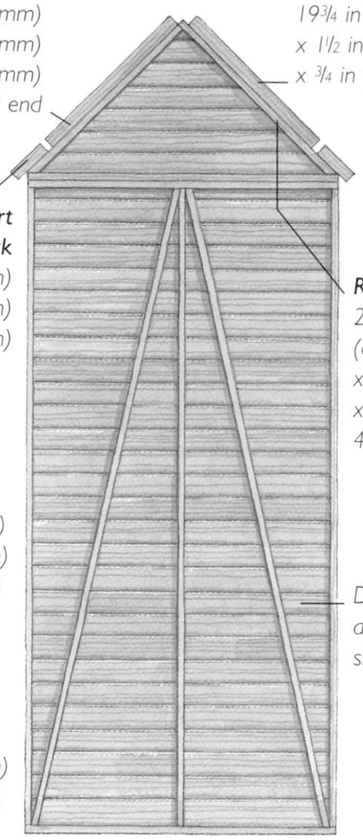
Roof frame
24 in (608 mm)
x 1 1/2 in (35 mm)
x 3/4 in (20 mm)
45° end
Roof support block
19 3/4 in (500 mm)
x 1 1/2 in (35 mm)
x 3/4 in (20 mm)
Roof support block
9 1/2 in (240 mm)
x 1 1/2 in (35 mm)
x 3/4 in (20 mm)
Roof frame
24 3/4 in
(628 mm)
x 1 1/2 in (35 mm)
x 3/4 in (20 mm)
45° end
Dimensions are as for side panel

INSIDE VIEW OF A SIDE PANEL

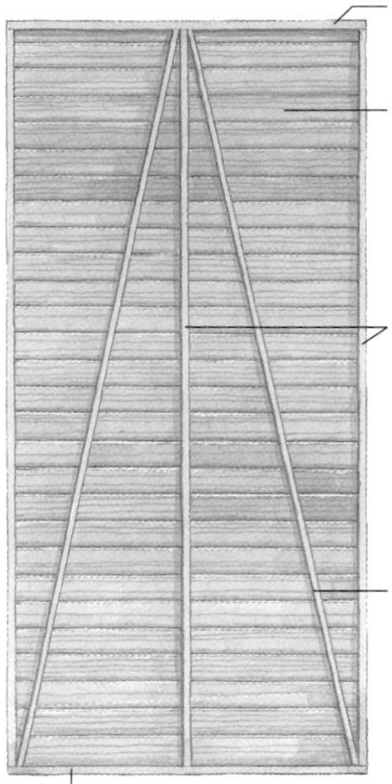
35 in (888 mm)
x 1 1/2 in (35 mm)
x 3/4 in (20 mm)
Siding
35 in (888 mm)
x 4 in (100 mm)
x 3/8 in (13 mm)
Central vertical bra
71 in (1.8 m)
x 1 1/2 in (35 mm)
x 3/4 in (20 mm)
Diagonal brace
72 3/4 in (1.846 m)
1 1/2 in (35 mm)
3/4 in (20 mm)
78° ends
35 in (888 mm) x 1 1/2 in
(35 mm) x 1/2 in (13 mm)

INSIDE VIEW OF A ROOF PANEL

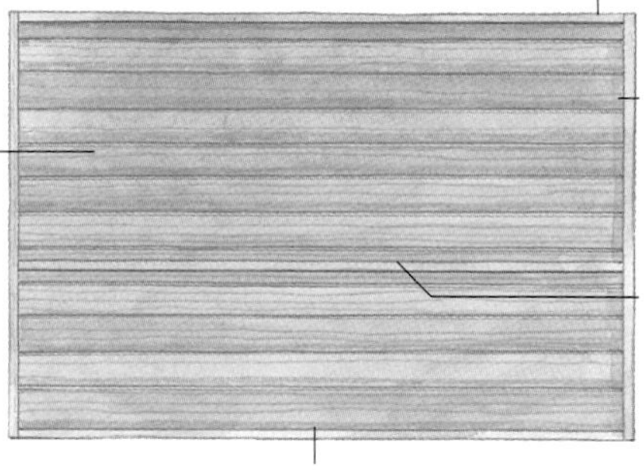
Roof frame
45 1/4 in (1.15 m) x 1 1/2 in (35 mm)
x 3/4 in (20 mm)
Bevel-edged board
46 7/8 in (1.19 m)
x 4 in (100 mm)
x 3/8 in (13 mm)
Roof frame
31 1/2 in (800 mm)
x 1 1/2 in (35 mm)
x 3/4 in (20 mm)
Roof location bar
45 1/4 in (1.15 m)
x 1 1/2 in (35 mm)
x 3/4 in (20 mm)
45 1/4 in (1.15 m) x 1 1/2 in
(35 mm) x 3/4 in (20 mm)

UNDERSIDE OF THE FLOOR PANEL

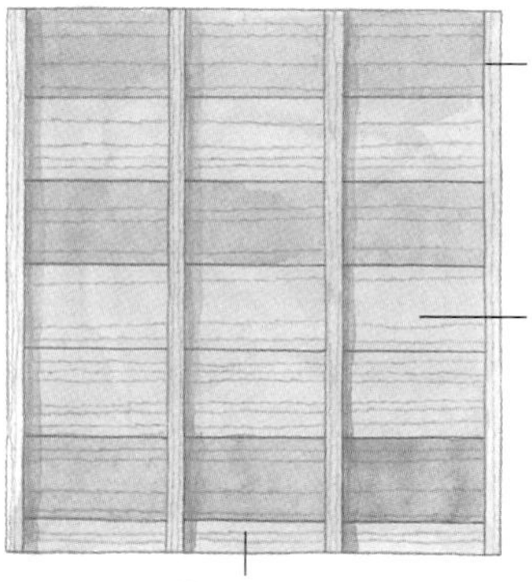
Floor joist
37 3/4 in (958 mm) x
2 in (50 mm) x
1 1/4 in (30 mm)
Floorboard
35 in (888 mm) x
6 in (150 mm) x
3/4 in (20 mm)
Floorboard
35 in (888 mm) x 2 in (50 mm)
x 3/4 in (20 mm)

CROSS-SECTION OF THE ROOF RIDGE BOARDS

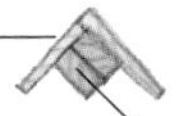
46 7/8 in (1.19 m) x 4 in
(100 mm) x 1/2 in
(13 mm) (siding)
46 7/8 in (1.19 m)
x 1 1/2 in (35 mm)
x 3/4 in (20 mm)

FINIAL

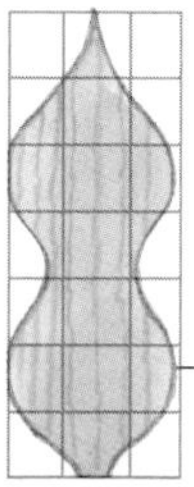
13 3/4 in (350 mm) x 5 in
(130 mm) x 3/4 in (20 mm)
1 grid square equals 2 in (50 mm)

DECORATIVE BARGE BOARD

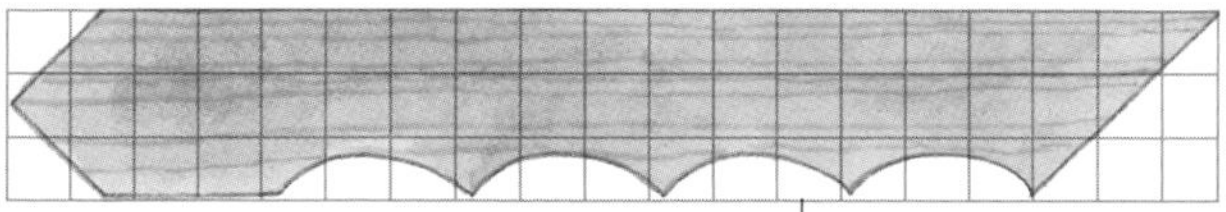
13 3/4 in (350 mm) x 5 in
(130 mm) x 3/4 in (20 mm)
1 grid square equals 2 in (50 mm)

EXPLODED VIEW OF THE VICTORIAN TOOL SHED

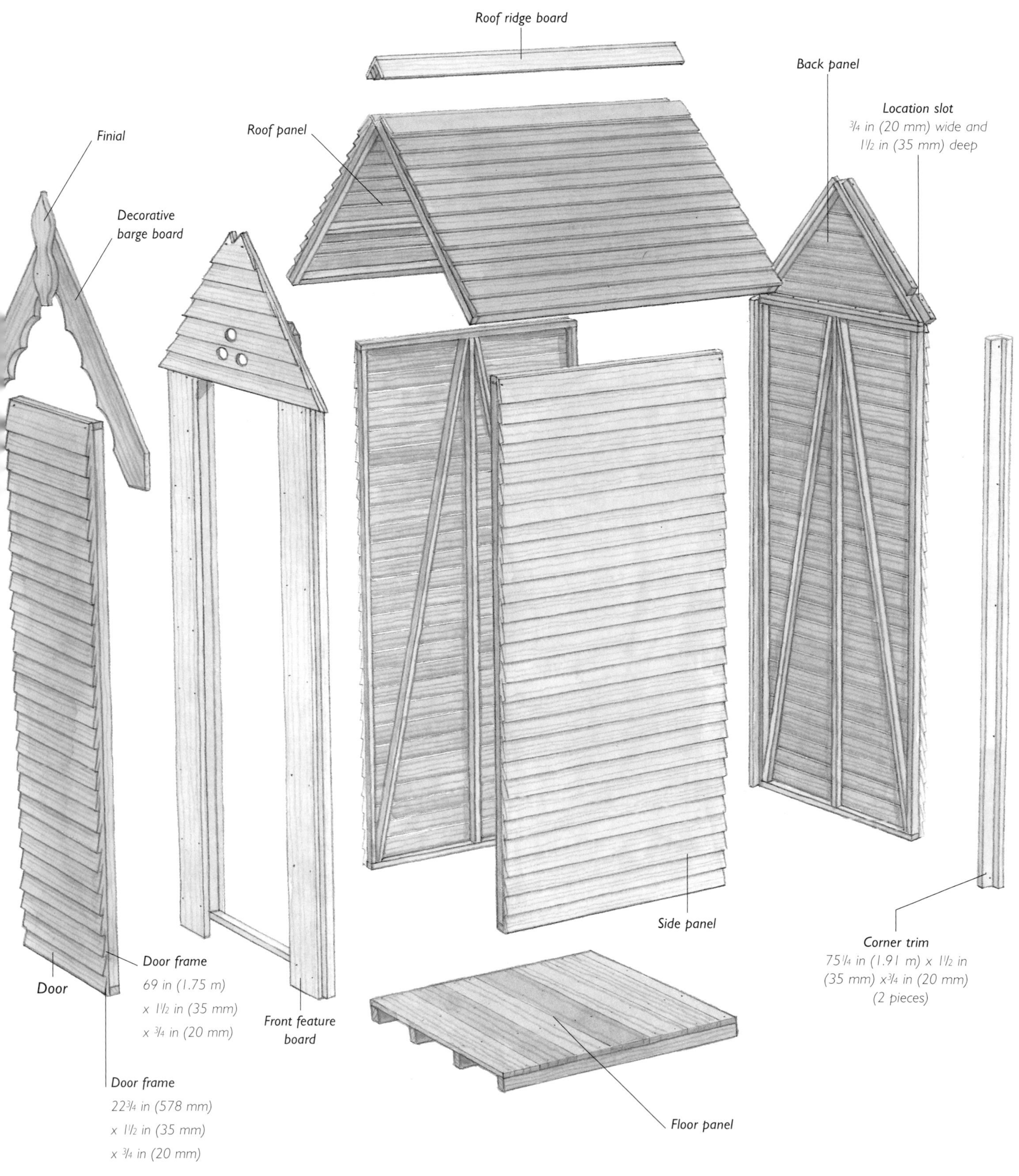
Roof ridge board
Back panel
Location slot
3/4 in (20 mm) wide and
1 1/2 in (35 mm) deep
Finial
Roof panel
Decorative
barge board
Side panel
Corner trim
75 1/4 in (1.91 m) x 1 1/2 in
(35 mm) x 3/4 in (20 mm)
(2 pieces)
Door frame
69 in (1.75 m)
x 1 1/2 in (35 mm)
x 3/4 in (20 mm)
Door
Front feature
board
Door frame
22 3/4 in (578 mm)
x 1 1/2 in (35 mm)
x 3/4 in (20 mm)
Floor panel

Step-by-step: **Making the Victorian tool shed**

Knot-free wood
Make sure that the door frames are free from knots

Uprights
Set the front frame and door frame pieces (for supporting the front feature board) 6 in (150mm) apart at the outside edges

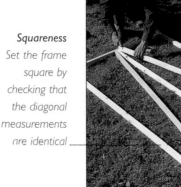

1 Cut the wood to size. Take the wood for the front panel, and butt join them with $1\frac{1}{2}$ inch (38 mm) screws. Set the two 6-inch-wide (150 mm) front feature boards on the front of the frame and fasten with $1\frac{1}{2}$ inch (38 mm) screws. Screw the doorway battens on the back of the frame with $1\frac{1}{2}$ inch (38 mm) screws.

Screwholes
Drill holes to take the screws

Squareness
Set the frame square by checking that the diagonal measurements are identical

Tight fit
The braces should be cut to fit perfectly within the squared frame

2 Build the back frame in much the same way as already described, only this time, fit a central vertical flanked by two diagonal braces. Aim to make the braces fit tightly into the frame. Build two identical side panel frames complete with central, vertical, and diagonal braces, as described for the back frame.

Roof location bar
Set $19\frac{3}{4}$ in (500 mm) from the ridge side of the frame

Screws
Have two screws at each joint

Roof frame
Choose an extra good bit of wood for the eaves

3 Build the door frame with the two sections of wood, using $1\frac{1}{2}$ inch (38 mm) screws, and 2 inch (50 mm) screws for fastening the diagonal brace pieces. Make two identical roof frames, each including a roof location bar, using two $1\frac{1}{2}$ inch (38 mm) screws at each joint.

Check angles
Make sure the frame is a right-angled triangle

Roof support block
Fasten each block with two $1\frac{1}{2}$ in (38 mm) screws

Location slot
Use an offcut of wood to ensure that the location slot will take the roof panel

4 Make two identical triangular gable frames with roof support blocks positioned to make location points for the roof frames. An offcut is used to ensure that the location slot is the correct size.

Siding
The siding needs to be level with the top of the plate

Coping saw
Cut the siding clear of the roof location slot

5 When you have covered the gable frames by nailing on the bevel-edged boards (a technique for positioning the boards is described in the Rabbit Hutch project on page 98), use the coping saw to cut through the siding to make a roof location slot, 3/4 inch (20 mm) wide and 1 1/2 inches (35 mm) deep, on the two elevated sides of the gable triangle.

Jig
Use a simple jig to help you space the siding properly

Nail holes
Drill holes before nailing, to avoid splitting the wood

Parallel
Check with a tape measure occasionally to make sure that the boards are still parallel

6 Cover the other frames with bevel-edged board. Use a simple jig to ensure that the overlap of the boards is constant. Drill holes for the nails, making sure that the nail doesn't pass through an underlying bevel-edged strip. Use the jigsaw to make the decorative barge boards. Sand all the panels and paint them on the outside.

Fastening panels
Run screws down through the side panel and floorboards and into the floor joists

7 Set the wall panels on the base and fasten with 2 inch (50 mm) screws running into the floor joists. Locate the roof panels and screw in place with 2 inch (50 mm) screws. Wrap felt over the joint between the two roof panels and fasten with nails. Use 1 1/2 inch (38 mm) screws to fasten the ridge board on top of the felt. Screw the decorative barge boards to the front edges of the panels, and the finials to the barge boards, with 1 1/2 inch (38 mm) screws. Drill three vent holes in the front gable. Fit the hinge and latch. Give all surfaces a coat of preservative. The floor panel should have an extra coat of preservative on the underside and on the ends of the joists.

Treehouse

Children love climbing trees and will be absolutely delighted with this hideaway. In their imaginations it may become anything from a hilltop castle to a pirate ship on the high seas to a magic carpet gliding over cities and deserts. It also makes a perfect retreat for adults! Select a sturdy, established tree.

TIME

Two long weekends – about twelve hours to prepare the tree and get the support beams in place, and the rest of the time for building the frames and lifting them into the tree.

SPECIAL TIP

You will need the help of four people to get the frames up into the tree.

FRONT VIEW OF THE TREEHOUSE

Panels

The roof and wall panels are constructed from 2½ x 1¼ in (64 x 32 mm) sections and then covered with bevel-edged board

Support structure

This is constructed to suit the shape of the tree

A BIRD'S-EYE VIEW

The treehouse is made from seven primary frames – two for the front, one for the back, one for each side, one for the base, and one for the roof. They are all made from 2½ x 1¼ inch (64 x 32 mm) sections covered in bevel-edged board. The roof slopes down towards the front, so that the overhang protects the inside of the house from wind and rain. The base is supported directly on beams that are attached to the tree with lag screws if required. We were able to create a stable support structure with just three horizontal beams and two vertical poles, but you will need to build a support arrangement to suit the shape of your chosen tree. The whole structure is designed so that the frames can be built on the ground and then moved up into the tree.

The actual business of getting the structure into the tree is not only tricky, but also potentially very dangerous. You will need at least four strong people to help, plus a pair of ladders and lots of thick rope. You must all wear gloves and sturdy boots, and you should elect one person to lead operations. In the interests of safety, children and pets must be kept at a distance.

YOU WILL NEED

Materials *for a treehouse 89 in (2.267 m) wide, 75½ in (1.918 m) deep, and 75¼ in (1.910 m) high. (All rough-sawn pine pieces include excess length for wastage.)*

- Pine: 25 pieces, 10 feet (3 m) long, 2½ in (64 mm) wide, and 1¼ in (32 mm) thick (long members for the frames for the walls, roof and floor)
- Pine: 20 pieces, 10 feet (3 m) long, 3 in (76 mm) wide, and ⅝ in (16 mm) thick (floorboards)
- Pine bevel-edged board: 30 pieces, 10 feet (3 m) long, 4 in (100 mm) wide, and ½ in (13 mm) thick (siding)
- Pine bevel-edged board: 17 pieces, 10 feet (3 m) long, 4 in (100 mm) wide, and ½ in (13 mm) thick (roofing)
- Pine: 2 pieces, 30 in (764 mm) long, 4 in (100 mm) wide, and ½ in (13 mm) thick (sills)
- Rope: 80 feet (20 m), ⅝ in (10 mm) in diameter (for lashing the floor panel to the support frame)
- Galvanized lag screws: 6 in (150 mm) long, quantity as necessary (optional)
- Zinc-plated, countersunk Phillips screws: 200 x 2 in (50 mm) no 8, 200 x 2½ in (65 mm) no 8
- Galvanized nails: 2 lb (1 kg) pack of 6d box (50 mm x 2.65 mm)

Tools

- Pencil, ruler, tape measure, marking gauge, square, and carpenter's level
- Two portable workbenches
- Ladder (length to suit site)
- Bolt wrench (if using lag screws)
- Crosscut saw
- Hammer
- Electric drill
- Cordless electric drill with a Phillips screwdriver bit
- Countersink drill bit to match the screw sizes
- Drill bit to match nail sizes
- Drill bit to match the diameter of the rope
- Electric sander with a pack of medium-grade sandpaper
- Pair of clamps

Treehouse

UNDERSIDE OF THE FLOOR PANEL

Frame
84¼ in (2.138 m) x 2½ in (64 mm) x 1¼ in (32 mm)

Frame/joists
57⅜ in (1.456 m)
x 2½ in (64 mm)
x 1¼ in (32 mm)

Floorboards
84¼ in (2.138 m)
x 3 in (76 mm)
x ⅝ in (16 mm)

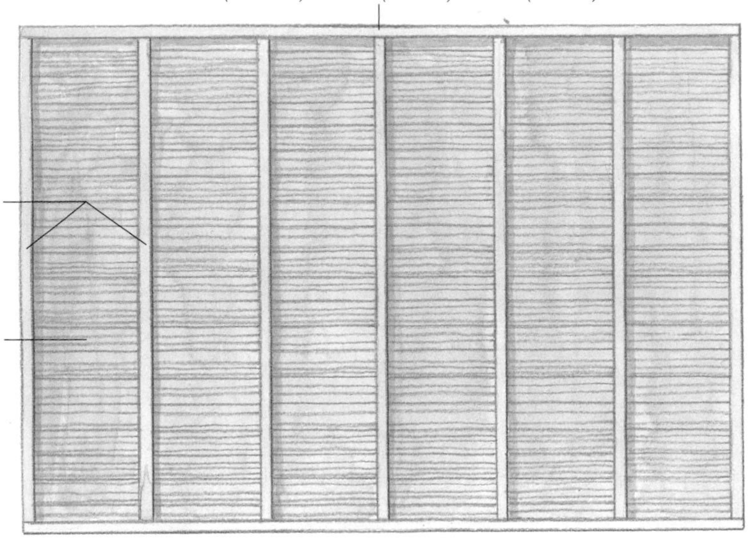

INSIDE OF A
FRONT PANEL

25 in (635 mm) x 2½ in (64 mm)
x 1¼ in (32 mm)
Top edge 33¼ in
(843 mm) up
from the base

51¼ in
(1.302 m)
x 2½ in
(64 mm)
x 1¼ in
(32 mm)

37½ in (954 mm)
x 2½ in (64 mm)
x 1¼ in (32 mm)
Ends angled to fit

Siding
30 in (764 mm) x
4 in (100 mm) x
½ in (13 mm)

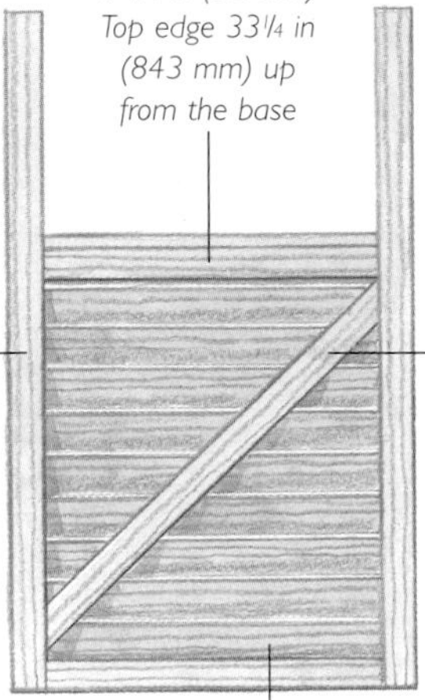

INSIDE OF THE BACK PANEL

79½ in (2.01 m) x 2½ in (64 mm) x 1¼ in (32 mm)
Top edge 33¼ in (843 mm) up from the base

51¼ in (1.302 m)
x 2½ in (64 mm)
x 1¼ in (32 mm)

37¼ in (944 mm)
x 2½ in (64 mm)
x 1¼ in (32 mm)
Ends angled to fit

Siding
42 in (1.69 m) x 4 in (100 mm) x ½
in (13 mm)
Joined at center

2½ in (64 mm)
x 1¼ in (32 mm)
Length and ends cut to fit

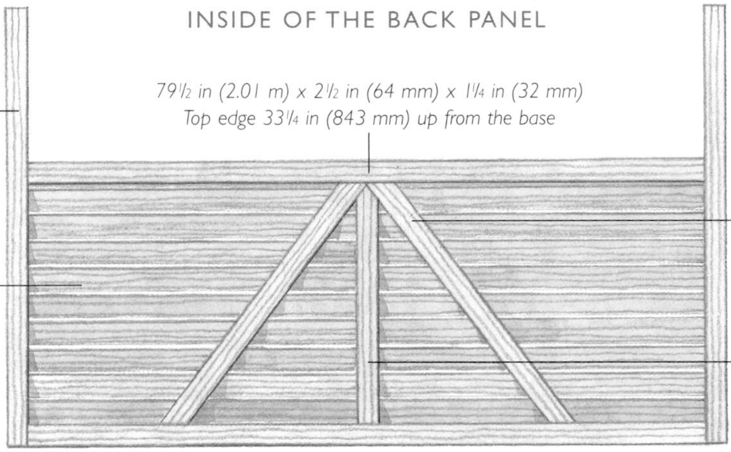

INSIDE OF A SIDE PANEL

51¼ in (1.302 m)
x 2½ in (64 mm)
x 1¼ in (32 mm)

57⅜ in (1.456 m) x 2½ in
(64 mm) x 1¼ in (32 mm)
Top edge 33¼ in (843 mm) up from the base

38 in (962 mm)
x 2½ in (64 mm)
x 1¼ in (32 mm)
Ends angled to fit

Siding
62⅜ in (1.584 m) x 4 in (100 mm) x ½ in (13 mm)

SIDE VIEW OF THE ROOF ASSEMBLY

Roofing

69 in (1.75 m)
x 2½ in (64 mm)
x 1¼ in (32 mm)

19° ends

26½ in (672 mm) x 2½ in
(64 mm) x 1¼ in (32 mm)

Pointed end cut
and angled to fit

62⅜ in (1.584 m) x 2½ in (64 mm) x 1¼ in (32 mm)

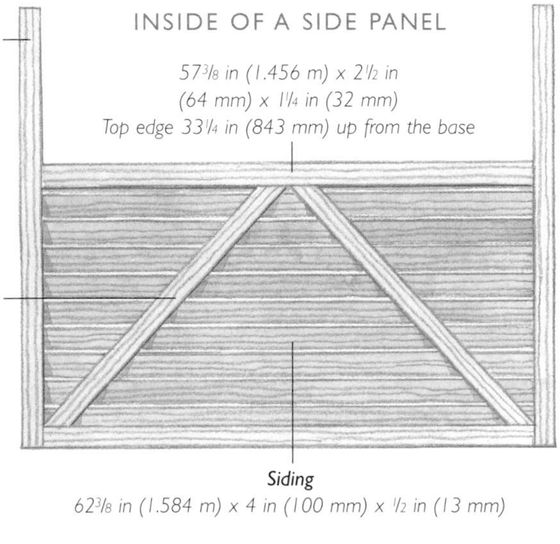

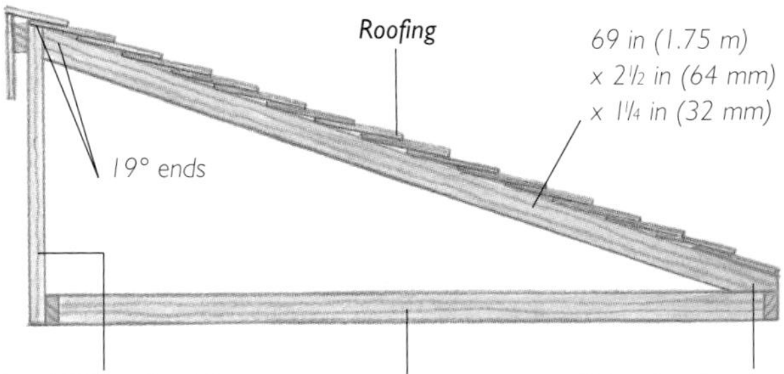

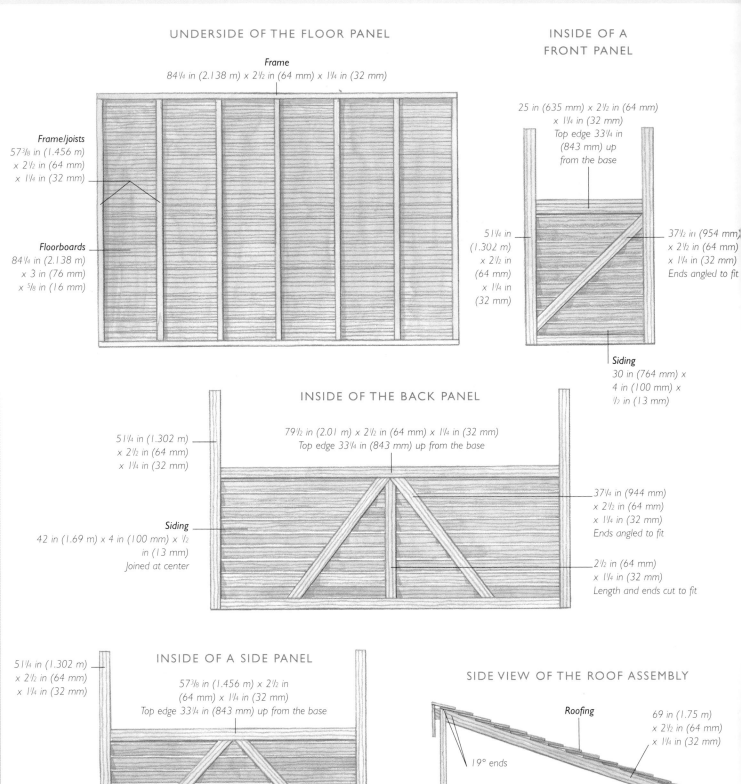

EXPLODED VIEW OF THE TREEHOUSE

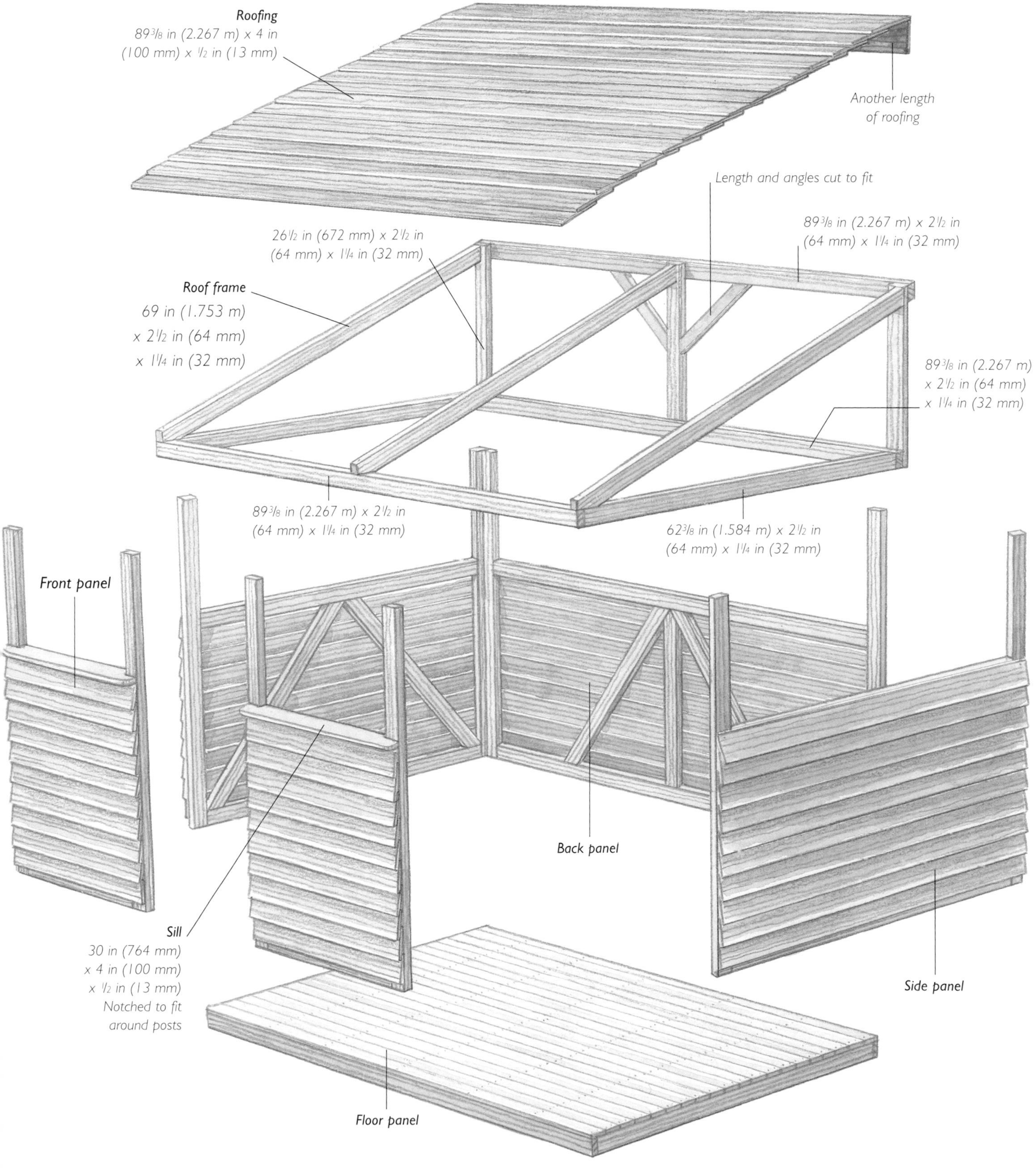
Roofing
89 3/8 in (2.267 m) x 4 in
(100 mm) x 1/2 in (13 mm)
Another length
of roofing
Length and angles cut to fit
26 1/2 in (672 mm) x 2 1/2 in
(64 mm) x 1 1/4 in (32 mm)
89 3/8 in (2.267 m) x 2 1/2 in
(64 mm) x 1 1/4 in (32 mm)
Roof frame
69 in (1.753 m)
x 2 1/2 in (64 mm)
x 1 1/4 in (32 mm)
89 3/8 in (2.267 m)
x 2 1/2 in (64 mm)
x 1 1/4 in (32 mm)
89 3/8 in (2.267 m) x 2 1/2 in
(64 mm) x 1 1/4 in (32 mm)
62 3/8 in (1.584 m) x 2 1/2 in
(64 mm) x 1 1/4 in (32 mm)
Front panel
Back panel
Sill
30 in (764 mm)
x 4 in (100 mm)
x 1/2 in (13 mm)
Notched to fit
around posts
Side panel
Floor panel

Step-by-step: **Making the treehouse**

Support poles
Attach three or more poles to the tree to make a horizontal platform

Branches
Trim off branches that will be in the way

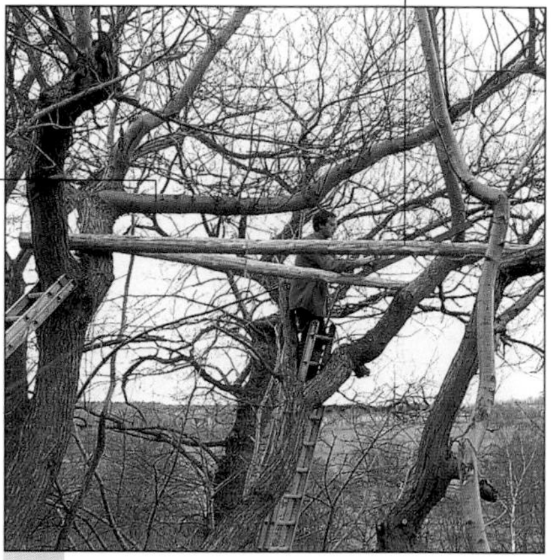

1 Choose a strong, established tree with suitable branches. Prepare the site (the area within the tree) by cutting back branches if necessary. Build a sturdy support frame to make a platform for the treehouse. Wedge it between the branches or attach to the tree with lag screws if needed. Check that the supports are level.

Rope-attachment points
Drill holes through the floor joists at points for roping the floor to the tree

Square frame
Check the frame is square by comparing the diagonal measurements

Floorboards
All the boards need to be screwed to the joists – one 2 in (50 mm) screw at each intersection

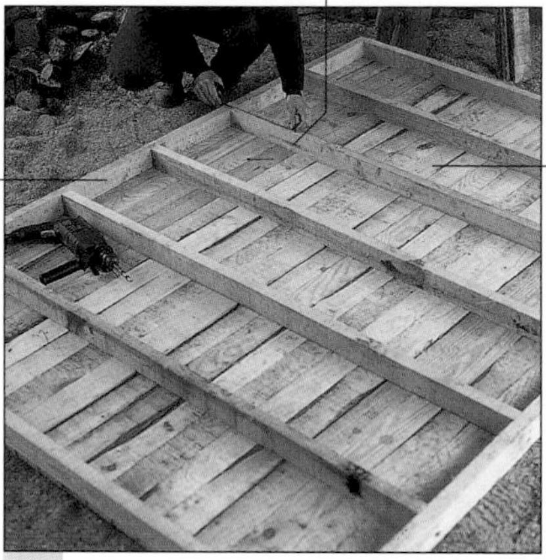

2 To make the floor panel, first build a frame about $84\frac{1}{4}$ inches (2.138 m) long and $59\frac{7}{8}$ inches (1.520 m) wide, complete with secondary joists, using $2\frac{1}{2}$ inch (65 mm) screws. Screw on the 4-inch-wide (76 mm) floorboards with 2 inch (50 mm) screws. Drill rope holes through the joists at points where they will be useful for lashing the floor to the support frame.

Bracing
The diagonal struts reinforce the frame and hold it square

Corner joints
Attach the frame together using two screws at each corner

3 Using $2\frac{1}{2}$ inch (65 mm) screws, build the back wall frame, making it $84\frac{1}{4}$ inches (2.138 m) wide and $51\frac{1}{4}$ inches (1.302 m) in total height. Brace the bottom of the frame with two diagonals that center on the underside of the top of the frame at sill level (no sill on back).

Siding
Keep the boards evenly spaced and parallel (overlap the boards by at least $\frac{3}{4}$ in (20 mm)

Nailing
Nail the siding to the frame at every intersection (drill holes for nails that occur near the end of a piece of wood)

4 Attach the 4-inch-wide (100 mm) bevel-edged board on the back wall frame. Working from the bottom upwards, and stopping short of the level of the sill, drill pilot holes through the boards and nail them to the frame with 6d (50 mm) nails.

Diagonals
Measure the diagonals to determine whether the frame is square

Brace
Fit a diagonal brace to hold the frame square

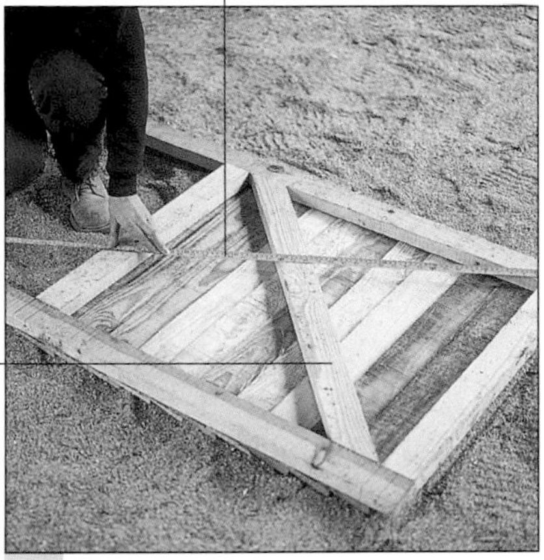

5 Build the frames for the other walls and roof in much the same way as already described, all the while double-checking that the measurements add up and the frames are square. Cut and fit two sills to the front frames with $2\frac{1}{2}$ inch (65 mm) screws.

Levelling
If necessary, add wedges under the base to make it level

Attaching
Thread rope through the holes in the joists and around the support beams

Additional support
We added vertical posts for extra strength

6 Heave the base up into the tree and lash it in place with rope. The rope allows the structure to flex in the wind without either the treehouse or the tree coming under too much stress.

Joining the panels
Screw the uprights to each other near the top, middle and bottom

Attaching to the base
Drive screws through the wall panel frames and into the base frame

7 Lift the two side wall frames up into the tree and clamp them firmly to the base. Screw them in position with $2\frac{1}{2}$ inch (65 mm) screws. Remove the clamps. Repeat the procedure with the back wall frame.

Temporary stays
Remove stays after the roof is secured

Attaching the roof
Screw the roof frame to the top corners of the wall frames

Safety
Make sure that the ladder is positioned safely and ask a friend to help hold it in place

8 When the back and the two side frames are securely in place, hoist the roof frame into position and screw it to the corner uprights of the wall frames. Finally, screw the two front frames to the side walls and to the roof. Use $2\frac{1}{2}$ inch (65 mm) screws throughout.

Children's playhouse

This playhouse has wonderful decorative details, making it look as though it is straight out of *Grimm's Fairy Tales*, and is therefore guaranteed to stimulate children's imaginations. If you have children or grandchildren aged up to about twelve, they will find the playhouse great fun and you will get much enjoyment from the project.

TIME

Two long weekends (one weekend for building the frames, about twelve hours for building the door and window, and the rest of the time for finishing).

USEFUL TIP

For safety reasons, plastic is used for the window "glass".

YOU WILL NEED

Materials *for a playhouse 6 feet 3¼ in (1.91 m) high, 6 feet (1.844 m) wide, and 5 feet 4½ in (1.635 m) deep.*

- Pine: 40 pieces, 8 feet (2 m) long, 1½ in (35 mm) wide, ¾ in (20 mm) thick (frames, small trimmers, roof location bar, roof support blocks)
- Pine tongue-and-groove: 5 pieces, each 8 feet (2 m) long, 3½ in (90 mm) wide, and ½ in (8 mm) thick (stable door, decorative shutters, beading to fasten window)
- Pine: 12 pieces, each 8 feet (2 m) long, 6 in (150 mm) wide, and ⅞ in (22 mm) thick (floorboards, decorative barge boards, decorative trim, back finial; window sill, door handle and door surround)
- Pine: 4 pieces, 8 feet (2 m) long, 2½ in (65 mm) wide, and 1¼ in (30 mm) thick (floor joists, front finial)
- Pine: 4 pieces, 8 feet (2 m) long, 2½ in (65 mm) wide, and 1½ in (35 mm) thick (for covering the corners)
- Pine: 1 piece, 8 feet (2 m) long, 3 in (75 mm) x 3 in (75 mm) triangular section (roof ridge board)
- Pine bevel-edged board: 100 pieces, each 8 feet (2 m) long, 4 in (100 mm) wide, and ⅜ in (10 mm) thick (siding; wall plates)
- Zinc-plated, countersunk Phillips screws: 200 x 1½ in (38 mm) no. 8, 100 x 2 in (50 mm) no. 8, 100 x 2½ in (65 mm) no. 10
- Galvanized nails: 8 lb (4 kg) x 4d (40 mm x 2.65 mm)
- Galvanized flat-headed ⅜ in (10 mm) roof tacks
- Polycarbonate sheet: 13 in (330 mm) x 13½ in (345 mm) (window)
- Piano hinges: 20 in (512 mm) and 26 in (672 mm) long, with screws to fit
- Water-based, exterior paint: white and blue
- Roof felt: 8 feet (2 m) long and 1 foot (300 mm) wide (for under roof ridge board)

Tools

- Pencil, ruler, tape measure, marking gauge, and square
- Two portable workbenches
- Crosscut saw
- Cordless electric drill with a Phillips screwdriver bit
- Drill bits to match screw sizes
- Coping saw
- Electric compound miter saw
- Hammer
- Electric sander with a pack of medium-grade sandpaper
- Paintbrush 1½ in (40 mm)
- Pair of clamps

FRONT VIEW OF THE PLAYHOUSE

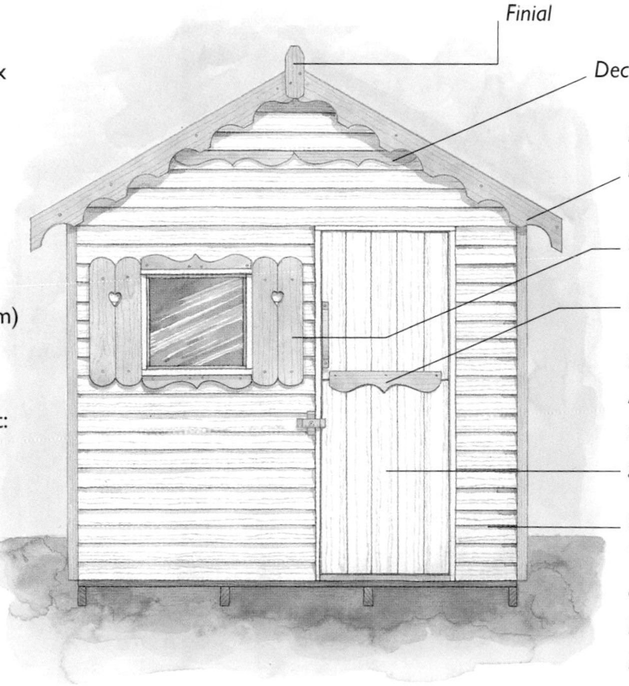
Finial
Decorative trim
Decorative barge board
Decorative shutter
Decorative trim
Dutch door
Made from tongue-and-groove boards
Siding
The panels are covered with bevel-edged boards

A MINI HOUSE FOR MINORS

If you want to delight your children or grandchildren, this is the playhouse that children dream about. It is high enough to stand upright in, the Dutch door can be shut from the inside, it has a proper weather-tight window, and there is plenty of space. The floor base measures 5 feet (1.525 m) x 49½ inches (1.255 m), so there is enough room for three or four children to spread out their sleeping bags. We have detailed the playhouse to suit children aged four to eight – with lots of fairy-tale trim and soft colors – but, for older children, the details can be changed and stronger colors used.

We have envisaged that you will make the frames outside your garage or garden workshop, and then move them to the site. We have fitted piano hinges because they close the gap between the door and the frame, preventing children from serious accidents to their fingers. Children can close the Dutch door from the inside, but you can also open the playhouse from the outside.

Children's playhouse

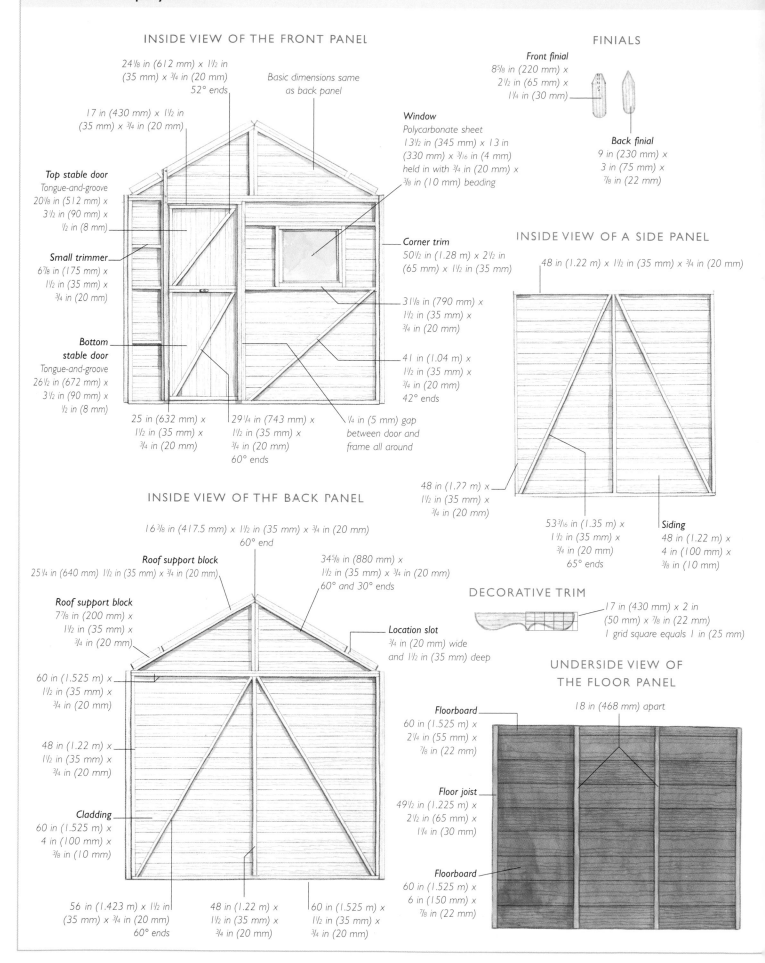

INSIDE VIEW OF THE FRONT PANEL

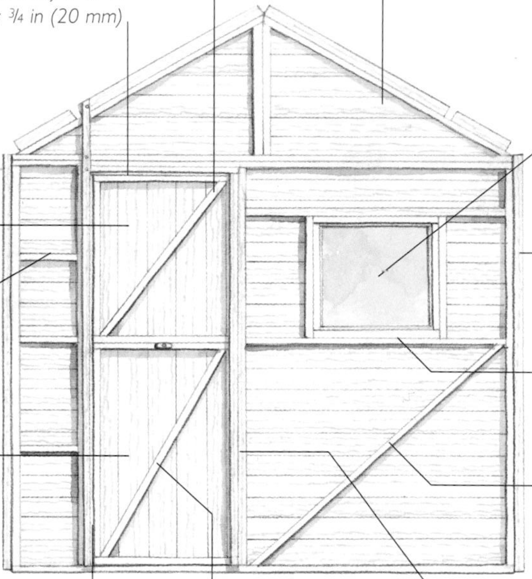
24 1/8 in (612 mm) x 1 1/2 in (35 mm) x 3/4 in (20 mm) 52° ends
Basic dimensions same as back panel
17 in (430 mm) x 1 1/2 in (35 mm) x 3/4 in (20 mm)
Window
Polycarbonate sheet 13 1/2 in (345 mm) x 13 in (330 mm) x 3/16 in (4 mm) held in with 3/4 in (20 mm) x 3/8 in (10 mm) beading
Top stable door
Tongue-and-groove 20 1/8 in (512 mm) x 3 1/2 in (90 mm) x 1/2 in (8 mm)
Small trimmer
6 7/8 in (175 mm) x 1 1/2 in (35 mm) x 3/4 in (20 mm)
Corner trim
50 1/2 in (1.28 m) x 2 1/2 in (65 mm) x 1 1/2 in (35 mm)
31 1/8 in (790 mm) x 1 1/2 in (35 mm) x 3/4 in (20 mm)
Bottom stable door
Tongue-and-groove 26 1/2 in (672 mm) x 3 1/2 in (90 mm) x 1/2 in (8 mm)
41 in (1.04 m) x 1 1/2 in (35 mm) x 3/4 in (20 mm) 42° ends
25 in (632 mm) x 1 1/2 in (35 mm) x 3/4 in (20 mm)
29 1/4 in (743 mm) x 1 1/2 in (35 mm) x 3/4 in (20 mm) 60° ends
1/4 in (5 mm) gap between door and frame all around

FINIALS

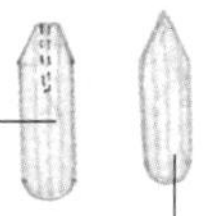
Front finial
8 5/8 in (220 mm) x 2 1/2 in (65 mm) x 1 1/4 in (30 mm)
Back finial
9 in (230 mm) x 3 in (75 mm) x 7/8 in (22 mm)

INSIDE VIEW OF A SIDE PANEL

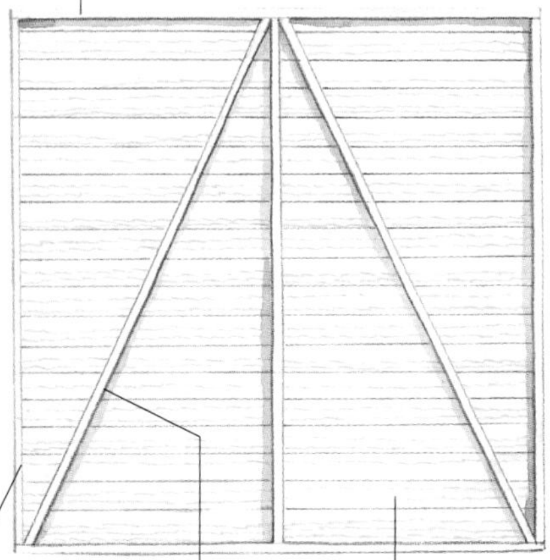
48 in (1.22 m) x 1 1/2 in (35 mm) x 3/4 in (20 mm)
48 in (1.22 m) x 1 1/2 in (35 mm) x 3/4 in (20 mm)
53 3/16 in (1.35 m) x 1 1/2 in (35 mm) x 3/4 in (20 mm) 65° ends
Siding
48 in (1.22 m) x 4 in (100 mm) x 3/8 in (10 mm)

INSIDE VIEW OF THF BACK PANEL

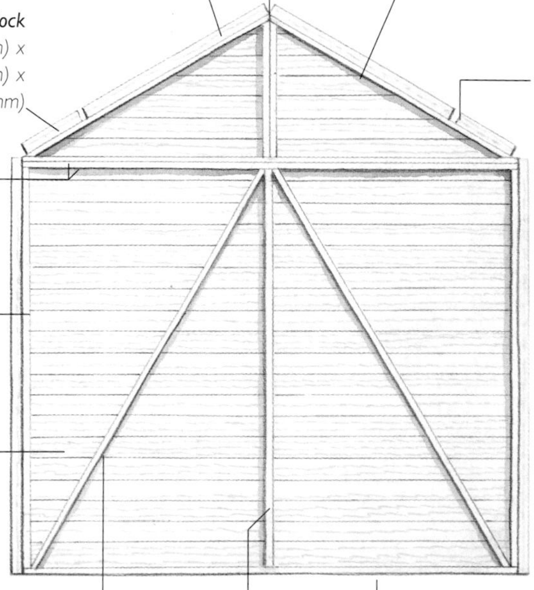
16 3/8 in (417.5 mm) x 1 1/2 in (35 mm) x 3/4 in (20 mm) 60° end
Roof support block
25 1/4 in (640 mm) 1 1/2 in (35 mm) x 3/4 in (20 mm)
34 5/8 in (880 mm) x 1 1/2 in (35 mm) x 3/4 in (20 mm) 60° and 30° ends
Roof support block
7 7/8 in (200 mm) x 1 1/2 in (35 mm) x 3/4 in (20 mm)
Location slot
3/4 in (20 mm) wide and 1 1/2 in (35 mm) deep
60 in (1.525 m) x 1 1/2 in (35 mm) x 3/4 in (20 mm)
48 in (1.22 m) x 1 1/2 in (35 mm) x 3/4 in (20 mm)
Cladding
60 in (1.525 m) x 4 in (100 mm) x 3/8 in (10 mm)
56 in (1.423 m) x 1 1/2 in (35 mm) x 3/4 in (20 mm) 60° ends
48 in (1.22 m) x 1 1/2 in (35 mm) x 3/4 in (20 mm)
60 in (1.525 m) x 1 1/2 in (35 mm) x 3/4 in (20 mm)

DECORATIVE TRIM

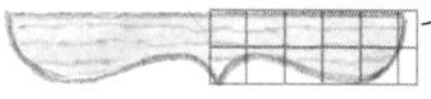
17 in (430 mm) x 2 in (50 mm) x 7/8 in (22 mm)
1 grid square equals 1 in (25 mm)

UNDERSIDE VIEW OF THE FLOOR PANEL

18 in (468 mm) apart
Floorboard
60 in (1.525 m) x 2 1/4 in (55 mm) x 7/8 in (22 mm)
Floor joist
49 1/2 in (1.225 m) x 2 1/2 in (65 mm) x 1 1/4 in (30 mm)
Floorboard
60 in (1.525 m) x 6 in (150 mm) x 7/8 in (22 mm)

INSIDE VIEW OF A ROOF PANEL

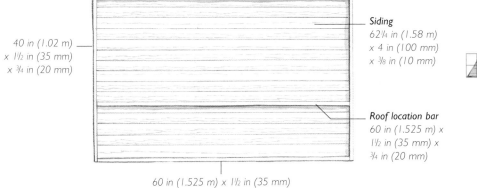

40 in (1.02 m)
x 1½ in (35 mm)
x ¾ in (20 mm)
Siding
62¼ in (1.58 m)
x 4 in (100 mm)
x ⅜ in (10 mm)
Roof location bar
60 in (1.525 m) x
1½ in (35 mm) x
¾ in (20 mm)
60 in (1.525 m) x 1½ in (35 mm)
x ¾ in (20 mm)

DECORATIVE BARGE BOARD

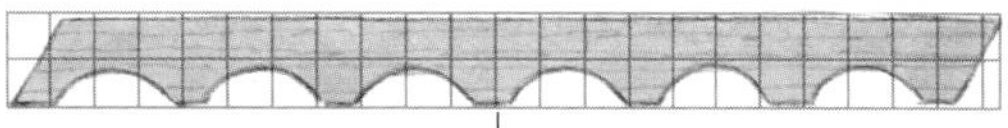
44⅛ in (1.121 m) x 4 in (100 mm) x ⅞ in (22 mm)
60° ends
1 grid square equals 2 in (50 mm)

EXPLODED VIEW OF THE CHILDREN'S PLAYHOUSE

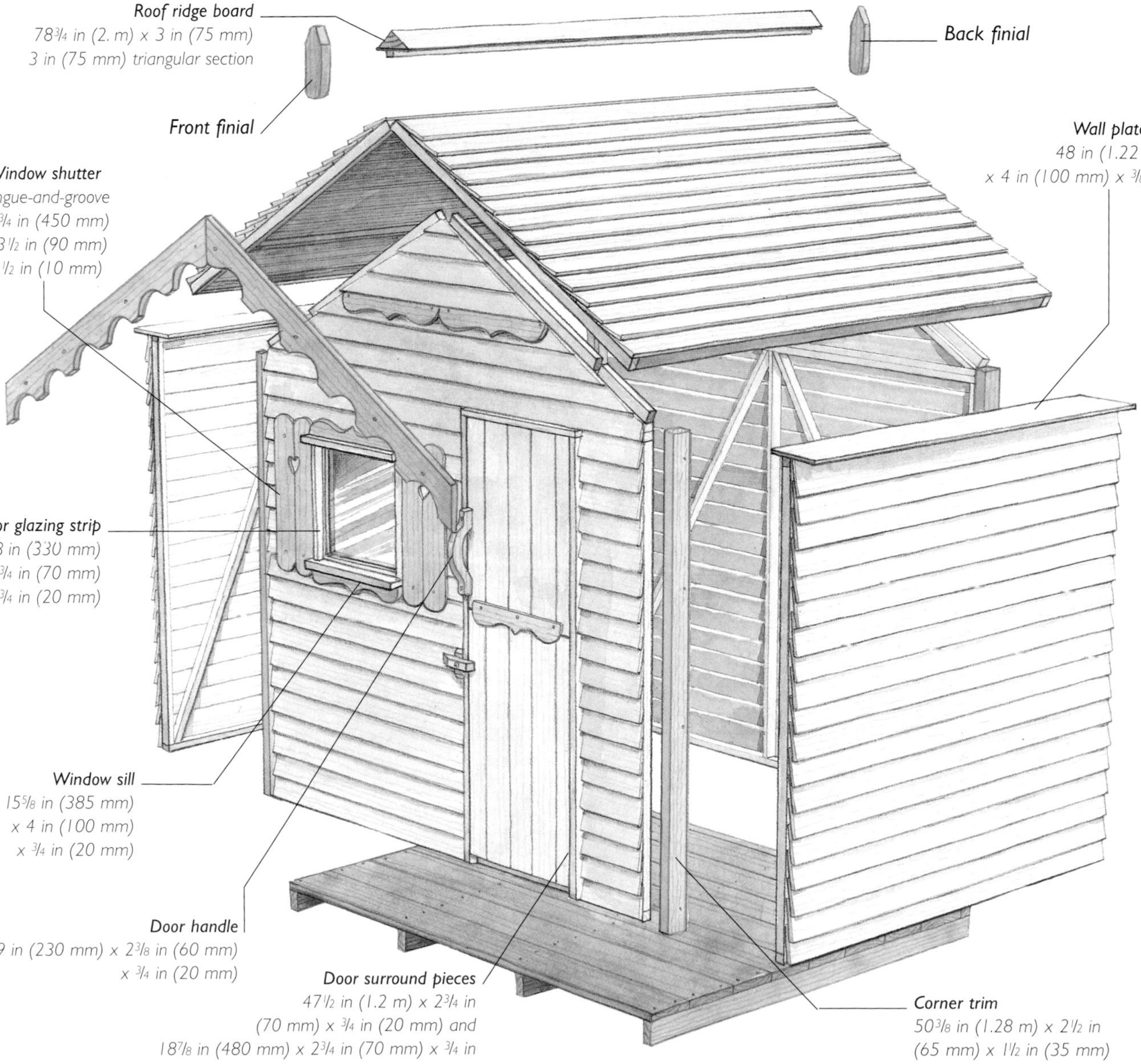
Roof ridge board
78¾ in (2. m) x 3 in (75 mm)
3 in (75 mm) triangular section
Back finial
Front finial
Wall plate
48 in (1.22 m)
x 4 in (100 mm) x ⅜ in (10 mm)
Window shutter
Tongue-and-groove
17¾ in (450 mm)
x 3½ in (90 mm)
x ½ in (10 mm)
Exterior glazing strip
13 in (330 mm)
x 2¾ in (70 mm)
x ¾ in (20 mm)
Window sill
15⅝ in (385 mm)
x 4 in (100 mm)
x ¾ in (20 mm)
Door handle
9 in (230 mm) x 2⅜ in (60 mm)
x ¾ in (20 mm)
Door surround pieces
47½ in (1.2 m) x 2¾ in
(70 mm) x ¾ in (20 mm) and
18⅞ in (480 mm) x 2¾ in (70 mm) x ¾ in
Corner trim
50⅜ in (1.28 m) x 2½ in
(65 mm) x 1½ in (35 mm)

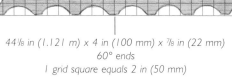

Step-by-step: **Making the children's playhouse**

Working area
Find an area of level ground to work on

Screwholes
Drill holes at the ends of the boards to take the screws

1 Use the crosscut saw to cut all the wood to size. First, make the floor. Set the four floor joists about 18 inches (468 mm) apart and screw the 6-inch-wide (150 mm) floorboards in place with 2 inch (50 mm) screws so that you finish up with a base that measures 60 inches (1.525 m) across and 49½ inches (1.255 m) from front to back.

Wood selection
Make sure that the pieces that make the door frame are perfectly straight

Joints
Use two screws at the joints where possible

Reinforcement
Use lengths of spare wood to strengthen the hinge side of the frame

2 Set out the overall size of the front frame and then divide it up, first with the two verticals for the door, then the two horizontals for the window. Finish with the diagonal braces and the small trimmers at the side of the door. Fasten everything with 1½ inch (38 mm) screws.

Verticals
Double up the verticals for strength

Roof support blocks
The blocks are for locating the roof panel and need to be placed accurately

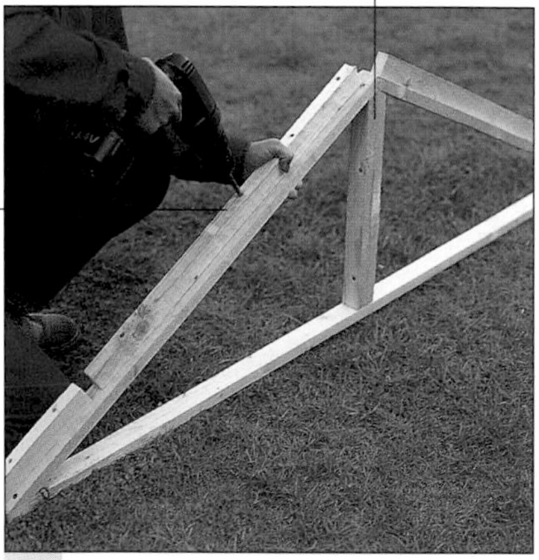

3 Build the gable triangles, complete with the roof support blocks (use 2 inch (50 mm) screws) for locating the roof frames. For the verticals, have two thicknesses of wood set back to back, in order to strengthen the frame and prevent it from twisting.

Overhang
The roof should mostly overhang at the front and only a little at the back

Location slot
The roof panel should drop into position and not need to be forced

4 Screw the wall frames together with 1½ inch (38 mm) screws and build the roof frame to fit. Locate the roof frame in the location slots that you have created on top of the gable frames. Dismantle the frames and lay on the ground in readiness for covering with bevel-edged board.

Window frame
Cut the frame from 6-in-wide (150 mm) offcuts
Appearance
Make sure that the short lengths of siding are free from knots

5 First frame the window with exterior glazing strips cut from the 6-inch-wide (150 mm) offcuts, and then set to work covering the frame with bevel-edged board, nailing it on with 4d (40 mm) nails. Clad the rest of the frames as described in other projects (a technique for positioning the boards is described in the Rabbit Hutch project on page 98).

Turnblock
Make a turnblock from a piece of spare wood
Hinges
Put screws in all the holes of the hinges, as they need to be firmly attached
Gap
Maintain a 1/4 in (5 mm) gap between the two doors

6 Build the frames for the doors (using 1½ inch (38 mm) screws) complete with the diagonal braces, and cover them with the tongue-and-groove boarding. Hang the doors with the piano hinges and make the stops and turnblocks from offcuts of 6-inch-wide (150 mm) wood (size and design to suit).

Heart detail
Push the two pieces together to make the heart shape
Screwholes
Drill holes for 1½ in (38 mm) screws through the siding and into the frame behind

7 Make the window shutters. Cut the heart detail 2½ inches (65 mm) long and 2 inches (50 mm) wide on the edges of the boards prior to assembly, using the coping saw. Cut the polycarbonate for the window and attach it with glazing beading strips taken from the tongue-and-groove.

Painting
Sand and paint all the panels inside and out before assembling
Placing
Make sure that you align the framework of the panels (rather than the siding) with the base
Floor attachment
Screw down through the panel frame, through the floorboard and into the floor joist

8 Set the floor on site. Clamp and screw the walls in place with 2½ inch (60 mm) screws. Position the roof frames. Screw on the wall plates with 1½ inch (38 mm) screws. Nail the felt over the ridge and screw on the ridge board with 2 inch (50 mm) screws.

Glossary

Aligning Setting one piece of wood against another (or one part of a structure against another) in order to obtain a good alignment or fit.

Butting The action of pushing one piece of wood against another to obtain a good flush fit, with both faces touching.

Centering Setting a measurement or component part on the center of another, or measuring a length or width to find the center.

Colorwashing The technique of mixing paint with water and brushing the resultant wash on wood in order to achieve a delicate, stained finish.

Dry run Putting all the parts of a project together without glue, nails or screws, in order to see whether the components are going to fit. The procedure can also be used to check that the design is going to work.

Finishing The procedure of sanding, painting, staining, and fitting hardware (wheels, latches, handles, and hinges) in order to complete the project.

Hinging Attaching one part to another by means of a hinge, pivot, or rotating part.

Laying out Using a pencil, rule, square and compass to draw lines on a piece of wood in readiness for cutting.

Levelling Using a carpenter's level to decide whether a structure or component part is perfectly horizontal or vertical, and then making adjustments to bring the component into line.

Preserving The procedure of painting wood with preservative in order to protect it against mold and rot. Preservative may be purchased as a colorless liquid, or it can form part of a paint or stain treatment. Some wood is pre-treated with preservative.

Sawing to size In this book, the term mostly refers to the procedure of taking the sawn wood – meaning wood that has been purchased pre-cut to width and thickness – and cutting it to length.

Siding The procedure of clothing a frame with wood (such as a sheet of plywood, or a pattern of individual boards), as with the shed projects.

Siding boards Used to cover the outside of a building.

Sighting To judge by eye. Also to look down a tool or down a length of wood in order to determine whether a particular cut, joint, or structure is level or true.

Squaring The technique of laying out with a set square or carpenter's level, and cutting and fastening wood so that surfaces or structures are at right angles to each other.

Tamping The act of using a length of wood to compact and level wet concrete.

Trial run Setting out a structure – all the pieces of wood and the various fixtures and fittings – in order to ascertain whether the envisaged project or technique is feasible.

Trimming Using a cutting tool to bring a piece of wood to a good finish; also the act of using short lengths of wood to brace or strengthen a frame.

Index

Reading List

Other Storey Titles You Will Enjoy

Fences for Pasture & Garden, by Gail Damerow. The complete guide to choosing, planning, and building today's best fences includes plans for wire, rail, electric, high-tension, and other fences. 160 pages. Paperback. ISBN 0-88266-753-X.

Garden Retreats: A Build-It-Yourself Guide, by David and Jeanie Stiles. Inspiring projects for outdoor living spaces, including a garden swing, rose arbor, gazebo, and potting shed. 160 pages. Paperback. ISBN 0-58017-149-4.

Home Made: 101 Easy-To-Make Things for Your Garden, Home or Farm, by Ken Braren and Roger Griffith. Save time and money with projects that are easy to build, even with only hand tools and limited experience. Includes fireplace front, root cellar, fences, gates, animal shelters, window greenhouse, solar drier, and more. 176 pages. Paperback. ISBN 0-88266-103-5.

Making Bentwood Trellises, Arbors, Gates & Fences, by Jim Long. Learn to collect limbs from a wide variety of trees and then craft and install trellises, gates, arbors, fences, and more. 160 pages. Paperback. ISBN 1-58017-051-X.

Making Bent Willow Furniture, by Brenda and Brian Cameron. Includes techniques and instructions for projects such as a quilt ladder, plant stand, hanging basket, chair, porch swing, headboard, and more. 144 pages. Paperback. ISBN 1-58017-048-X.

Outdoor Stonework: 16 Easy-To-Build Projects for Your Yard & Garden, by Alan and Gill Bridgewater. This complete primer on working with stone covers everything from choosing materials to safety considerations, and features step-by-step construction methods. 128 pages. Paperback. ISBN 1-58017-333-0.

Outdoor Water Features: 16 Easy-To-Build Projects for Your Yard & Garden, by Alan and Gill Bridgewater. It's never been easier for gardeners to add the sparkle and serenity of water to their landscapes. Offers explanatory photographs, clear instructions, and helpful tips and techniques. 128 pages. Paperback. ISBN 1-58017-334-9.

Renovating Barns, Sheds & Outbuildings, by Nick Engler. Learn to save money, history, and architecture by renovating and restoring rather than replacing. 256 pages. Paperback. ISBN 1-58017-216-4.

Rustic Retreats: A Build-It-Yourself Guide, by David and Jeanie Stiles. A complete guide to building sturdy, inexpensive, and beautiful backyard and woodland shelters. 160 pages. Paperback. ISBN 1-58017-035-8

Acknowledgments

AG&G Books would like to thank *Garden and Wildlife Matters Photographic Library* for contributing the pictures used on pages 50, 51, 74, 75, 106, and 107.